BUTCHER BIRD

Hauptmann *Josef Wurmheller*, Staffelkapitän *of 9.JG 2, standing by his Fw 190 in July 1943. His rudder depicts his Knight's Cross and Oakleaves, awarded after sixty victories, and an additional ten RAF and four USAF victory bars taking his score, at that time, to 74. Wurmheller went on to win the Swords with a final score of 102 and became* Kommandeur *of III./JG 2.*

Butcher Bird
THE FOCKE-WULF Fw190

EDWARD SHACKLADY

CERBERUS

First published in 2003

PUBLISHED BY:
Cerberus Publishing Limited
Penn House, Bannerleigh Road,
Leigh Woods, Bristol BS8 3PF, U.K.
Telephone: ++44 117 974 7175
Facsimile: ++44 117 973 0890
e-mail: cerberusbooks@aol.com

British Library Cataloguing in Publication Data.
A catalogue record for this book is available from the British Library.

ISBN 1 84145 103 7

PRINTED AND BOUND IN ENGLAND

Contents

		Page
Introduction		*vii*
Prologue		*ix*
Chapter One	A Company is Born	1
Chapter Two	Kurt Tank – The Fw 190's Mastermind	9
Chapter Three	The New Generation Fighter	25
Chapter Four	The 'Butcher Bird' Enters Service	39
Chapter Five	The Fw 190 in Action	57
Chapter Six	'Wilde Sau'	83
Chapter Seven	An Aircraft to fit the Rôle	103
Chapter Eight	The Battle for Germany	127
Chapter Nine	In Search of High Performance	151
Chapter Ten	The Long-Nosed 'Dora'	179
Chapter Eleven	Notable Fw 190 Pilots	197
Chapter Twelve	Kurt Tank's Focke-Wulf Ta 152	209
Appendix A	Service Markings & Colour Schemes	221
Appendix B	Armament carried by the Fw 190 and the Ta 152	230
Appendix C	Fw 190 and Ta 152 Projects and Variants	234
Colour Plates	Between pages	52/53, 116/117, 148/148
Black & White Plates	Between pages	212/213

Introduction

THE FOCKE-WULF Fw 190, the *'Würger'* or 'Butcher Bird', is recognized as one of the most aesthetically attractive, and functionally successful, aircraft of the many that appeared during the course of the Second World War. Dipl. Ing. Kurt Tank, the Technical Director of the *Focke-Wulf Flugzeugbau GmbH.*, achieved success when combining a bulky radial engine with a lightweight, refined, airframe. And that deadly combination was to almost sweep the Supermarine Spitfire Mk V from the skies of Northern Europe in 1941/42. Such was its initial impact on the Royal Air Forces' Fighter Command, that Air Marshal Sholto Douglas, its Commander-in-Chief, issued orders that all sorties over France would be suspended until new tactics could be evolved to deal with the new menace.

In any study of this fighter, arguably the finest produced by Germany for service in the Second World War, there are few people who cannot fail to be impressed by the extraordinary similarity of its development with that of the contemporary British fighter, the Hawker Typhoon. Both were conceived as 'second generation' interceptors with a maximum speed requirement of over 400-mph. Yet while Sydney Camm, a staunch supporter of the liquid-cooled in-line engine, persisted with designs around the Rolls-Royce Vulture (the Hawker Tornado) and the Napier Sabre (the Typhoon) engines, Kurt Tank's successful tender was based on the BMW 139 radial air-cooled engine. An alternative design, with the Daimler-Benz DB 601 in-line, was discarded – almost certainly so as to avoid over-straining the production of that engine, which was already in use with the Messerschmitt Bf 109.

From the outset Tank recognized and achieved the benefits of a thin wing aerofoil section, with the result that the performance and flying characteristics of the Fw 190 bestowed a marked superiority over contemporary Allied fighters in a wide altitude band. The thick wing of the Typhoon proved an impossible handicap in the interceptor rôle above 15,000 ft, and when the development potential of the Sabre engine failed to reach expectations it was decided to change the aircraft's rôle, almost exclusively, to that of ground-attack. It should also be remarked that while the Typhoon excelled in its later rôle, the Focke-Wulf Fw 190 proved readily adaptable in, and master of, a wide range of combat duties.

Before the war had started studies were being made of two Supermarine Spitfire variants which, if the Battle of Britain had not started, would have been ready to cope with the Fw 190. Perhaps, in this context it was fortunate for Focke-Wulf that the campaign of 1940 halted all development of new British fighters. This included the Spitfire Mk III, powered by the Rolls-Royce Series 60 engine for which large contracts were placed, the Spitfire Mk IV, powered by the Rolls-Royce Griffon engine and which, Air Marshal Freeman had declared, would be the next generation fighter after the Spitfire I.

Prologue

Pre-War Strategy

IT WAS a British politician, Stanley Baldwin, Prime Minister of Britain in the years preceding the Second World War, who stated 'The bomber will always get through', and this dogma was widely accepted by the nations of Continental Europe. This statement was also in accord with the military strategy that influenced the leaders of Nazi Germany from their observations of the operations of *Luftwaffe* bombers that had gained their skills when taking part in the air war of Spain's agony of the civil war in the late 'thirties.

These skills were gained at the cost of the slaughter of hundreds of innocent civilians, particularly in the overcrowded cities of Spain. They were further honed during the early months of the Second World War when again the *Luftwaffe* swept from the skies over Poland and destroyed, almost unopposed, that hapless country's small air force. When Germany invaded France in May 1940 the French Air Force suffered a similar fate, albeit they managed to challenge the *Luftwaffe* more successfully.

When the victorious German forces were ready to challenge their strongest opponent, Britain, the German leaders, in particular Adolf Hitler and his commander of the *Luftwaffe*. Hermann Göring, decided that by crushing the Royal Air Force an invasion would be virtually unopposed.

The intention of this decisive campaign, known as the 'Battle of Britain', had been anticipated in the years between the wars and

Baldwin's statement had also taken notice of *Marshall* Douhert's theory. This was that the bomber would get through to its target with an acceptable level of loss, and this was to lead to the establishment of a defence based around the so-called 'Metropolitan Interceptor'.

As a result of this, 'British Interceptor' designs of the period had concentrated on a fighter with the smallest airframe, heavy armament and a fast climbing speed with a combat range limited to a maximum of 250 miles. This philosophy virtually dictated the design of the two British fighters that were to defend primarily the cities of Great Britain, in particular those located in the southern areas. The German bombers did get through, but they paid a heavy price due to a well-planned and organized defence. Britain had inaugurated an infrastructure that established complete support for putting the fighters into the air at the correct moment in time. It also provided bases from which the aircraft could be maintained to the highest levels to support long-term operations. It was this that proved decisive for the successful outcome of the Battle of Britain. Fighter Command was strained to the limit to maintain a strong fighter defence and the battle was hard fought until the *Luftwaffe* accepted defeat and acknowledged that the bomber could be repelled.

The German General Staff had adopted a different approach and used their fighters for duties other than that of pure interceptors. They were also capable of carrying out offensive action for the German army by providing ground-support and attack. This strategy was first tested during World War One with little obvious result and, during the learning period of the Spanish Civil War, the *Luftwaffe* fighters continued to operate the Messerschmitt Bf 109 in that dual rôle.

The ground-support/fighter rôle theory worked well when Germany launched the 'Lightning War', the *Blitzkrieg*, against Poland, Holland, Belgium and France. It was only when the *Luftwaffe* met the RAF Fighter Command over Southern England that the theory was called into question.

The attacking *Luftwaffe* bombers were despatched in great 'waves' over Britain with support from the fighters. Initially the Messerschmitt Bf 109s successfully fought the Spitfire and Hurricane interceptors that had, nevertheless, caused considerable damage to the bombers. The *Luftwaffe* was slowly grinding down the British fighter force but, at a critical moment, Göring altered his tactics by directing his bomber *Geschwaderen* to carry out the destruction of Britain's cities.

The bombers had a long flight from their bases in France to reach the main target London. They had an even longer journey for their attacks on other cities which neccessitated a close fighter support. By the time the target had been reached and after dealing with the RAF forces, the accompanying German fighters were so short of fuel that they had to turn for home before the bombers could press home their attack. This gave RAF Fighter Command the time to assemble its squadrons and the resulting destruction to the attacking bomber forces decimated whole *Geschwaderen* and drastically limited their effectiveness.

When finally the Battle of Britain came to an end the positions of the RAF and German fighters were reversed when Fighter Command launched its sweeps over France. The *Luftwaffe* commanders had absorbed the lessons of the Battle of Britain and early in 1941 had established a strategy of developing fast, well armed interceptors to battle with the attacking British air forces.

CHAPTER ONE

A Company is Born

THE story of the Focke-Wulf Fw 190 and its successor, the Ta 152, is largely the story of designer Kurt Tank. Unlike the enthusiastic support given by the German aviation authorities to his contemporary, Willi Messerschmitt, Tank had a continual 'up-hill' struggle to gain acceptance for his concept of what a fighter's rôle should encompass. Conflict and problems persisted throughout the development of this redoubtable fighter, which, but for its designer's indomitable confidence and tenacious belief, may never have reached the *Luftwaffe* units and achieve the success it did.

A study of the personnel behind the Focke-Wulf company and its history reveals how an idea can be pursued to fulfilment of an ambition.

The company's founding partner, Henrich Focke, was born in Bremen, a port on the northern coast of Germany, on October 8, 1890. Born into a middle-class family – his father, *Dr* Johann Focke was a member of the Senate of Bremen, Henrich had the advantages of a good education and showed a distinct aptitude for practical and technical subjects. When he was of an age to decide his future career he chose engineering, being awarded a coveted place at the Technical High School in Hanover.

Focke graduated in 1913 but his first introduction to aviation was in 1909 when, at the age of eighteen, he aided his brother Wilhelm to design and build a prototype 'pusher-type' aircraft. By September of that year the new machine was ready for its first flight at the Bornstedt Field on the outskirts of Potsdam. The flight was not a success and the aircraft could only leave the ground in a series of ungainly hops. It was back to the drawing board and Henrich's second attempt was his first design, a small glider. This was followed in 1910 by a second powered 'pusher', again designed by his brother, and financed by a couple of friends. It was a small aircraft powered by a tiny eight horse-power NSU engine that had been acquired from yet another friend, Oscar

Henrich Focke in 1909.

Müller. Henrich Focke's technical training had not, apparently, taught him that the weight of the aircraft governs the horse-power required for the engine and it was no surprise when this aircraft also failed to get off the ground.

Although this second attempt at powered flight was a failure Henrich, nevertheless, persisted in his efforts and in 1911, with the aid of a friend, built a new machine. This time the design was a 'tractor' with the engine intended to pull the aircraft rather than push. Unfortunately, Henrich had not learnt from his previous experiences and still persisted in utilising the same NSU 8-hp engine. Although the little plane managed to taxi around the airfield it refused, to Focke's growing dismay, to leave the ground. What was significant about this design, however, was that he had the aid of a young man by the name of Georg Wulf who, at the age of seventeen, was an apprentice engineer. It was the subsequent partnership of these two men that would give the company its name.

With the realisation that flight would never be achieved unless they substantially increased the power of the engine, the two young men were able to persuade Focke's old friend, Oscar Müller, to again come to their rescue. He made available a more powerful Argus 50-hp unit but there was no immediate aircraft in which to install it as, the Argus engine being much heavier than the NSU it required a larger, heavier airframe.

Like many of the aspiring young aeronautically minded young men of the period Focke and his friend Wulf lacked sufficient finance with which to build such an airframe and they had to acquire the funding by hoarding the money they earned during their spare time.

Eventually, in 1912, they were finally successful in accumulating the necessary money and, in the absence of their own design,

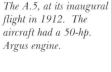

The A.5, at its inaugural flight in 1912. The aircraft had a 50-hp. Argus engine.

decided to take over an aircraft that was being built by other would-be aviators. This aircraft was based upon the *Taube* (Dove), a small, monoplane tractor design and which, after long hours and hard work, was ready for its first flight in November 1912. It was given the designation A.5 (presumably because it was the fifth in their endeavours) and, with the aid of the more powerful engine and the gained experience of design and construction, the new aircraft to their gratification took to the air. With an old friend, Kolthoff who had helped out on Henrich's previous attempts, the A.5 achieved a height of sixteen feet!

Wulf was the first of the duo to learn to fly the A.5 and, despite damaging the monoplane on several occasions and with necessary rebuilding, he gained his pilot's certificate. The two young engineers also took the opportunity of modifying the monoplane between crashes.

At the time when the First World war started Focke had designed and built four new types and after a few months service with the German Army he was posted to the German Flying

Georg Wulf in the cockpit of the A.7.

Corps. He served with the Corps until 1917 when he was invalided out to a post in the Aircraft Ministry as an engineer working on the development of many types of aircraft and gaining valuable experience which was to serve him well in later years.

His partner and friend, Wulf, had also joined the Flying Corps and in 1916 transferred to the prestigious *Flieger-Abteilung 40*. He ended the war, however, in a bomber squadron. Both men had kept in touch and they decided to return to the Technical High School in Hanover where they took advanced engineering studies. Despite the victorious Allies' prohibition on the construction of aeroplanes the two engineers designed and built their first post-war design but it took three long years before they were able to make it public in 1921.

During the aircraft's construction in a cellar of the Focke-Museum in Bremen someone had reported to the French authorities, who had jurisdiction for the Allied administration in that part of Germany, that the 'machine' could well contravene the regulations imposed after the war. Whether Focke and Wulf had time to 'disguise' their efforts or, and rather more plausibly, the French control officer was not totally aware of what they were building, the pair received a hand-written note stating that what they were building 'did not come within Article 202 of the Peace Treaty'. So nonplussed was the French officer, when he had inspected the 'aircraft', he was overheard to say in his fractured German that he could not understand how anyone could possibly fly in such a mess!

The A.16, powered by a 75-hp Siemens engine, was the Focke-Wulf company's first production aircraft. It carried a pilot and three passengers.

After three years of construction, and now armed with an 'official' piece of paper, Focke and Wulf took the new aircraft for its first flight in November 1921. It had been named the A.7 and although the team had difficulty in starting the Argus engine because of the cold Wulf, who was piloting, managed to get it off the ground and reach an altitude of 650 feet. Nothing to the height they had both been used to during their flying experience in the war but, to them, it was the achievement of their dreams. During a storm, some weeks later, the aircraft was damaged but by the summer of the following year it was rebuilt and they resumed flying. Although they considered the Argus engine too heavy for the airframe the aircraft performed satisfactorily and it was registered in December 1922 for 'personal transport'.

This aircraft was to lead to the foundation of the *Focke-Wulf Flugzeubau* when in the latter part of 1923 a group of Bremen businessmen decided to find the funding for a company to build transport aircraft. One of the financiers was *Dr* Ludwig Roselius, the owner of a well-known coffee import and export company called *Kaffee-Hag*. With the company's foundation, on January 1, 1924, Focke was appointed Technical Director and Wulf the company test pilot. Another businessman from Bremen, *Dr* Walter Naumann, became the Commercial Director and it was his business acumen that

The secretly developed S.39 reconnaissance aircraft.

laid the foundations for the company's later success. *Dr* Roselius remained the company's influential Chairman until his death in 1943.

The company's first design, the A.16 completed on June 23, 1924, was a small personal transport that could carry a pilot and three passengers with the aid of a Siemens 75-hp engine. It could reach a speed of 84 mph and, after gaining its civil certificate, it was put into regular service.

Throughout the intervening years until 1932, when he relinquished his position as Technical Director, Focke was responsible for designing 35 types of aircraft which included the clandestine W.4 reconnaissance seaplane for the German military. This was followed by the W.7, the S.39 and the S.40, all reconnaissance land-planes.

Henrich Focke (left) *standing beside the F.19a* Ente. *It was in this aircraft that Georg Wulf lost his life in September 1927.*

In addition the company had produced the A.17 *Möwe* (Gull) and this name was given to its successors the A.29 and the A.38. The original A.16 was succeeded as a personal transport aircraft by the A.20 and A.28 *Habicht* (Hawk), the A.32 *Bussard* (Buzzard), followed by the A.33 *Sperber* (Sparrowhawk). The original A.7 two-seater light-plane spawned the S.1, the S.2 and the S.24. This latter aircraft proved very successful and although only powered by a 60-hp Siemens engine won an endurance flight record of 994.8 miles and a long-range record of 826.4 miles.

In 1926 Focke decided to utilise his brother's designs for the 1908 'pusher' and redesigned it with twin-engines using two Siemens 75-hp engines. This extremely unusual configuration was designated the A.19a *Ente* (Duck) and it was while flying this that Georg Wulf died when the aircraft crashed on September 29, 1927. An air investigation into the accident determined that the crash was caused by the controls breaking and not the eccentric design.

Henrich Focke's last designs for the company were the A.43 *Falke* (Falcon) and the A.47 weather-observation aircraft.

As can be seen it was traditional for all the company's aircraft to be given a bird's name in addition to their designated number and this practice continued throughout Focke-Wulf's existence.

Over the last few years Focke had made it clear to the management of the company that he was more interested in research than design and resigned in November 1931. However, he did not sever his connections with his old company but was appointed a professor of a research centre, within the Focke-Wulf organization, to study the potential of helicopter flight. For this purpose Focke formed a company, the *Focke-Achgelis* Company, with a former German aerobatics champion, Gerd Achgelis.

Focke's increasing preoccupation with helicopter designs led to the appointment of a new Chief Designer, Kurt Tank. At around the same period the company had also taken over the old *Albatros* company that had found themselves in continuing financial difficulties. This proved a very successful marriage as Focke-Wulf's management were commercially sound and soon turned the situation around. In addition to the traditions and ethos of building 'fighter' aircraft Focke-Wulf also acquired new engineers and designers, such as *Dr* Cassens and *Dr* Müller as well as *Dipl. Ing.* R Blaser who eventually became head of the Fw 190 development.

The Focke-Wulf company was suddenly developing into a major aircraft manufacturer and needed to get their operational structure streamlined to meet all eventualities. His qualities recognized, Kurt Tank was soon made Technical Director to replace Henrich Focke and it was he who was to transform the activities of the company. Under his guidance the company grew from a small, under-capitalised concern into a giant that became one of the main suppliers of military aircraft to the newly formed *Luftwaffe*.

CHAPTER TWO

Kurt Tank – The Fw 190's Mastermind

ALTHOUGH, it can be said, the Focke-Wulf company had proved to be a success over the first eight years (1924 – 1932) of its existence, output of aircraft was relatively low key and while many different aircraft were being designed and produced individual production figures were quite small. Now, with the inclusion of the Albatros company, the accompanying acquisition of first-rate designers and engineers, it was necessary to turn what had been a workshop into a factory.

Kurt Tank, the Chief Designer Focke-Wulf had appointed the year previously, was now given the position of Technical Director to replace Henrich Focke. Tank's dynamism was to infect the company and he exerted great influence on its future operations. Through him Focke-Wulf entered into new designs and manufacturing that, over the subsequent years, turned the company into a leading and innovative producer of aircraft that culminated with the Fw 190.

Tank was born in Bromberg, West Prussia, on February 24, 1898. His father, until 1905, had been a professional soldier in a grenadier regiment and retired from active service as a sergeant to became a hydraulic engineer. His father's new career was to have a great influence on Kurt Tank especially his youthful observations on how the currents of water, flowing in the local river, affected the flow of objects floating on the surface. Soon his imagination led him from paper boats to paper 'planes as he realised that air had similar properties to that of water.

At the age of sixteen, at the outbreak of The Great War (1914 – 1918), Kurt volunteered for the German Army. During his four years service he was wounded several times, received innumerable

decorations and, when hostilities ended, had become an officer
with the 71st Infantry Regiment. The Treaty of Versailles had,
amongst many other conditions, redrawn the boundaries of
Germany and what had once been the Tank family home was now
in Polish territory. His father was able to obtain a position as a
hydraulic engineer based in Potsdam, a small town close to Berlin,
and it was here that Kurt returned to study engineering at the
Technical High School in Berlin-Charlottenburg.

His choice would have been aerodynamics but as this was not
recognized as a subject at the time he decided to study electrical
engineering. In 1919 he attended the Technical High School as a
full time student with Professor Moritz Weber being his senior tutor
in mechanics. At the same time, to gain practical experience, he
worked at *Orenstein u. Koppel*, a locomotive factory based in the
Spandau suburb of Berlin. It was during this time that he met his
future wife, Charlotte Teufel – they married in September 1923.

Kurt Tank

Kurt's first interest, aerodynamics, was never far from his thoughts and although the Versailles Treaty had banned powered flying he and three fellow students of similar mind decided that a glider would enable them to study their cherished subject.

Mainly because of the prohibitions of the peace treaty many would-be aviators in Germany formed or joined glider clubs. So prolific did these clubs become that, during the 'twenties and 'thirties, Germany could boast many international champions and a large number of the young members subsequently formed the backbone of the *Luftwaffe* when it was established following Hitler's take-over of power in 1933.

Tank and his friends soon obtained permission from their High School authorities to convert one of the unused rooms into a workshop where they could design and build, in model form, the gliders that would, hopefully, be converted into full-scale. Although, at first, little more than a discussion group with ideas floating about, the 'club' revelled under the name of *Akademische Fliegergruppe Berlin*, but its members conducted their affairs with professionalism and enthusiasm.

Within a short space of time Kurt Tank had designed his first glider. It was aerodynamically tested in model form and all that was left was to convert this into a full-scale glider. Being students the required finance for such a project was not available and so Tank and a friend, Gillert, decided that they would approach an established manufacturer and *allow* them to build their 'brain-child'. The company chosen was the redoubtable *Albatros Werke* based in the Johannisthal suburb of Berlin and who, after their past glories, were now producing gliders.

Dipl. Ing. Rudolf Schubert was the Technical Director of Albatros at the time, having replaced *Dipl. Ing.* Robert Thelen on the latter's retirement. Both these men had been responsible for the design and development of the Albatros C- and D- series of aircraft that had been flown by many of Germany's 'aces', to great effect, during The Great War. Unfortunately, Schubert lacked the drive and vision that Thelen had shown and although he was an excellent designer he was clearly more at home as a subordinate. It was largely due to his direction, or lack of, that the Albatros company started to decline.

True to form he professed to see no merit in Tank's design or, more likely, the company's financial situation would not allow funding for a project that was from an untried and as yet untested group of young men. Tank made several more attempts at convincing Schubert but, after much prevarication on the latter's behalf, he could see it was of no use.

Not to be daunted Tank had now named his glider *Teufelchen* (Little Devil) after his fiancée, Charlotte Teufel, and approached another aircraft manufacturer. The LFG (*Luftfahrzeug Gesellschaft*) company had gained a reputation in The Great War for their Roland aircraft and they quickly took up Tank's designs and decided to build it at their Stralsund factory. In its constructed state, in 1923, the glider was taken to a competition where, with Tank flying, it achieved success. Unfortunately, it subsequently crashed in bad weather and LFG declined to rebuild it.

However, Tank had proved to himself and to his tutors that his designs were viable, and it gave him the impetus to finish his education and qualify. With the help of his mechanics tutor, Weber, he secured a position as an aerodynamics engineer with the Rohrbach Aircraft Company and was soon involved in his earlier interests, hydrodynamics. The company had, for some time, been

A Turkish example of the Rohrbach Ro IIIa built in Denmark.

engaged in designing and building flying-boats and one of Tank's first projects with his new company was to improve the performance of the Ro III's hull. This new design was to be called the Ro IIIa or, phonetically, 'Rodra' (Ro-drei-A).

Again under the Versailles Treaty agreement no German company was allowed to build powered aircraft and so, in common with other companies, Rohrbach manufactured the parts in Berlin and shipped them to their subsidiary company in Denmark for assembly. In many ways the Treaty was a nonsense, as most of the signatories were aware. These 'backdoor' operations were not only tolerated they were positively encouraged as it was not considered

Ernst Udet

'unethical' for any country, even those that had defeated Germany in The Great War and imposed the restrictions, to supply necessary parts. In the case of the 'Rodra' Rohrbach were supplied with the Rolls-Royce 'Eagle' engines by Britain who, further, purchased two completed aircraft.

Tank was sent to Denmark to supervise the aircraft's construction and it was during this time that he learnt to fly. He was considered an excellent pilot and, not content with merely designing the machine, he insisted also on test flying them. In Denmark at that time, also testing aircraft, was an '*Alte Adler*' of The Great War, Ernst Udet. Tank and Udet became firm friends and this friendship lasted until Udet's untimely death in 1941.

It was while at Rohrbach that Tank introduced several new concepts that would revolutionise aircraft manufacture and earn him the gratitude of pilots then and in future years. Many civil aircraft had, hitherto, been equipped with open cockpits, which were, inevitably, susceptible to all elements of the weather. The pilots continually complained of this but it was left to Tank to construct the first 'greenhouse' canopy and attach it to the Rohrbach 'Roland'. He approached *Lufthansa*, the national airline, only to be told by its senior management that it was undesirable and the pilots would not be able to operate the aircraft properly! A number of the canopies were constructed by Rohrbach but, with the failure to get them accepted by *Lufthansa*, they were put into stock. Almost forgotten and gathering dust the canopies remained

The Rohrback 'Roland' showing the enclosed 'greenhouse' cockpit that Kurt Tank designed to protect the pilots.

in the company's storeroom until a chance remark made by Hans Baur to Tank resurrected the idea. Baur, who became Hitler's personal pilot, was, at this time, a flight captain with *Lufthansa* flying the Rohrbach 'Roland' and had told Tank how cold it became in the cockpit when flying over the Alps. Tank informed Baur that he already had the solution to this but that *Lufthansa* had turned it down. The 'Greenhouse' was in stock but the only way Baur could get one was to order it privately. Baur ordered two and when other 'Roland' pilots were made aware that they too could fly in relative comfort and warmth they also put in their orders. Soon all 'Rolands' were equipped with cockpit canopies forcing other manufacturers to do likewise.

Another innovation that was to become standard on aircraft was Tank's design for wheel-brakes, first fitted on the Beardmore-Rohrbach 'Inflexible'. This aircraft although of German design was built in Scotland by William Beardmore and was considered, at the time, to be the largest aircraft in the world.

Although Tank was happy at Rohrbach and achieved great success for their civil flying-boat development it became increasingly obvious that he wanted to put his ideas on the design of 'land-planes' into operation. He left Rohrbach in 1929 but remained good friends with the company's founder *Dr* Rohrbach for whom he had the greatest admiration. Leaving Denmark, from where he had been operating over the last few years, Tank returned to Germany as Chief Designer for the *Bayerische Flugzeugwerke* in Augsburg, Bavaria. Unfortunately, this coincided with the post-war financial difficulties that were to effect most countries and result in the Depression period. Because of its economic fragility Germany was one of the first countries to experience the inflationary aspects and many companies either disappeared or had to make swathing cuts in personnel and operations. Fortuitously, as it turned out, Tank made yet another move when, on November 1, 1931, he joined Focke-Wulf.

When Focke-Wulf had taken over the Albatros company they found that many of the aircraft designs were now obsolete. One that had survived, the L.101, had originally been designed by the aforementionrd Rudolf Schubert, but it was found to have a weakness in the wing construction. After modification this aircraft went into limited production to become a trainer for the new

Luftwaffe. Similarly the L.102, although this aircraft had an inauspicious start when it crashed while being flight-tested by Kurt Tank. The crash occurred when Tank experienced violent vibrations of the ailerons. This resulted in an extreme distortion of the starboard wing and this, in turn, effected the aerodynamics of the aircraft. As with the L.101 the wings were strengthened and it too became a trainer for the *Luftwaffe* under the designation Fw 55.

With the Nazi take-over of power in 1933 and the open establishment of a national air force, Focke-Wulf, in common with other aircraft manufacturers, lost no time in contacting the new Minister of Aviation, Erhard Milch. Impressed by the new team of

The Fw 44 'Steiglitz'. This aircraft was Focke-Wulf's first big success. it was used as a trainer by the Luftwaffe *and many flying clubs throughout the world.*

design and construction engineers that Tank was putting together for Focke-Wulf, Milch made it clear that the company would, in due course, receive orders for development.

In the meantime Tank kept the company busy by looking at some of the designs that Henrich Focke had been working on just prior to his departure. Some like the Fw 40, the Fw 43 and the Fw 47, a weather observation aircraft, had limited appeal but the Fw 44 had much more potential.

The first prototype of the Fw 44 '*Steiglitz*' (Goldfinch) had originally been flight-tested by Gerd Achgelis prior to his leaving the company to form a new one with Henrich Focke. After Tank had carried out his own flight-tests – over a hundred hours – he was greatly impressed with the aircraft's capabilities and decided that it should go into production. The aircraft was a great success and toured with a German aerobatics team that visited the United States. With Ernst Udet, the veteran pilot and friend of Tank, singing its praises the Fw 44 soon became the choice for many aerobatics pilots throughout the world. The Steiglitz made Focke-Wulf's reputation in the mid-'thirties with over 1,000 aircraft being produced. So popular was this aircraft with aerobatics pilots that some were still performing twenty-five years after the end of World War II.

While developing some of the designs he had inherited, Tank was also working hard on his own ideas. His first design for Focke-Wulf was the Fw 56 '*Stösser*' – a bird of prey. This high-wing

The Fw 56 'Stösser'
Kurt Tank's first design for
the Focke-Wulf company.
On Ernst Udet's
recommendation
this aircraft became the
fore-runner of
the dive bomber.

monoplane was again a success with the aerobatics teams as its high manoeuvrability and diving qualities proved valuable in competition and, indeed, was to play a part in the *Luftwaffe*'s decision to equip itself with dive-bombers.

In 1936 Tank's friend, Ernst Udet, had become *Generalluftzeugmeister* of the *Luftwaffe* with the rank of *Generalmajor*. This position meant that he was also in charge of their Technical

Office, the body that evaluated and recommended various types of aircraft for service use. The previous year Udet had been in the United States and was given a demonstration by the US Navy of their Curtiss 'Helldiver'. So impressed was he with the American dive-bombers and their ability to pin-point their targets that, on his return to Germany, he made recommendations to the Air Ministry that they too should consider this type for inclusion in the *Luftwaffe*'s armoury. At that time the suggestion was turned down

Generalmajor
Ernst Udet, the new
Generalluftzeugmeister,
seen here in conversation
with
Willi Messerschmitt.

by the air authorities as totally unorthodox and contrary to the strategies already in place. Knowing of Tank's new design Udet arranged to put it through its paces himself. With the help of Tank he had two bomb racks installed under the aircraft wings that would allow 110-lb. 'cement' bombs to be carried. Within a short period of time Udet was able to make repeated 'dive-bomb' attacks with great accuracy and thus the *Sturzkampfflugdeug* (Stuka) was conceived.

On his promotion Udet was in a position to resurrect these ideas and promptly invited *Generalleutnant* Walther Wever, the Chief of the Air Staff, and other senior officers to a demonstration of the Fw 56 'dive-bomber'. Although an advocate of the 'big bomber', Wever was impressed with the high accuracy of the bombing and conceded that it was greater than anything the 'big bomber' could achieve.

Following this several aircraft manufacturers, including Arado, Blohm & Voss, Heinkel and Junkers, were given development orders for a single-engine 'dive-bomber'. Focke-Wulf, although they had provided the demonstration aircraft, were not included as they had no previous experience of building all-metal aircraft. As is well known Junkers, from this start, went on to develop their Ju 87 which became notorious in the '*Blitzkrieg*' campaigns.

The Fw 57V1. Focke-Wulf's design for the RLM's requirement for a Zerstörer *(Destroyer) aircraft.*

Somewhat incensed by not being on the list of contractors Tank took the next opportunity available to produce an all-metal aircraft, the Fw 57. This was in response to a General Staff requirement for a 'heavy fighter' or '*Zerstörer*' (Destroyer). Although both Focke-Wulf and Henschel, who produced the Hs 124, were in the competition it was Messerschmitt with their Bf 110 that was eventually given the

The Fw 159V3.

contract.

Next, from the Focke-Wulf stable, came the Fw 58 '*Weihe*' (Harrier), the first German trainer with a retractable undercarriage. This was soon followed by the Fw 159, Tank's response to the Air Staff's requirement for a single-seat fighter.

The specifications for this new fighter called for an all-metal, single-seat, monoplane with retractable undercarriage. Tank was perfectly aware that the competing manufacturers, Arado (Ar 80), Heinkel (He 112), and the ultimate winner, *Bayerische Flugzeugwerke* with their Bf 109, were building aircraft with a low or mid-wing construction. But, on the suggestion of the air authorities, he

The Fw 159V1.

decided to utilise the configuration of the successful Fw 56 'Stösser' – a parasol one-piece wing.

Tank's design and development team, led by *Ing.* Blaser who subsequently headed the team responsible for the Fw 190, incorporated many refinements that, in many ways, were in advance of those provided for the ultimate winner, the Bf 109. But one problem that the parasol wing presented was where to house the retractable undercarriage? The only position available was on the forward underside of the fuselage and this had great limitations. The design team came up with an extremely ingenious method of 'double-jointed' main legs that enabled them to retract within a space in the fuselage no bigger than the circumference of the wheel. Although this was successfully tested on the bench time and time again, when it came to the flight trials an inherent weakness was found. The aircraft had taken off and the undercarriage had retracted perfectly within its housing in the fuselage. Wolfgang Stein, the pilot, then proceeded to carry out all the flying tests and prepared to land. Stein lowered the undercarriage, which to the onlookers on the ground appeared successful, but a light in the cockpit indicated that the legs had failed to lock. Stein immediately gained height and made several more attempts at lowering the wheels, but to no avail. Stein had only completed 30 minutes of flying time and still retained enough fuel for another 90 minutes flight. With no means to jettison the remaining load Stein had to circle the airfield until the fuel-tank was practically empty. In the meantime, and with no R/T equipment, Tank and others on the ground tried to relay some suggestions to the pilot by writing them with white-wash on the concrete surface of the airfield. It was with trepidation that Stein landed the aircraft with the undercarriage still only partly extended and the inevitable happened. On contact with the ground the legs snapped causing the aircraft to somersault and finally come to rest on its back. Stein, miraculously, was not injured but the prototype Fw 159 was completely destroyed.

Thus ended Tank's first endeavours to provide the *Luftwaffe* with a single-seat fighter although the lessons learnt proved invaluable when the next opportunity to build a fighter came along.

Three more notable pre-war designs came from Tank's drawing board, the Fw 187, the Fw 189 and the Fw 200. The Fw 187 *'Falke'*

The Fw 187A-0 prototype.

(Falcon) was an elegant twin-engine, single-seat fighter that although resembling the Me 110 had superior speed and comparable armament. Unfortunately, at that time, the Air Ministry's requirement was for a two-seater and the team at Focke-Wulf enlarged, slightly, the 'greenhouse' cockpit in order to accommodate the additional crew member. Although the *Reichsluftfahrtministerium* (RLM) ordered several of this aircraft for evaluation purposes they ultimately decided that the Me 110 would continue to satisfy their requirements and that there was no need to introduce a replacement.

The Fw 189 '*Eule*' (Owl) was Focke-Wulf's answer to the RLMs specification for a tactical reconnaissance aircraft that could carry three crew members and offer all-round defensive cover. Although the requirement was for a much higher performance, the new designs were intended for the replacement of the Heinkel He 46. To the surprise of RLMs Technical Office, who had envisaged a single-engined aircraft, Kurt Tank submitted designs for a *twin*-engined, *twin*-boomed machine with a centrally positioned fuselage nacelle that could certainly be called a 'greenhouse'. After the initial shock it was pointed out that the specifications merely stated the

The Fw 189V1

desired power level but not that it could only be achieved with a single engine. However, it was shown, in a flying demonstration to the *Luftwaffe* authorities, just how versatile and adaptable Tank's unorthodox configuration could be and a development contract was awarded to Focke-Wulf in April 1937 – although the RLM, by way of 'hedging-their-bets', also awarded a similar contract to Arado for its more conventional design, the Ar 198.

After a number of prototypes that included many modifications a production order was given, in the spring of 1940, for the Fw 189A. This aircraft did, indeed, prove versatile and its variants performed invaluable service, for the next four years, in all theatres of operations conducted by the German forces.

The Focke-Wulf Fw 200 '*Condor*' was conceived as an idea in early 1936 when Kurt Tank held discussions with *Dr* Stüssel, a director of *Deutsche Lufthansa*. Tank had long believed in the viability of transatlantic passenger travel and talked of such to Stüssel who could readily see the advantages for his own airline. The subsequent designs took shape, by the summer of that year, in the form of a fuselage mock-up that included high aspect ratio wings able to carry four engines. Tank had so convinced the directors of *Lufthansa* that in July of the same year a development contract, signed by *Freiherr* von Gablenz, the chief executive of *Lufthansa*, and *Dr* Stüssel, its technical director, was placed with Focke-Wulf. On the successful completion of the first prototype's flight trials a production order was given to the company by *Lufthansa*.

The Fw 200V3 Immelmann III which became Adolf Hitler's personal transport.

Several Fw 200 '*Condors*' were successfully employed as transatlantic, and other 'long-haul', airliners but with the coming of the war the RLM could also see the potential of this large, four-

One of the early Fw 200C-0 transport Condors (Nr 021) taken over by the Luftwaffe.

engined aircraft. The Fw 200C series was developed for military use and many of the early production aircraft saw service with *I Gruppe/Kampfgeschwader* 40 (I./KG40), a *Luftwaffe* unit formed to bomb shipping in the North Sea and the Atlantic, particularly in the Bay of Biscay area.

CHAPTER THREE

The New Generation Fighter

As the National Socialist Party, under Adolf Hitler, gradually usurped power, the initially slow expansion of the military now increased rapidly, in particular that of the new *Luftwaffe*. Focke-Wulf was one of the many companies that applied to the new Government for orders, and was eventually awarded a contract for the design and development of three prototype advanced trainers. It was successful, as has been related, and a total of 1,000 were delivered before production ended. Kurt Tank had also established himself as a successful designer.

His most famous, and well-known design was, without question, the superlative Fw 190 '*Würger*' (Shrike – also known as the 'Butcher Bird'). When the Messerschmitt Bf 109 entered mass production in 1936 the *Reichsluftfahrtministerium* (RLM) had also ordered design studies for its eventual replacement, little realising that the nimble fighter would remain in production longer than any other aircraft – fighter or bomber.

Kurt Tank's studies of Messerschmitt's design, the Bf 109, convinced him that he could produce a more superior fighter than any other company's submission by paying careful study to the aerodynamic advantages of a thin section wing and closely cowled engine. He also proposed to adopt a wide track, 'inward' retracting undercarriage, rather than the 'outward' one adopted by Messerschmitt and which was to prove a weakness of the Bf 109.

However, in 1937 the RLM had committed themselves to the development of the Messerschmitt Bf 109, that was to enter the *Luftwaffe* in 1938 and whose performance included a top speed of about 350-mph which was roughly equal to that of the British

Spitfire. The ever-advancing demands by the *Luftwaffe* authorities then centred upon increased performance and heavier gun armament. A specification was, therefore, issued in September 1937 by the RLM to *Focke-Wulf Flugzeugbau*, not committed at that

Oberingenieur
R Blaser

time to a major military project, that laid emphasis on performance and handling improvements over the Bf 109. Kurt Tank accordingly submitted project schemes for alternative designs of which one, incorporating the 1,550-hp. BMW 139 radial engine, was selected for prototype development. This, despite the RLM preference for an in-line, liquid cooled engine such as the Daimler Benz 601. Focke-Wulf subsequently received a contract for three prototypes and these were to be given the RLM number, 190.

The experimental design effort was led by *Oberingenieur* Blaser and commenced during the summer of 1938. With RLM still committed to the production of the Bf 109 for front-line service there was no initial haste required by Focke-Wulf although this was soon to change. As the Bf 109 became integrated with the *Luftwaffe*'s fighter groups and battle conditions were soon experienced serious problems with the aircraft became apparent. The *Reichsluftfahrt-ministerium* therefore gave Tank instructions to speed-up the development of the Fw 190 as it was becoming apparent that it may be required sooner than originally intended. So short was the period of development now given to Focke-Wulf that those involved with the project found themselves working around the clock. Although these extreme pressures had a detrimental effect on Blaser's health he managed to complete the first prototype within the time-scale insisted on by the RLM.

The Fw 190V1 ready for its second test flight. It has been fitted with machine-guns in the wing roots and now carried the civil registration D-OPZE.

On June 1, 1939, the first prototype, the Fw 190V1 with the *Werk Nr* 0001 and the civil registration D-OPZE, was taken for its first test flight with Focke-Wulf's chief test pilot Hans Sander at the controls. Despite its bulky engine cowl, which housed the 18-cylinder, two-in-row, 1,550-hp BMW 139 radial engine with a ducted spinner, the aircraft was designed very much with aerodynamics in mind. The thin leading-edge cantilever wing allowed for speed and high manoeuvrability in the air. The overall wingspan for this first prototype was 31 ft 2½ inches giving a total wing area of 160.67 sq. ft. The length, from spinner to the trailing edge of the rudder, was 28 ft 7 inches and a gross weight of 6,100 lbs.

After this initial flight four more were made, during which period Sander reported that he considered the engine performance to be below par. It was decided to replace the ducted spinner with a normal smooth one thus giving the Fw 190 its highly recognisable profile. The aircraft was, on completion of these flight tests, handed over to the *Luftwaffe* for service trials at their Rechlin *Erprobungsstelle* (test centre) and given the *Luftwaffe* registration FO+LY. The *Luftwaffe* pilots were favourably impressed with the Fw 190's handling qualities and acceleration capabilities but also encountered the inherent problem of poor forward visibility when taxiing, a problem that was to prove fatal

The Fw 190V1 in early 1940 with its replacement spinner and now with Luftwaffe *markings and registration FO+LY.*

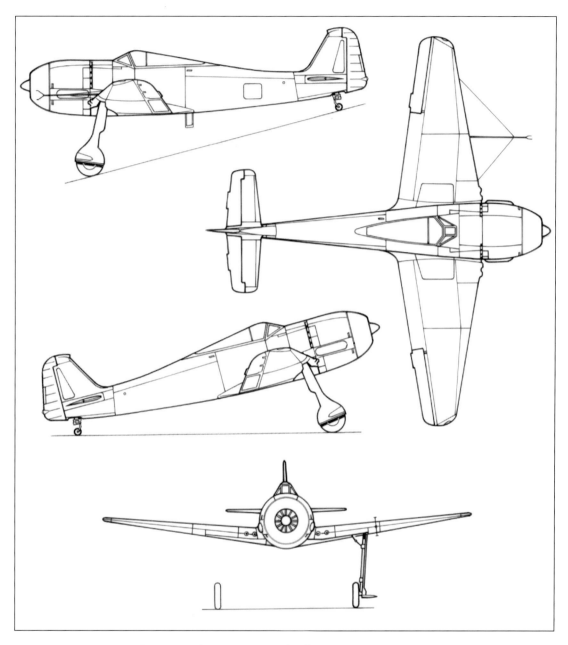

for some inexperienced pilots.

The second prototype, the Fw 190V2 with the *Luftwaffe* registration FO+LZ, was ready for flight in October 1939. It was armed with two 7.9-mm MG 17 and two 13-mm MG 131 guns, but this aircraft was lost following a crankshaft failure after 50 flying hours. Continuing flight trials with the Fw 190V1, which achieved

a top speed of 370-mph, were of sufficient promise to prompt a development contract for the manufacture of eighteen pre-production Fw 190A-0 aircraft and further development of prototypes. After the V2, subsequent aircraft were powered by the 14-cylinder BMW 801C engine of 1,600-hp which necessitated a strengthened mounting structure. At the same time the cockpit was located approximately eleven inches further aft to compensate for the increased engine weight. While this went some way in alleviating the high cockpit temperatures that were

The Fw 190V5k with the reduced wing span.

Fw 190V5g (Werk Nr 0015) with the increased wing span. The aircraft was fitted with the ill-fated BMW 801 engine and smoke discoloration can be seen around the engine cowling due to overheating.

Another view of the Fw 190V5k also showing smoke discoloration.

noted during the earlier trials it did, unfortunately, add to the already restricted ground vision for the pilot.

Development of the Fw 190V3 and V4 was discontinued as, with the arrival of the BMW 801C engine, there were too many modifications to be made which made both projects impractical. The engine was, therefore, first installed in the Fw 190V5k (k – *kleine Flügel*, small wing), this prototype retained the 31 ft 2½ inches (short) span of the earlier aircraft. The V5k was flown during the spring of 1940 (at about the same time as the Typhoon prototype) and was followed quickly by the V5g (g – *große Flügel*, large wing) which featured wider wings of 34 ft 5½ inches span. The latter possessed a top speed of 408-mph, about six mph less than that of the V5k, but the increased wingspan allowed for better flying characteristics in both handling and manoeuvrability.

Following the order for eighteen pre-production Fw 190A-0 fighters Focke-Wulf had extended their assembly line and started to manufacture the airframes. Two of these airframes, based on the configuration of the V5g and numbered 0006 and 0007 respectively, were designated Fw 190V6 and Fw 190V7. The V6 was initially unarmed but the V7 was fully representative of the initial *Luftwaffe* version, and was fitted with two 7.9-mm MG 17 machine-guns located on the upper fuselage and forward of the cockpit. Both guns were synchronised to fire through the propeller and could be directly sighted by the pilot through the

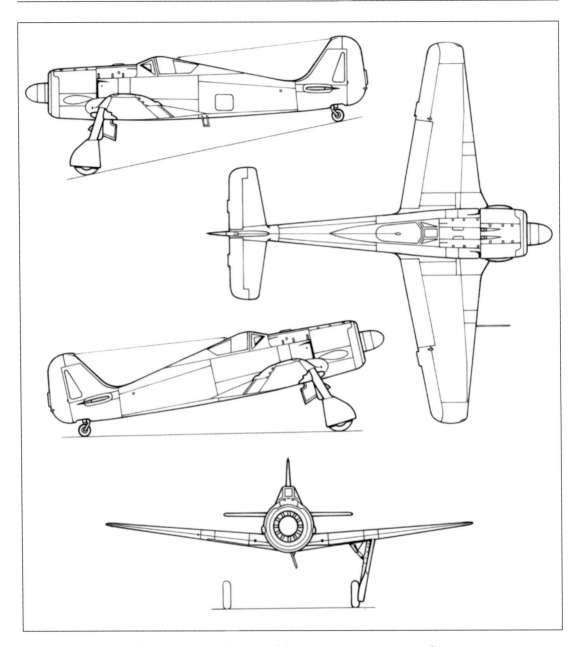

windscreen. In addition two similar machine-guns were mounted, one each side, in the wing-roots for which a Revi C/12C reflector sight was fitted. After successful flight trials in October 1940 the V7 entered firing trials at the *Waffenprüfplatz* (weapon proving grounds) at Tarnewitz. Manufacturer's trials continued on this aircraft while the V5g came to be used as an engine development

Fw 190A-0 was applied to the first seven airframes. This plan shows the reduced wing surface.

test bed for such power-plants as the BMW 801D and E, the Daimler Benz 603A and G, and the Junkers Jumo 213A and F. The V5k was destroyed in a take-off collision with a tractor, an accident almost totally attributable to the poor forward vision. Meanwhile, manufacture and assembly of the remaining sixteen Fw 190A-0 pre-production aircraft got under way towards the end of 1940, the first seven aircraft (*Werk Nr* 0008 to 0014) displaying the short-span wings. Thereafter, and throughout the production of the Fw 190A-1, the 34 ft 5½ inches wings were standardised. However, only the first two Fw 190A-0 aircraft were fitted with the BMW 801C-0 engine, 0010 and subsequent A-0s were fitted with the production BMW 801C-1 engine.

Construction

Wings. Cantilever monoplane built in one piece with the front spar continuous and passing through the fuselage to which it was attached at three points, two on the upper flanges and one to the lower. The rear spar was built in two sections, the roots attached to the fuselage sides by pin-joints. A two spar wing structure with widely spaced flange plate rib formers. Span-wise 'Z' section and a stressed metal outer skin. The spars were built up of flanged plates *'Small wing' Fw 190.* which, inboard from the ailerons, were reinforced by 'L' section

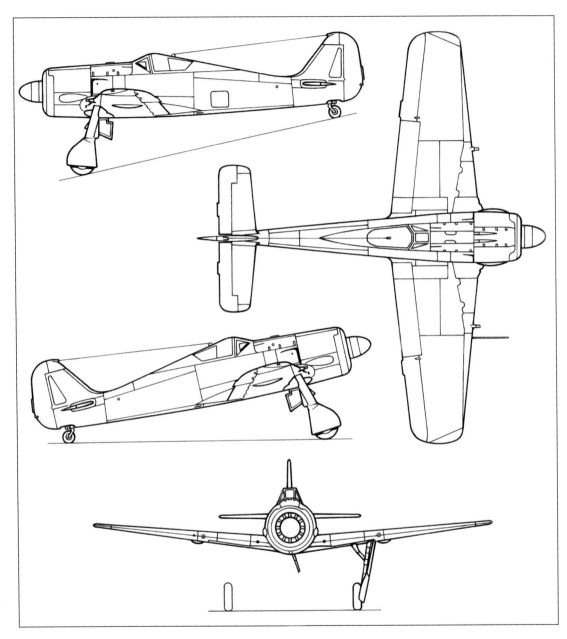

extrusions and progressively thickened cap-strips to form 'T' *Fw 190A-0*
section members. Outboard of the ailerons the spars had single *with its final*
airframe
integral flanges. The front spar from the points of attachment of the *configuration.*
landing gear to the upper attachments to the fuselage cranked
inwards. The undercarriage when retracted lay ahead of the front
spar. The guns and landing gear had specially strengthened ribs.
Both the ailerons and split trailing edge flaps were metal-framed

and fabric covered. The flaps were electrically operated and contolled by three buttons on the left of the cockpit console. At take-off a yellow button was selected to give a 10-degree elevation while for landing a green button initiated a 60-degree angle. The third button, coloured red, was used to raise the flaps to a normal flying position. To achieve these preset flap settings the buttons had to be totally pressed and locked but intermediate settings could be made by depressing the relevant buttons without locking them.

Fuselage. All metal monocoque structure built up from bulkheads, flanged formers, 'Z' section stringers and a smooth, riveted stressed outer skin. The front inverted 'U' shaped bulkhead was attached to the upper flanges of the front spar, and on the front face of the bulkhead and spar were five attachments for the engine mounting, three on the spar and two on the bulkhead. All other bulkheads and frames conformed to the cross section. The extreme rear section was integral with the fin and detachable from the main structure in one piece. Large detachable panels in the underside of the fuselage extended from the engine bay to the rear of the cockpit to allow installation and removal of the fuel tanks. The pilot seat was armoured, the cockpit canopy could be jettisoned and had a bullet-proof windscreen. Fuel 272-gallons.

Tail Unit. Cantilever monoplane type with the fin integral with the rear fuselage. Electrically operated, adjustable, single spar tailplane. All metal frames with metal covered tailplane and fin.

A pre-production Fw 190A-0 (Werk Nr 0025) being evaluated by II./JG 26.

Fabric covered elevators and rudder. Fixed, perforated trim tabs in rudder and elevators. Fin rear fuselage section housed the electrical incidence gear for lowering rear landing-gear wheel.

Undercarriage. Electrically operated retractable type with main undercarriage legs hinged ahead of the front wing spar. It retracted inwards. Fairings on legs and on wheels and on under surface of the wings closing the apertures when the wheels were raised. The tail-wheel was partially retractable by a cable attached to the starboard oleo leg. The tail-wheel had a spring centering and a centre lock, the latter operating when the control column was pulled back hard.

Engine. One 1,600-hp BMW 801C fourteen cylinder, two-in-row radial, air-cooled geared and supercharged unit in low drag cowling with induced fan cooling. The engine unit, complete with oil cooler, was attached to the front bulkhead and spar face by five bolts. Protected fuel tanks beneath the cockpit floor. Oil tank holding 10 Imperial gallons in fuselage. Reverse flow oil coolers in annular ring forming the cowling leading edge. VDM propeller with electrical pitch change and three metal blades.

After the Fw 190A-0s testing at the *Luftwaffe*'s *Erprobungsstelle* at Rechlin the RLM decided that before it entered operational service it should be further tested by experienced pilots from a front-line unit.

Two pilots from *Jagdgeschwader* 26 '*Schlageter*', then commanded by *Oberstleutnant* Adolf Galland, were selected. *Oberleutnant* Otto Behrens, the *Staffelkapitän* of 6./JG 26, and *Oberleutnant* Karl Borris, together with approximately thirty engineers and mechanics, arrived in Rechlin towards the end of March, 1941. Two more experienced pilots could not have been chosen as they had both started their careers in the *Luftwaffe* as mechanics, going on to become pilots and promoted officers.

They immediately started a program of intensive flight-testing and soon became impressed with the aircraft's undoubtable handling and performance capabilities. One problem that did persist was with the engine as its reliability was 'temperamental' at best. On innumerable occasions Behrens and Borris were forced to cut their flight test short as the engine started to overheat and emit smoke that billowed from the cowling vents. The early BMW

801 engines, when they first came into service, had not been fitted with cooling fans and, after about twenty hours of flying time, the engines started to seriously overheat and misfire. A cooling fan was fitted which provided considerable improvement but still did

Karl Borris, seen here as a Hauptmann, *later became* Kommandeur *of I./JG 26 and went on to win the Knight's Cross with a victory score of 43.*

not allow for total reliability – this was only achieved two years later with the installation of a 'command' device, or *Kommandogerät*.

A large wing Fw 190A-0 (Werk Nr 0022) fitted with a SC 250 bomb for Jabo tests.

This ingenious and brilliantly engineered device was electro-hydraulically operated and automatically adjusted the fuel flow and mixture proportions to suit the altitude at which the aircraft was flying. In addition it also adjusted the ignition and propeller pitch settings, and automatically allowed for the second stage cut-in of the supercharger. All this could be operated by a single throttle control that also incorporated a switch that allowed the pilot to over-ride it should he want to manually adjust the propeller pitch setting.

Unfortunately, this control unit was some time in the future and the continuing problems of the overheating engine soon had the RLM considering whether to abandon the Fw 190 fighter program. It was largely due to the unreserved enthusiasm of Benrens and Borris, who had included comparison flight-tests against a number of captured Allied fighters, that the Air Ministry finally relented when they considered the reports that showed the Fw 190s superiority.

CHAPTER FOUR

The 'Butcher Bird' Enters Service

By MID-1941 the war situation of the Third Reich represented the zenith of Nazi fortunes. Hitler was about to embark upon his ultimately catastrophic Russian adventure in the East. Axis fortunes in North Africa were at least temporarily loaded in Germany's favour, and maritime pressure on the British Isles was gaining a stranglehold that seemed capable of eliminating any threat of attack in the West. The German daylight air attacks on Britain had been blunted in 1940, and the night *Blitz* against British cities was discontinued in May 1941 with the redeployment of *Kampfgeschwaderen* to the East in readiness for Operation *Barbarossa*.

The only two fighter units deployed in Western Europe were *Jagdgeschwader* 2 '*Richthofen*', at that time commanded by *Oberstleutnant* Harry von Bülow-Bothkamp and based in the north-west Brest/Cherbourg sector, and Adolf Galland's *Jagdgeschwader* 26 '*Schlageter*'. These two *Geschwaderen* were equipped with Messerschmitt Bf 109Fs, an excellent aeroplane, but one of no more than parity with the Spitfire Vb, of which RAF Fighter Command had large numbers. It was the shift towards RAF ascendancy in the skies over France and the Low Countries that prompted the *Oberkommando der Luftwaffe* (OKL) to urgently request delivery of the early Fw 190A-1s to JG 26, based at the Abbeville/St Omer airfield complex in north-east France during July 1941.

Oblt Borris and *Oblt* Behrens were instructed, in August 1941, to fly a number of the Fw 190A-1s to Le Bourget, an airfield on the outskirts of Paris. With the help of *Stabsingenieur* Ernst Battmer, the Technical Officer of JG 26, the aircraft were soon made available for a number of *Geschwader* pilots to test under operational conditions. Not surprisingly, Adolf Galland, the

Kommodore of JG 26, was the first to test the new aircraft and was soon to become impressed with its performance although the troubles that beset the BMW 801 engine still continued.

An early production Fw 190A (KB+PV) being prepared for evaluation by Oblt *Behrens.*

Practically every test flight at Le Bourget experienced overheating of the engine. In some cases aircraft encountered engine trouble even before they were able to take off when a normal engine 'run-up' had to be shut down for fear of damage, on occasion resulting in total blow-up. In other instances the extreme overheating caused the ammunition for the nose-mounted MG 17 machine-guns to explode in their storage compartments. All-in-all the situation was becoming critical when, predictably, Focke-Wulf blamed BMW for designing an engine that had no practical use for powering a fighter aircraft. In retaliation BMW accused Focke-Wulf of not incorporating adequate engine cooling systems in their airframe designs.

Relationships between the two companies became strained, to say the least, with a certain amount of truth in both arguments. More prosaically the difficulties arose over RLM's insistence that the aircraft be made available to front-line *Geschwaderen* before the manufacturers had adequate time to make full tests, both independent and co-operative. At one stage, during these difficulties, a delegation from the RLM visited Le Bourget to investigate why these delays were being incurred. Encountering intransigence from representatives of both companies the RLM officials seriously considered recommending that the whole Fw 190 program be aborted. By the persuasive efforts of JG 26's technical staff, who clearly saw the great potential of the aircraft, the officials decided to delay their final recommendation and

Oblt Behrens flying KB+PV during the test flight.

allow them a little more time to rectify the problems.

Working day and night *Oberleutnant* Behrens and the technical staff of JG 26 adjusted, adapted and modified the engine cooling ducts and cowling and it was their efforts that finally brought the aircraft up to front-line capability.

Luftwaffe records suggest that JG 26, which, for the moment, retained its Bf 109s in I *Gruppe* and in the 1st *Staffel* of III *Gruppe*, flew its first Fw 190s, with II *Gruppe* commanded by *Hauptmann* Walter Adolph, on defensive sorties during September, 1941. It was during this month, on the 18th, that Adolph was killed while his *Gruppe* was providing an escort to a ship convoy. During an aerial combat with British fighters his aircraft was hit and fell into the Channel. His body was later recovered after being washed ashore on the Belgian coast. Adolph became one of the earliest operational victims while flying the new Fw 190. The first hint, however, from RAF records that a new fighter had entered service emerged from erroneous reports of encounters with the 'Curtiss Hawk 75A', presumed to have previously belonged to the French *Armée de l'Air*. The following month if any allied pilot seriously believed these reports of the appearance of the old American fighter they were soon to suffer a rude shock as numbers of the 'Butcher Bird' quickly increased. Confidence in the Spitfire V was quickly vanishing as the true identity of the enemy fighter became known. Compared to the Spitfire's maximum speed of around 370 mph, the Fw 190A-2 was capable of 389-mph, although the Spitfire's weight of armament was still roughly twenty per cent more than that of the new German fighter.

After completing extensive modifications Oblt Behrens lands after the first test flight. With great relief it appears that the engine trouble has been overcome.

Moreover, the manoeuvrability of the Spitfire, while not surpassed by the Fw 190, was of little consequence as the German fighter could break off an engagement at will and escape with its superior level or diving speed. Unfortunately the nature of operations in Northern Europe was such that the RAF could not glean much more information about the Fw 190 and could only rely upon reports from pilots who had encountered the fighter, and had been fortunate to escape. Not unnaturally these reports

Ground staff of JG 26 admiring one of the first Fw 190s to be delivered.

over emphasised the qualities of the Fw 190.

By November 1941 Galland and the JG 26 *Geschwader Stab* personnel had their Bf 109Fs replaced with the new fighter. Although he retained an affection for the Messerschmitt and would return to it when the 'Gustav' was available, Galland had every confidence in the abilities of the 'Butcher Bird' in combat.

While the Fw 190A-1 continued to be produced and supplied to JG 26 Focke-Wulf had already instigated the production of the Fw 190A-2 which was considered by the RLM to be the first *true* production model of the new fighter. An order for 426 of the A-2 had been given and these were to be similar to the A-1 but with some minor refinements and, more importantly, the newly available BMW 801C-2 engine was to be installed with the armament upgraded. The two 7.9-mm MG 17 machine-guns were retained in the upper fuselage/nose position but the two, previously housed in the wing roots, were replaced by two 20-mm MG 151 cannons. Even this was deemed to be insufficient and a 20-mm MG FF cannon was also mounted on each wing.

With this increased production requirement Focke-Wulf now encountered yet another problem as they had insufficient factory space to accommodate the new output. It was, therefore, necessary to arrange for other aircraft manufacturers to produce

the new series, and subsequent ones, under licence. After looking at various companies *Arado Flugzeugwerke GmbH.*, based in Brandenburg, and *AGO Flugzeugwerke*, based in Oschersleben, were chosen. Ultimately, after Focke-Wulf themselves, AGO went on to become the largest producer of the Fw 190 in all its various series. It was, however, recognised by the personnel who flew and maintained them that those manufactured by Arado were superior – interestingly Arado was also the 'licensed' manufacturer of most of the production Ju 88 bombers.

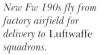

Line up of Fw 190A-1s recently delivered to II./JG 2, France, 1941

New Fw 190s fly from factory airfield for delivery to Luftwaffe squadrons.

The battle cruisers
Gneisenau *and*
Scharnhorst
viewed from
Prinz Eugen
during their
'Channel Dash'.

On February 12, 1942, the A-2s were given their first real test of aerial combat when Adolf Galland, now promoted to Inspector of Fighters on Werner Mölders death, was ordered to provide air cover for the two battle cruisers, the *Scharnhorst* and the *Gneisenau* together with the heavy cruiser the *Prinz Eugen*. Under the *Luftwaffe* code name Operation *Thunderbolt* the battleships were to attempt to leave the French port of Brest to a safer anchorage in Germany. Surprisingly, the *Kriegsmarine* used their own code name, *Cerberus*, for the same operation but this could well have been required to avoid confusion between the two military arms.

The French port, where the three ships had sought refuge from the determined efforts of the Royal Navy and RAF, had now become the centre of the Allies objective to destroy these 'flagships' of the German Navy. The plan was for the three ships, initially under the cover of darkness, to make a 'Channel Dash' through the Straits of Dover and on to Kiel and Wilhelmshaven where they could be protected by the heavy defences of those

Fw 190A-2 at Bordeaux-Merignac airfield, France, 1942.

ports. Galland had 252 aircraft available to him for the operation and these consisted of Bf 109Fs culled from JG 1, JG 2 and the fighter school based at Paris, Bf 110 night-fighters from NJG 1 and Fw 190A-2s from JG 26 (although a number of Bf 190Fs were also from JG 26).

The ships successfully reached their destinations, although both the *Scharnhorst*, and the *Gneisenau*, were damaged by mines. The operation was hailed, by the *Luftwaffe* and the *Kriegsmarine*, as an outstanding success with official reports showing forty-nine British aircraft destroyed, with an additional thirteen 'probables', at the cost of seven German aircraft lost.

The next variant to be delivered to the *Luftwaffe* was the Fw 190A-3 and began appearing in operational units towards the end of 1941 – although mainly for evaluation purposes. The new version represented efforts to remedy early service weaknesses that included the unreliability of the BMW 801C engine.

The A-3 series was to be powered by the new 1,700-hp BMW 801D-2, which, although similar to the C-2, now had an increased compression ratio of 7.55:1 (up from 6.5:1) and minor increases in the supercharger drive ratios. With the additional horse-power the engine also provided increased thrust for take-off and emergencies. The armament, that became standard, remained the

190A-3 of 3./JG 26 undergoing maintenance, France, 1942.

same as that installed in the final version of the A-2 series, namely two MG 17, two MG 151 and two MG FF cannons.

The external changes of the Fw 190A-3 were minor and this series model is difficult to identify from the previous A-2. The engine cowling had modified inspection panels and access latches. It also included a re-contoured fairing for the supercharger air trunk and louvered outlets to air-cool the motor. An additional outward change was to the vertical tail fin that incorporated a new attachment for the aerial antenna.

Due to the Fw 190s success as a fighter aircraft it was decided, by the RLM, to adapt it for different rôles. At least seven modifications of the A-3 were made and identified with the inclusion of a 'U' in the type designation (this stood for *Umrüst-Bausätz*, or *Umbau* for short, which in English translates to 'factory rebuild'). So, for instance, the first modification, the Fw 190A-3/U1,

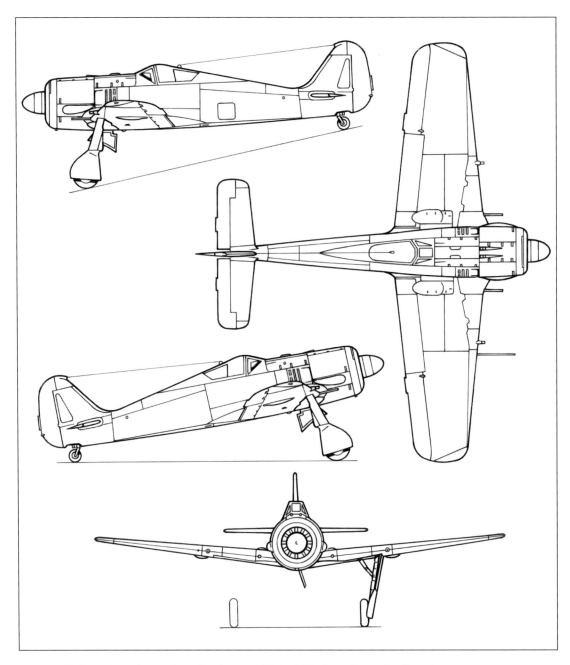

The Fw 190A-3

was a fighter/bomber that had an ETC 500 bomb-rack fitted beneath the fuselage and could carry a 551-lb or 1,102-lb bomb. The rack could also be fitted with an adapter that allowed the fitting of four 110-lb bombs. As a consequence it also lost its two wing-mounted MG FF cannons.

190A-3 with bomb on ventral carrier but empty racks under wing.

Fw 190A-3 of 9./JG 2 'Richthofen.

Jagdgeschwader 2 started to receive the Fw 190 in April 1942 to replace their Bf 109Fs and, for several months, JG 2 and JG 26 were the only operational fighter units equipped with the new fighter. JG 26, by early 1942, had been fully equipped with the Fw 190A-2 but during March and April of that year II./JG 26 had started to receive the new A-3. During this time the first fighter-

(above) Fw 190A-3 of JG 26 stationed in France 1942.

(left) Fw 190 at rest on airfield in France, 1943.

(above) Fw 190A-4/U3 of 10 (Jabo) JG 26, 'Schlageter' 1942.

(right) Fw 190A-4s of JG 26 'Schlagater'. Standard Luftwaffe colour scheme.

school, based at Werneuchen, also introduced the Fw 190 into their training program when a number of Fw 190A-1s were delivered.

Oblt Arnim Faber, Adjutant of III./JG 2 'Richthofen' landed his aircraft at RAF Pembrey on June 23, 1942.

After their initial familiarisation with the new front-line fighter pilots were unanimous in their praise for this welcome addition and although aerial battles with the British fighters increased the Fw 190 appeared to give the German pilots an edge. This, however, started to change when RAF squadrons, hitherto equipped with Hurricanes, appeared in the sky with the new series Spitfire.

On June 23, 1942, the RAF had the opportunity of inspecting and evaluating their first intact Fw 190 when *Oberleutnant* Arnim Faber, the adjutant of III./JG 2, landed his aircraft at Pembrey in South Wales. Such a lapse of airmanship was difficult to explain but could have resulted from a compass failure as the pilot had only shortly before been in action against Spitfires over the English Channel, more than a hundred miles to the south. The raid in which he had been involved extended up to the Bristol Channel and it is thought that, in his disorientation, he mistakenly took this for the English Channel. His aircraft, a Fw 190A-3, was immediately taken to the Royal Aircraft Establishment (RAE) at Farnborough, Hampshire, where it was exhaustively examined,

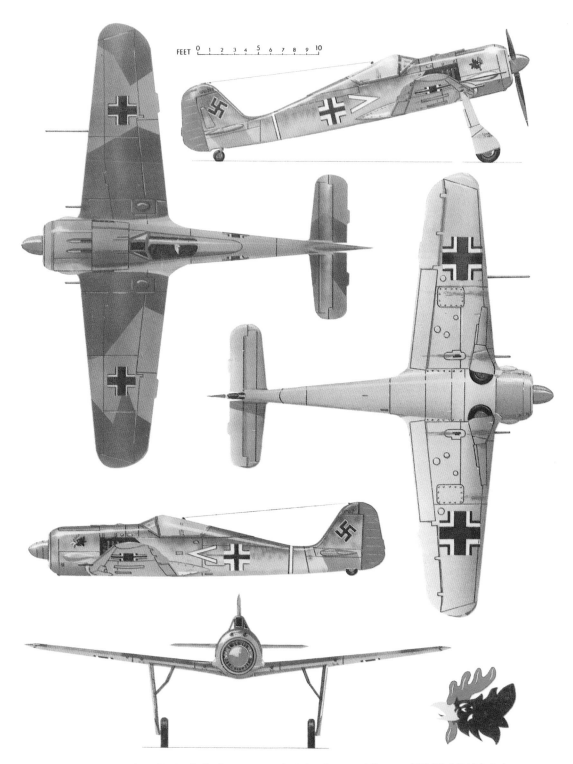

FEET

Fw 190A-3 (Werk Nr 0313) of Oberleutnant *Arnim Faber,* Gruppe Adjutant *of III./JG 2 'Richthofen'.*

*Fw 190A-3 of 5./JG 1 'Oesau',
Northern France, 1943.*

*Fw 190A-3 with the markings of
the Adjutant of I./JG 1, 1942.*

*Fw 190A-3 of 7./JG 2 'Richthofen',
Northern France, Autumn 1942.*

*Fw 190A-3 of 8./JG 2 'Richthofen',
Northern France, 1942*

Fw 190A-3 of 6./JG 3 'Udet'.

Fw 190A-3 of 5./JG 3 'Udet'.

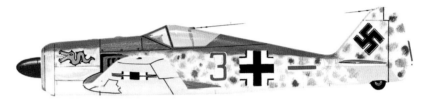

Fw 190A-3 of 5./JG 3 'Udet'. Although the 'Tatzelwurm' was usually painted in the Staffel *colours of the* Geschwader's *II* Gruppe *this aircraft carries a variation.*

Fw 190A-3 of III./JG 2 'Richthofen'. This aircraft was flown by Oblt *Arnim Faber, the* Gruppe *Adjutant.*

Fw 190A-3 of 8./JG 2 'Richthofen' with additional 66-gal. fuel tank.

Fw 190A-3 of 9./JG 2 'Richthofen' flown by Ofw. *Hartmann, Cherbourg, France, July 1942.*

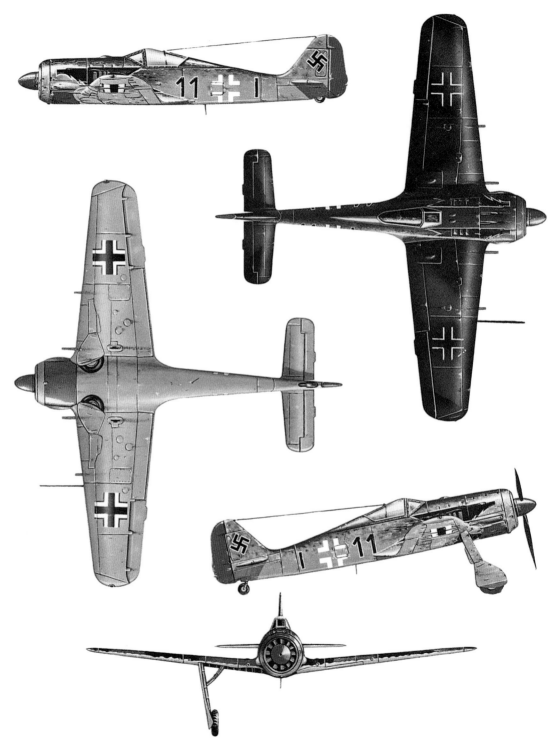

Fw 190A-3 (Werk Nr 2187) of 8./JG2 'Richthofen', Northern France, July 1942.

*Fw 190A-3 of 7./JG 2 'Richthofen',
France, August 1942.*

*Fw 190A-3 of 14.(Jabo)/JG 5 'Eismeer',
Finland, 1943.*

*Fw 190A-4 of 1./JG 1 'Oesau',
Denmark, October 1943.*

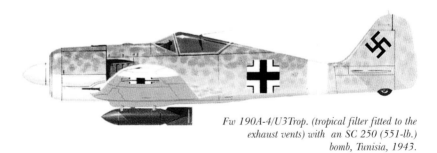

*Fw 190A-4/U3Trop. (tropical filter fitted to the
exhaust vents) with an SC 250 (551-lb.)
bomb, Tunisia, 1943.*

Fw 190A-4 of I,/JG 54 'Grünherz', Russia,1943.

Fw 190A-4/U3 of 10.(Jabo)/JG 26 'Schlageter'.

Fw 190A-4 flown by Hauptmann *Siegfried Schnell,*
Staffelkapitän *of 9./JG 2 'Richthofen', Vannes, France, February 1943.*

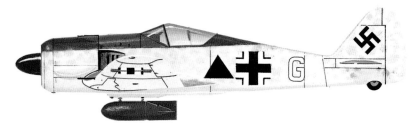

Fw 190A-4/U3 of I./SKG 10, Amiens, France, 1943.

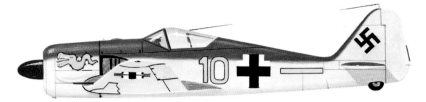

Fw 190A-3 of 6./JG 3 'Udet'.

*Fw 190A-4/R6 (fitted with Wfr Gr. 21 mortars beneath
each wing) with the insignia of a* Gruppe *Technical Officer.*

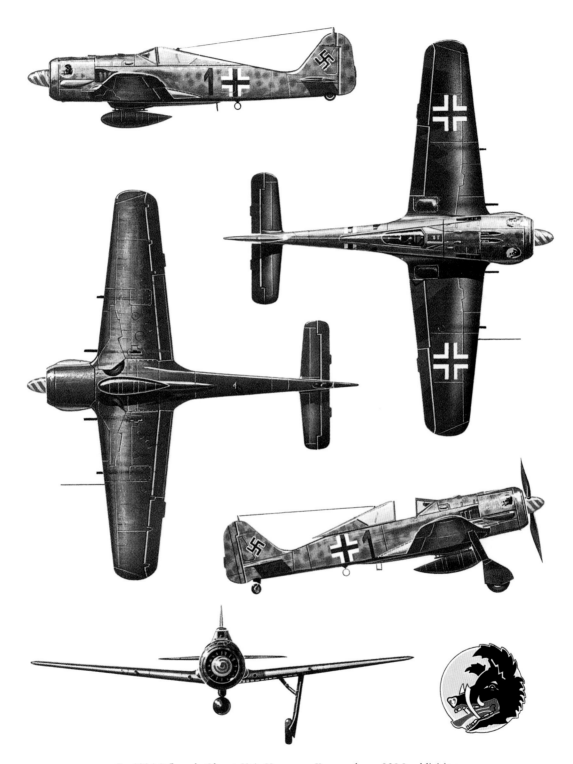

Fw 190A-5 flown by Oberst *Hajo Herrmann,* Kommodore *of 30* Jagddivision.

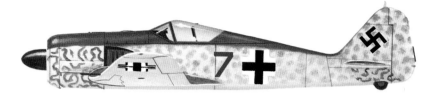

Fw 190A-4, Northern France, 1943.

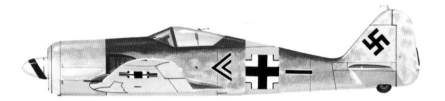

Fw 190A-4 of JG 26 'Schlageter', Northern France, 1943

Fw 190A-4, of 9./JG 2 'Richthofen', Northern France, 1943

Fw 190A-4, France, 1943.

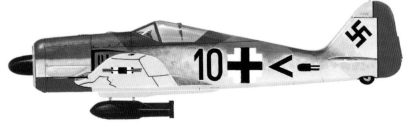

Fw 190A-4/U3 'Jabo'. Northern France, 1943

Faber's Fw 190A-3 now with British markings and being test flown by the RAF.

tested and evaluated. There is no doubt that its study and that of the engine measurably assisted in the development of the Centaurus installation design of the Typhoon II (later to become the Tempest II, and eventually the Hawker Fury). Nevertheless its capture in no way compromised the appearance of the much faster A-4, and no doubt gave false confidence in the Spitfire IX's ability to out-fly the Fw 190.

After the war a number of theories were given for Faber's actions in landing his aircraft. One, a persistent rumour, was that he was attempting to desert but this was never borne out by his subsequent interrogation or, in fact, his later behaviour. When he was settled into a prisoner of war camp he successfully convinced the British authorities that he suffered from epilepsy. With a little more thought to the matter the British authorities might have wondered how an epileptic pilot could rise to be a senior member of a front-line fighter unit. But, nonetheless, in 1944 they allowed his repatriation and, shortly after his return, he was again flying in fighter operations.

As the production of the A-3, in 1942, was still in full swing an additional model the Fw 190A-4 was introduced. This model differed from the previous only in the introduction of a methanol-water injection system, the MW 50. This allowed the BMW 801D-2 engine to be 'boosted' for short periods to an output of 2,000-hp. The boost was obtained by injecting water and methyl-alcohol which acted as an anti-detonant. It was observed, however, that this injected mixture had an extremely detrimental effect on the life of the engine's spark plugs. With this change of model the FuG 7a radio was replaced with the FuG 16Z and, consequentially, a short vertical aerial was installed at th top leading edge of the fin – the only outward visual sign of the change in model.

As with the A-3 the Fw 190A-4 was also subject to *Umbau* modifications which ranged from heavier armament and bomb

loads, to the addition of variable capacity external fuel tanks. The A-4 also saw the introduction of a new designation letter, 'R', which was intended to show the type of 'add-ons' a particular aircraft carried. The letter denoted the German word *Rüstsätz* and showed that the aircraft had been modified, usually after its delivery to an operational unit, by a 'stock' part that allowed it to

Fw 190A-4 of I./JG 51, Russia, January 1943. Hastily applied White camouflaged.

carry a whole range of weapons. Hence, the Fw 190A-4/R6, which came into service in 1943, had attachments that allowed it to carry two Wfr. Gr. 21 mortars beneath each wing.

Delivery of the Fw 190A-4 to operational units started in the summer of 1942 when JG 26 were again selected to be the first *Geschwader* to receive them. JG 2 were shortly to be re-equipped with the A-4 and during August and September JG 51 '*Mölders*', commanded by *Major* Karl-Gottfried Nordmann, was also re-equipped with the new fighter. I./JG 51 was the first *Gruppe* to receive the A-4 when they were transferred from the Eastern Front to Jesau on the home front. In October it was the turn of II./JG 51

190A-4 of I./JG 54 'Grünherz', Russia.

to receive Fw 190s followed in November by III./JG 51, although
this *Gruppe* were again re-equipped with the Bf 109G in March
1943. IV./JG 51 were to receive their Fw 190s in January 1943.

Towards the end of 1942 I and II *Gruppen* of JG 1, at that time
commanded by *Oberstleutnant* Dr Erich Mix and based in Holland
and north-west Germany, received the Fw 190A-3. III *Gruppe* was
also to be updated but because the new aircraft was in short supply
they continued to use the Bf 109.

In February 1943 the *Stabstaffel* and I *Gruppe* of JG 54 'Grünherz',
with *Major* Hannes Trautloft as the *Kommodore*, received delivery of
the Fw 190A-3 and from their base in Krasnogvardeysk took on
aerial combat with Russian aircraft and low-level attacks with
renewed vigour.

CHAPTER FIVE

The Fw 190 in Action

B Y THE middle of 1942, the mass production of the Focke-Wulf
Fw 190 substantially increased. The operational experience
gained by JG 26 with the early Fw 190s gave impetus to the
development of the new A-3 series. Two of the earlier A-0
production aircraft were given the designation Fw 190V8 to serve
as prototypes for this new series and were fitted with the BMW
801D-2 engine which, together with the redesigned engine
cooling configuration of the airframe, now proved extremely
reliable.

In addition to equipping *Luftwaffe Geschwaderen* seventy-five
Fw 190A-3s had also been ordered and exported to Turkey, whose
pilots expressed a marked preference for the German fighter over
the Supermarine Spitfire V, supplied by Britain. Manufacture and
assembly was then, or shortly to be, undertaken at Mecklenburg,

*A large wing
Fw 190A-0
(Werk Nr 0022)
equipped for* Jabo *tests
with a SC 250 bomb.*

Marienburg (both heavily attacked by the RAF and USAAF),   *Line up of new Fw 190s.*
Cottbus, Eschwere, Einswarden, Gydnia, Sorau, Halberstadt,
Neubrandenburg, Schwerin and Wismar, as well as the AGO
aircraft factory at Oschersleben, and the Fieseler works at Kassel.
No fewer than 1,850 Fw 190A-3s and A-4s had been delivered
during 1942, in contrast to 266 Typhoons.

    Also by 1942 both the Allied air forces of Britain and the United   *An early production
Fw 190A-3*

States were despatching over the Continent and Germany an ever growing number of fighters and bombers. The US 8th and 9th Air Forces based in England were operating fighter escorts to British and American bombers. One attack was typical of that period when a force of twelve Bostons and B-17s with fighter escort bombed Abbeville airfield.

The bombers and their escorts crossed into France, located their target and prepared for the run-in. The bombers successfully attacked the airfield and were turning for home when they were pounced upon by a *Staffel* of Fw 190s. During the ensuing fight the 133rd Squadron, USAAF, lost three fighters. A few days later 133rd Squadron and 65th Fighter Command were flying as escorts to twenty-two B-17s that were on their way to bomb Dunkirk when they were met by ten Fw 190s flying at 10,000 feet. The bombers and their escort were immediately attacked by the fighters but both

Fw 190V8 (an A-0 prototype for the A-3) undergoing Jabo *trials. The aircraft is armed with eight 250-lb. ventral fuselage and wing bombs.*

sides, after a short engagement, broke off combat with no losses

This was the prelude to a sustained Allied bombing campaign against targets on the Continent, in general, and Germany, in particular, which lasted for 995 days and nights, and during which

Fw 190V8 undergoing Jabo trials.

the 8th Air Force alone would drop 4,337,984 bombs and 25,556,978 four pound incendiaries, a total of 71,300 tons. The US 8th Air Force lost 41,786 men, dead or missing. To that number can be added the losses sustained by the 9th Air Force and RAF Bomber Command. It was a high price to pay but was without any doubt the pivotal action that led to the eventual collapse of Germany.

In addition to these set pieces both American and RAF fighters would conduct attacks such as a 'Rhubarb' which consisted of two aircraft attacking targets of opportunity in France. The fighters approached at high speed and shot up trains, vehicle road traffic and fixed installations. There was always a price to pay such as wandering over a flak site to be shot at with machine-guns, 20-mm flak guns and anything that could fire at the invaders.

One such 'set piece' was Operation *Jubilee*, the attack on Dieppe, which was planned in the spring of 1942. It was virtually a rehearsal for the Normandy invasion but, on this occasion, was

launched against a port. The plan was not to risk a frontal attack but to land infantry and tanks at Quiberville, six miles west of Dieppe. The airfield was to be captured and, following this, two battalions of infantry would land two miles west of the port supported by two additional battalions a mile east of the harbour.

It was decided that in order not to arouse the defences before time the heavy bombers would not bomb the port the night before. However, due to bad weather, the attack had to be postponed and the waiting troop's moral suffered. On the night of August 18, 1942, 252 ships carrying 6,096 officers and men, mostly Canadians, left England and headed to the northern coast of France under the protection of escort shipping. The plan was to neutralise eleven miles of the French coastal area by air and sea bombardment, which would follow commando landings the night before to destroy defences.

The infantry force and tanks were landed just before dawn at six beaches and at first light a force of Bostons dropped smoke bombs to blind the enemy shore batteries. However, the defences had been alerted by the commando raid the night before, and the bombers came under heavy flak with nine of them being damaged. Throughout the day the aircraft bombed and strafed

enemy positions while the Royal Navy kept up a constant
bombardment on shore installations, but the German batteries
had been unscathed and returned heavy fire.

By now the Allied fighter screen had arrived and provided a
protective umbrella at considerable cost as they could not stay in
the area for very long and reinforcements were constantly arriving
over the beach-head. A number of Fw 190s with Yellow noses from
Abbeville appeared carrying bombs and launched a low-level
attack with limited success as two of them were shot down. The
German aircraft belonged to 10.(*Jabo*)/JG 26.

During the course of August 19, both 10.(*Jabo*)/JG 2 and
10.(*Jabo*)/JG 26 flew numerous sorties against Allied positions,
landing craft and supporting ships with their new Fw 190
Fighter/Bombers. The remaining *Gruppen* of the two *Geschwaderen*,

with their more conventional fighters, endeavoured to tackle the Allied fighter 'umbrella' and with success accounted for the majority of the RAF's loss of 106 aircraft.

The *Jabo* units had been created on March 10, 1942, following orders by *General der Flieger* Hugo Sperrle, who commanded *Luftlotte* 3. He intstructed the two *Jagdgeschwaderen* remaining in the West, JG 2 and JG 26, to each form a *Jagdbomber* (fighter/bomber) or '*Jabo*' *Staffel*. Although initially equipped with bomb-carrying Messerschmitt Bf 109F-4/Bs these wcrc to be replaced in June 1942 with the Fw 190A-3/U1 (Heavy Fighter/Bomber). 10.(*Jabo*)/JG 2, based at Caen, performed shipping strikes in the English Channel, while 10.(*Jabo*)/JG 26 mounted snap low-level strikes against industrial plants, railways and harbours on the English South Coast. By the autumn of that year the first Fw 190A-4s were being delivered to 10.(*Jabo*)/JG 26. Although early aircraft were not fitted for bomb-carrying they were soon to receive the specially equipped Fw 190A-4/U1 (Heavy Fighter/Bomber), fitted with two ETC 501 bomb racks, and the Fw 190A-4/U3 (Ground Support Fighter), fitted with a single 551-lb. SC 250 bomb, beneath the fuselage.

Fw 190A-4/U3, 10.(Jabo)/JG 26, 'Schlageter', France 1942. The 500-lb bomb is destined for the south coast of England.

It was the appearance of the A-4/U8 (Long Range Fighter/Bomber) sub-variant that heralded bombing attacks in September 1942. These aircraft were on the operational strength of both the *Jabo Staffeln* with JG 2 and JG 26. Retaining the inboard wing-mounted MG 151 cannon and the cowling machine-guns, the A-4/U8 had provision to carry a single SC 500 (1,100-lb.) bomb on a centre-line rack under the fuselage, as well as a 66-gallon fuel tank under each wing. A variation on this

Fw 190A-3 (Werk Nr 511) used for various test purposes by Focke-Wulf.

Fw 190As at dispersal for servicing and maintenance.

armament was to locate a single 66-gallon ventral fuel tank with four 110-lb. SC 50 bombs on wing racks.

Although *Jabo Staffeln* were fully utilised on various bombing raids, as a unit of a fighter *Geschwader* they remained under the control of the *Jagdfliegerführer* or *Jafü* (fighter leader) of all fighter units within the *Luftflotte*.

Throughout the autumn and early winter of 1942 *Jabo Staffeln*

Fw 190A-3, III./JG 2 'Richthofen', France 1942. Aircraft is 'Red 15'.

provoked a response from the RAF out of all proportion to the threat posed. The Focke-Wulfs attacked 'targets of opportunity' in southern England including towns, airfields and trains. Usually flying in pairs, approaching the coastline at wave-top height and thereby escaping radar detection. In the early stages of this 'campaign' they were frequently on their homeward journey before RAF fighters could react. It was this situation that prompted the mounting of almost continuous standing patrols by Typhoons and Spitfire IXs on such a scale that not more than one patrol in 200 resulted in combat.

The *Jabo* raids were usually flown with one or two *Schwarm* – a unit of four aircraft, and it was rare for the whole *Staffel* to be involved in these sorties as, due to losses and other problems, it was seldom that more than a dozen aircraft were available.

In response to an estimated 360 *Jagdbomber* sorties the RAF flew slightly more that 52,000 defence sorties! Losses among the German pilots in this period amounted to fifteen in four months.

The lessons learned from Operation *Jubilee* allowed the allies to predict that any landing force into France would have to be self-contained and take its ports with them. This was successfully fulfilled on D-Day two years later. Airborne troops would have to be deployed before the main attack, plus as many battleships as possible using the heavy artillery to swamp local defences. Among the most potent of weapons was the 65-lb. rocket which was carried by the ships and LCTs.

The raids by air against Hitler's fortress continued, and in

New delivery Fw 190A-3 of III./JG 2 'Richthofen' is manhandled out of camouflaged barn, France, Winter 1941. Note leading edge scheme.

September 1942 a number of B-17s were despatched to the Focke-Wulf factory in Morlaix. They were escorted for part of the way by three squadrons of the Royal Canadian Air Force (RCAF) who

were flying the new Spitfire Mk IX, and one USAAF squadron, which was also equipped with the Mk IX Spitfire. They met the B-17s at 25,000 feet over the Channel and escorted them to the target and back during which twelve Spitfires were lost to German fighters and flak over the target.

In September 1942 the three American Eagle Squadrons of the RAF were transferred to the US 8th Air Force, commanded by General Spaatz. One of their first operations, flying Spitfires and P-38 Lightnings, was to support a formation of 108 B-17 Flying Fortress and B-24 Liberator heavy bombers during a raid against the French city of Lille. The P-38s were later transferred to the 12th Air Force to take part in Operation *Torch*, the invasion of North Africa. The Eagle Squadrons became the Fourth Fighter Group and, with the other fighters, they met the bombers over Beachy Head. The target was bombed but faced attacks by fifty Fw 190s and Bf 109s with the result that four bombers were lost. However, a large number of the heavy bombers aborted the raid due to mechanical troubles.

In December 1941 the decision was taken to attack the *Luftwaffe*'s main base just five miles from Paris, it was also the

Fw 190A-4, II./JG 2. Yellow '10' and fuselage bar.

servicing centre for all *Jagdgeschwaderen* based in France and the Low Countries. One hundred and one bombers were despatched with a fighter escort from the Fourth Fighter Group. Unfortunately, the escorting fighters had to turn back before the target was reached as it was beyond their tactical radius. As soon as the escort had left sixty enemy fighters, from JG 26, shortly to be joined by others from JG 2, appeared and attacked the bomber force. The *Luftwaffe* kept up the attacks until the bombers were returning to base where they were met by a number of Spitfire squadrons. Six American bombers were destroyed and twenty-nine severely damaged. The 12th Air Force was formed under General Doolittle in preparation of Operation *Torch* but he took with him the most seasoned bomber squadrons. In the four months that the 8th Air Force had started its campaign it had lost thirty-three aircraft out of a total of 1,053 but only 451 had reached their targets. The *Luftwaffe* considered they had the problem under control.

A new year, 1943, dawned and on January 13, the Lille locomotive works was attacked by eighteen bombers protected by

Fw 190A-4/U8 of SKG 10 in temporary night fighter finish for intruder operations inadvertently landed at West Malling, 16 July, 1943.

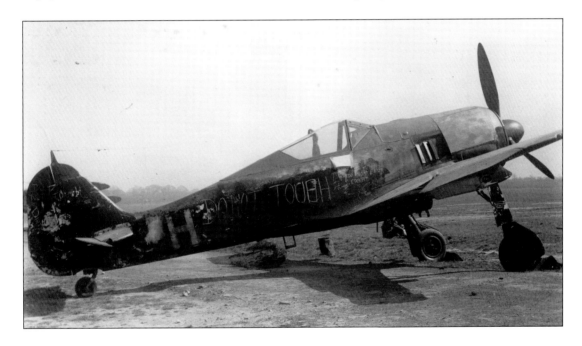

fighters but three bombers were lost.

The first P-47 Thunderbolt fighters were also delivered during this month but pilots had to record fifty hours flying time with them before they could fly on operations. The change from the Spitfire and Lightnings they had been flying was dramatic as the P-47 Thunderbolt was a large aircraft that could reach speeds of

429-mph, but it was heavy and took its time reaching altitude. Once there it was a great fighter that could out-dive any German machine.

The first operation with the P-47 took place on March 10, with a sweep over St Omer, where they came under attack by the Fw 190. Thirty German aircraft attacked the formation with the loss of one of the fighters which was shot down. On April 17, the 8th Air Force sent 115 B-17s into Germany to attack the Focke-Wulf works in Bremen and they were escorted by fifty-nine P-47 Thunderbolts. As they crossed into Europe they were spotted by a German observation aircraft and, alerted, the *Luftwaffe* sent a force of Fw 190s and Bf 109s who kept up a savage and concentrated attack. The factory was badly damaged at the cost of sixteen B-17s. During the bombing raid the USAAF flew a diversion sweep over Belgium without sighting any enemy aircraft, mainly because these had been concentrated on the

190A-4 of II./JG 26, France, later 1942. Handcart starter is interesting.

main attack.

The 8th Air Force was still in the learning stages and on May 4, 1943, an attack was launched upon Antwerp. Seventy-nine bombers made up the force which was protected by P-47 Thunderbolts. Although attacked by Fw 190s and Bf 109s the escorts kept them away from the bombers who returned to base without loss. A second attack on the city followed with forty-nine

Fw 190A-4 of 9./JG 2, July 1942.

B-17s and thirty fighters being despatched. The force, as soon as they crossed the coast of Holland, immediately encountered opposition when they were attacked by Fw 190s from JG 26 based at Abbeville, but this time the bright yellow-coloured nose had been roughly camouflaged with black. A few days later thirty-six P-47 aircraft flew into Europe at 30,000 feet to be met again by JG 26 yellow nosed fighters, and, for good measure, they were followed by fifteen red nosed Fw 190s from JG 2.

By the end of 1942 the increasing threat of daylight raids by USAAF heavy bombers had, however, forced withdrawal of the Fw 190s of JG 2 and JG 26 from these bombing attacks on Britain, and both *Geschwaderen* resumed full interception duties. Early in 1943 a new unit, SKG 10 (*Schnellkampfgeschwader* 10) was created and, equipped with approximately one hundred Fw 190A-4/U8 fighter/bombers, this *Geschwader* resumed the attacks on Britain after a brief spell on anti-shipping duties in the Bay of Biscay.

I *Gruppe*, SKG 10, continued to fly bombing raids against southern England throughout 1943 and into 1944 with most attacks being made at night. Among these attacks was a raid

Fw 190A-4/R6 with Wfr Gr. 21 rocket tubes mounted under each wing.

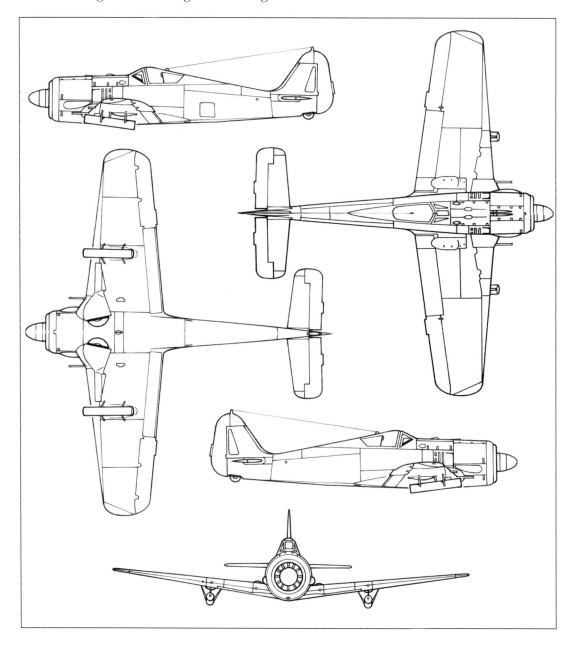

mounted by twenty-eight *Jabo* aircraft on the night of April 16/17, 1943, against London. Despite considerable planning the intended raid went sadly wrong. Carried out at high altitude, the aircraft encountered headwinds, the strength of which had been much underestimated, with the result that only two bombs fell in the entire Greater London area, with most falling over a two hundred square mile tract to the west. What was perhaps more serious for the Germans was that three of the raiders landed intact at the RAF airfield at West Malling and gave the RAF a 'golden' opportunity to study and evaluate this particular variant.

The majority of the allied fighters were flying three sorties each during the day and there to oppose them were *Luftwaffe* units JG 2 'Richthofen' from western France, JG 26 'Schlageter' from Belgium, and JG 5 'Eismeer' from Norway, the latter refuelling and rearming from the local *Luftwaffe* bases. The air above Dieppe was

The Fw 190A-4/R6 with Wfr Gr. 21 mortar-launching barrels.

crowded with fighters from both sides and added to this was the constant arrival of twin-engine bombers from England and similar German twins such as the Junkers Ju 88 and Dornier Do 17s which all carried bombs.

As previously stated the Allied raid was considered to be an abject failure with Hitler subsequently stating that any other allied incursion into Europe would suffer the same fate. The raiding

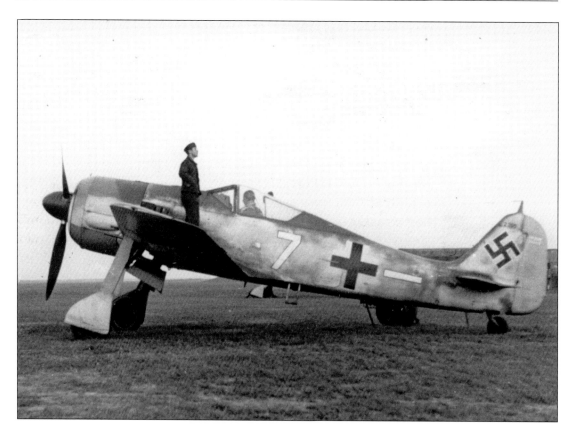

Fw 190A-4 of II./JG 26, France, late 1942.

force had taken a hammering and when it withdrew at around noon all the armour and other vehicles were left on the beach, which they never left owing to the steep sea wall. The Bostons were the principal allied aircraft and during the closing phases of the raid they covered the area with smoke.

The final fighters from England arrived over the beach-head around 13.00 hours to protect the allied troops crowded on the beach and awaiting evacuation to the waiting larger ships to carry them back to England. A furious battle was launched by the *Luftwaffe* who threw in *Staffel* after *Staffel* of Fw 190s, Bf 109s, Dornier Do 17s and Ju 88s. Both sides lost heavily and of the 6,086 officers and men who landed almost 3,000 were left behind, wounded or dead. The Allied naval forces lost 550 men, a destroyer and thirty-three smaller craft. The *Luftwaffe* claimed to have destroyed a large number of aircraft, as did the allies, with both sides exaggerating claims. In actual terms the RAF lost 106 aircraft, the Germans forty-eight, but their bombers were easily dealt with and destroyed.

In another theatre of operation reinforcement of the *Luftwaffe* in North Africa during the final months of the *Afrika Korps'* resistance in Tunisia resulted in the despatch of a single fragmented *Gruppe* of Fw 190A-4/Trop. fighters to bolster *Fliegerführer Tunis.* Surviving records suggest that these aircraft achieved a measure of success against American P-38 Lightnings, but almost all met their end on the ground when caught by raiding B-26 bombers. Sixty-eight 190A-4/Trop. sand-filter equipped fighters were built, the majority fitted with a fuselage bomb-rack capable of carrying a single SC 250 (550-lb.) bomb. The surviving Focke-Wulfs were evacuated to Sicily, each pilot frequently carrying one or even two ground crewmen squeezed into his rear fuselage.

With the collapse of Axis forces in North Africa in 1943, II, III and IV *Gruppen*, SKG 10, under the command of *Major* Temme, were hurriedly transferred to Sicily to counter the threat of invasion to that island. This, however, proved of little value in the face of overwhelming Allied air superiority.

The fortunes of the *Luftwaffe* faired no better during the Sicilian campaign with the tattered remnants of SKG 10's fighter/bombers

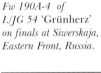

Fw 190A-4 of I./JG 54 'Grünherz' on finals at Siwerskaja, Eastern Front, Russia.

Ground crew work on a Fw 190A of I./JG51 on the Eastern Russian Front.

being forced to disperse among the airfields and emergency grounds around Gerbini. They attempted to attack Allied shipping and land installations in the south of the island after July 10, but were constantly harried by P-38 Lightnings and Spitfires. Once again they were withdrawn, this time to the Italian mainland, continuing almost to extinction in *Generalfeldmarschall* Albert Kesselring's *Luftflotte* 2 until 1944.

The only other service variation of the A-4 was the A-4/R6, introduced as a measure to counter the fast-growing formations of B-17 Flying Fortresses and B-24 Liberators over Western Europe.

This fighter retained the gun armament of the standard A-4 but also featured a Wfr Gr 21 (21-cm) mortar-launching barrel under each wing. When fitted with impact fuses the missiles were of little effect owing to the difficulty in aiming and the 'weather-cocking' tendencies of the single weapon fired from each barrel. It was however estimated that at one time in 1943 nearly 200

This view of bombing-up a Fw 190 of I./JG 51, using tractor and sledge, illustrates vividly the harsh Russian winter.

Fw 190A-4/R6s were deployed against USAAF bombers.

It is perhaps surprising that the Fw 190 was not delivered in any great numbers to support the German ground forces in the East until the early spring of 1943. A possible explanation may be that the aircraft was considered to be the only fighter capable of retaining a degree of parity with Western fighters. The marked inferiority of Russian aircraft encountered in the East had enabled traditional elements of *Luftwaffe* equipment to provide air superiority to cover the hitherto victorious German armies.

As stated earlier the Fw 190A-3 had been introduced in limited numbers in 1942 to two *Gruppen* in different *Geschwaderen* then operating on the Eastern Front. I./JG 51 'Mölders' had, in September of that year, been re-equipped at Jesau and in October had become operational. In December I./JG 54 'Grünherz' had also been similarly re-equipped and were soon operating in the Leningrad region then under the command of *Luftflotte* 1. By the end of 1942 both II and III *Gruppen* of JG 51 had received the Fw 190A and had become fully operational and IV./JG 51 reccived

theirs in March 1943. By March 1943, however, the aircraft of
III./JG 51 were replaced by the new Bf 109G.

One additional unit became partially equipped with the Focke-
Wulf, this time the Fw 190A-4/U3 was the type of choice for the
Schlachtgruppe, II./Sch.G 1, who were under the dual control of
Luftwaffenkommando Don and *Luftflotte* 4. However, the total
number of Fw 190s deployed on the Eastern Front at this time was
still less than 100 aircraft.

By 1943 the advances of the previously victorious German
armies in the East had all been checked as the Soviet giant war
machine grew in strength and numbers. The German panzers
and infantry had faltered because of the lack of new armaments
and manpower. German forces were widely scattered across
Europe and the Middle East, and the threat of the Anglo-
American invasion across the English Channel became a reality.

In the air, the Soviet commanders now threw caution to the
wind and flaunted every principle of war. Despite the German air
superiority over the battlefields, the Russians launched massive
swarms of aircraft, albeit of truly mediocre quality, to cover their

*Brand new Fw 190A-4
at the factory gate. The
aircraft is showing
service test group
markings 03+11.*

Fw 190A-3

Fw 190A-4 of I./JG 54 'Grünherz'

Fw 190A-4 of III./JG 54

Fw 190A-3 of I./JG 3 'Udet' showing a 20-mm
MG 151 cannon in the wing-root and a 20-mm
MG FF cannon, with the pitot tube outboard of these.

Two Fw 190As preparing for take-off.

armies, and hardly surprisingly these were shot out of the sky like flies. Later in 1943 a number of better aircraft types were being flown by the Russian airforce, among them some British and American aircraft that had been supplied under the Lease/Lend agreement, and losses among the venerable Junkers Ju 87 ground/support aircraft started to increase fairly quickly. Demands for the Focke-Wulf fighter/bomber by the German aircrew were now heard, with the result that additional quantities of the Fw 190A-4/U8 were delivered to *Schlachtgeschwader* 1 in the Orel-Bielgorod area in April that year.

Re-equipment of other *Schlachtgruppen* followed with the arrival of new sub-variants such as the Fw 190A-5/U3 capable of carrying a 2,200-lb. bomb (but with all wing cannon removed). Also the Fw 190A-5/U8 with a 1,100-lb. bomb, and the Fw 190A-5/U11 (with a 990-lb. bomb) which featured guns in all positions with the outboard MG FF replaced by the 30-mm Mk 103 cannon. Such was the success achieved by these fighter-bombers that in 1944 the Ju 87 Stuka was relegated almost entirely to night attacks, their place by day being exclusively undertaken by the Fw 190.

In the pure day fighting rôle the Focke-Wulf was introduced on the Russian front, not so much to replace but to strengthen existing fighter equipment. The planning of Operation *Citadel*, the Germans prodigious armoured punch aimed at straightening the area of the Kursk salient on the central front, included the reinforcement of both ground attack and fighter echelons of the *Luftwaffe*. To provide aerial cover Fw 190s were issued to eight *Jagdgruppen* including I, III and IV./JG 51 'Mölders' and III./JG 54 'Grünherz', and these units caused enormous damage among the Soviet 1st, 4th and 16th Air Armies during that disastrous campaign. Notwithstanding success in the air, the Panzer divisions were eventually stopped by the huge, in-depth defences bolstered by clouds of Soviet Sturmovic aircraft, and blasted to a halt. It was the beginning of the Armageddon that stretched from the Kursk salient to the fall of Berlin as the German offensive petered out with such losses that, coupled with tremendous defeats in the South, represented the turning point of German fortunes in the East.

CHAPTER SIX

Wilde Sau

The introduction of the Fw 190A-5 coincided with the climax of RAF Bomber Command's night offensive against major cities within Germany. Despite heavy losses to the bombers from night fighters the raids were reaching alarming strength and regularity. It was at this point that an ex-bomber commander, Hajo Herrmann, who had flown Junkers Ju 88s over Britain in 1940, suggested using day fighters on freelance night defence sorties and utilising flares in conjunction with ground searchlights.

At this time Herrmann was one of the most experienced pilots in the *Luftwaffe* and had seen action with the Condor Legion in the Spanish Civil War. He had flown operationally during the *Blitzkrieg* of Poland, the Norwegian campaign, the invasion of France, including the Low countries, and had continued during the Battle of Britain and the subsequent bombing of British towns and cities. His operational experience progressed with bombing attacks on Malta and targets during the Greek campaign. By early 1942, having reached the rank of *Hauptmann* and been awarded the *Ritterkreuz*, he was now stationed in the north of Norway where, as a *Staffelkapitän* with III./KG 30, he was attacking and harrying the Russian convoys.*

Somewhat surprisingly he was posted to a 'desk job' in Berlin during July of that year. Herrmann accepted this position with reluctance as he had, to his certain knowledge, given no reason to the *Luftwaffe* High Command that he was anything but an experienced and dedicated operational pilot. Herrmann's posting

---

* Extracts of Hajo Herrmann's career and the formation of 'Wilde Sau' have been taken, with the author's kind permission, from *The Other Battle* by Peter Hinchliffe, published by Airlife Publishing Ltd.

was to the *Luftwaffe* Command Staff based near Potsdam. The small section in which Herrmann now found himself was called *Gruppe T* and, staffed by a half-dozen junior officers like himself, was responsible for 'Technical/Tactical Requirements'. Separate operational activities were allocated to each officer on the section and Herrmann's specific task was to manage the 'Bomber Desk'. At this particular juncture of the war he found himself preoccupied more and more with the defensive aspects rather than offensive operations.

The demands for aircraft by the various *Geschwaderen* and *Luftflotten*, trying to stem the tide of increased Allied activity in all Theatres of Operation, fell squarely on the desks of *Gruppe T*. With the Russian Front showing a clear and obvious priority for fighters, fighter-bombers and bombers, Herrmann and his colleagues were desperately trying to juggle all requirements. Now that the war, for Germany, had entered into a critical defensive aspect, where British bombers were attacking the heartland of the Reich at night and American bombers were building up their daytime offensive, the strain on resources soon became evident.

Gruppe T had at their disposal the figures provided by German intelligence assessments of the Allies' aircraft production and this provided alarming reading. Britain and America, excluding estimated figures from other Allied countries, were producing over 29,000 bombers a year while the forecasted output for German fighters was 10,000.

As a bomber pilot himself Herrmann could well foresee the growing disadvantagies to the German fighters and, with this in mind, he was developing a number of ideas in an attempt to combat this. Traditionally the single-engine fighters flew only in the hours of daylight but, his proposal recommended, with suitable organisation the Bf 109s and Fw 190s of the *Tagjagd* (Day-Fighters) could perform around the clock. With specially trained pilots, who would take over the aircraft from their daytime comrades, the aircraft could be used at night to attack the Halifaxes, Lancasters and Wellingtons of the British Bomber Command.

Herrmann's proposal was not entirely a new concept as in the early stages of the war the Bf 109s of *Jagdgeschwader* 2 were tentatively used to intercept bombers before they reached their targets but, in his proposal, Herrmann suggested that greater

*Hajo Herrmann
seen here with the rank
of* Oberstleutnant

*Hajo Herrmann
seen here with the rank
of* Oberstleutnant

success would be achieved if the fast, highly manoeuvrable fighters attacked the British bombers when they were immediately above the targeted towns and cities. The searchlights and artillery flak, if the latter was kept to a pre-arranged ceiling, would give the fighters extra visibility and so enhance their chances of success.

Although Herrmann's proposal did not generate much enthusiasm with the *Luftwaffe* High Command he was able to persuade a senior *Luftwaffe* officer, *Oberst* Eschenauer, who was sympathetic to his idea, to provide him with a single-engine fighter to test his theory.

With a fighter aircraft available Herrmann also had the co-operation of the commander of the Berlin Flak Artillery, *General* Schaller. In addition he also obtained the services of a Heinkel He 111 bomber and its crew to act as a target for him in practices over the city of Berlin, flying from the day-fighter base at Staaken on the western edge of the German capital. He had no difficulty in finding other pilots with night-flying qualification and experience to join him in his scheme, the first coming from among the instructors at the flying school at Brandenburg/Briest, about seventy miles to the west of Berlin, men prepared to do their normal work by day and to join Herrmann in the hazardous occupation of flying day-fighters at night over cities being attacked by hundreds of RAF bombers. Herrmann extended his experiments to participation in live operations, despite an order originating from the *Führer* himself that there should not be any restriction on the height to which the anti-aircraft guns fired.

In April 1943 he and seven other pilots took off in single-seater fighters in an attempt to intercept a Mosquito that the radar had picked up approaching Berlin from the west. Herrmann himself was at 11,000 metres when he saw the Mosquito 2,000 metres below him, and he went in to attack among the dense flak that was surrounding the British machine, but although he fired at it he did not succeed in shooting it down. Two of his volunteer pilots also opened fire unsuccessfully.

Although the Mosquito had not been destroyed, Herrmann had shown that it was not the invulnerable 'miracle bird' it was reputed to be, although in some high quarters, among which *General* Kammhuber, of the *Nachtjagd*, and *Generalfeldmarschall* Milch were prominent, there was reluctance to believe his story. The respected *Generalmajor* Galland, however, who was *General der Jagdflieger* (General of Fighters), was favourably impressed both by Herrmann himself and by his theories, and he made further fighters available. Throughout May and June 1943, night after night, Herrmann and his volunteers practised their night flying and their tactics, in addition to carrying out their day-time jobs, waiting for a raid on Berlin so that they could prove their worth, but none came.

What sort of a man was Herrmann? He was, as his record

Fw 190A-5/U2 'large wing' with single SC 500 bomb.

proved, a brilliant, courageous pilot. He was a clear-thinking man impatient of bureaucracy and of inflexibility in his superiors, a man of great powers of leadership, an officer in the best tradition of the *Wehrmacht*. A regular officer of the *Luftwaffe* with an outstanding reputation, he was well connected and more influential than his comparatively lowly rank of *Major* – he had been promoted in April 1943 – might suggest. An officer who knew him in Berlin when he was first calling for volunteers, and who later commanded one of Herrmann's single-seater units, was Gerd Stamp, himself a *Major* at the time. Like Herrmann, Stamp too was a bomber pilot, and he had achieved considerable distinction in the eastern

Mediterranean, flying the Ju 88 with *Lehrgeschwader* 1:

  'In April 1943 I was sent home to Berlin to work on the Staff. It was there that I met Hajo Herrmann. It was a rest period from operations for me; I already had several hundred missions to my credit. Herrmann had been in Berlin since 1942, and in his spare time he went over to Brandenburg/Briest to practise night flying. It was at a

Major *Gerhard Stamp*

time when Bomber Command were coming increasingly frequently. People said a Messerschmitt 109 or a Focke-Wulf 190 couldn't be flown at night, but he said, "We'll see!" When I heard he wanted pilots I asked him if I could join him. At that time I already had the *Ritterkreuz*, so my ability was established, but I had never flown the Bf 109 before.

'You ask me what sort of a man Herrmann was. I must say that at

Fw 190A-5s 'large wing' with single 500-lb. bomb on ETC 250 rack and 66-gallon auxiliary fuel tanks under each wing.

first I didn't like him at all. He knew who he was – self-confident, assured, aloof, cold, arrogant. However, as I was the same rank as he I could speak to him on equal terms and I told him he was a flying calculating machine, and that he thought everyone should be able to do as well as he could. I told him that this was not so: "Not everyone is a flying genius like you are." He really was a flying genius.'

Herrmann's endeavours met with approval on the one hand, opposition on the other. Prominent among the sceptics was *Generaloberst* Weise, in overall charge of air defence (*Befehlshaber Mitte*), who refused categorically to issue orders limiting the Flak to a specific height 'for the sake of a handful of fighters'.

Major
Werner Baumbach

At a meeting chaired by Weise in Berlin to discuss the subject *Oberstleutnant* Boehm-Tettelbach referred to Herrmann's ideas in dismissive terms, calling them '*Wilde Sau*', which in German means crazy, bull-at-a-gate, irresponsible, a reference to the frenetic behaviour of the wild sow when cornered. It was a name that would stick. Despite Weise's opposition, however, it was arranged that Herrmann should outline his ideas personally to the *Reichsmarschall*, Hermann Göring, and he did so at Obersalzberg on 27 June, 1943. The Chief of Staff of the *Luftwaffe*, *Generaloberst* Jeschonnek, was also present at what was a small meeting. Herrmann was supported by his close associate in *Gruppe T*, *Major* Werner Baumbach, probably the greatest bomber pilot on the German side in the Second World War. The minutes of the meeting include the following passage:

'*Major* Hermann [sic] outlines his plans for freelance single-engined night fighting. As grounds for this plan he points out that the current building-up of a defensive belt and the control of individual fighters in small areas closely tied to the organisation on the ground is only appropriate to incoming flights that are widely separated. When the attacks are concentrated in space and time this system can only produce a set number of shootings-down. The establishment of a true defensive concentration by this means is impossible.

'*Major* Hermann therefore proposes: That in addition to the night-fighting method so far used, *helle Nachtjagd* should be carried out in the light of the searchlights in Flak areas provided with lights, using standard single-engined fighter aircraft. This will be particularly effective in that the searchlights coupled to *Würzburg* radars can hold their targets sufficiently long even in hazy weather. During major attacks in the Ruhr area (Düsseldorf, Essen etc.) there have regularly been fifty to 140 aircraft held in the searchlights for more than three minutes. That means that the conditions for interception are similar to those by day. Indeed, finding targets is probably easier than in daylight, because the targets are identified optically by the lights, so that target-finding by eye is easy without the necessity for radar control. By this method it is possible to carry out single-engined night-fighting over the target with between eighty and a hundred single-engined fighters and so achieve a considerable increase in the number shot down.

'In addition, because the system is not dependent upon the ground organisation, it is possible to alter the defensive focus rapidly as the bombers approach, so that single-engined night-fighter *Gruppen* positioned in the *Ruhrgebiet* and promptly scrambled to height when there are enemy penetrations from the west can cover individual targets in the *Ruhrgebiet* and further, should the bombers continue onward in the direction of eg, Berlin or Hamburg, accompany the bombers and then attack them over the target in the light of the searchlights.

'Co-operation with the Flak, already discussed with *General* Hintz, has been guaranteed. There is no question of stopping the Flak firing completely or by sectors, but it may be stopped by means of an optical signal indicating that a specific enemy aircraft is coming under fire from a friendly fighter attacking from astern. Recognition of friendly aircraft is guaranteed by the use of *Häuptling*.*

'The *Reichsmarschall* suggests as an extra means of optical identification, a 'cat's eye' type of reflecting system by means of a suitable paint or something similar. Recognition vis-a-vis friendly fighters can be ensured by means of a tail-light. It would be particularly advantageous if the fighter could remain in the darkness so that the rear gunner in the bomber would be dazzled by the searchlight and could not see the night-fighter.'

Göring liked Herrmann's ideas, and he and his volunteers became known as the *Nachtjagdversuchskommando*, or 'Night-Fighting Experimental Unit'. He was given permission to test his theories in the West, where his chances of action would be greater because the Ruhr was a more likely target than Berlin in the shorter nights of summer. Herrmann had already been in touch with the Commanding General of the *II. Flakkorps*, Hintz, responsible for the Ruhr area, who was co-operative and promised him that when an opportunity came for the *Wilde Sau* irregulars to go into action he would order the Flak to confine itself to 5,500 metres, or 18,000 feet.

Herrmann's chance came on 3 July, 1943, when in the early evening the air raid warning system forecast a heavy raid on the Ruhr area. Herrmann rapidly contacted his pilots, obtained permission from their superiors for them to join in his live experiment – he himself had no powers of command – and took off from Berlin/Staaken for the airfield at Mönchengladbach. When he arrived there nine of his volunteer pilots, who had flown on ahead of him from Berlin in their Bf 109s and Fw 190s, had already taken off and were circling as planned at between 6,000 and 7,000 metres above the centre of the sprawling Ruhr complex of towns.

Herrmann took off after them as soon as his machine had been refuelled. He was pleased to find that Hintz's agreement not to fire above 5,500 metres was obviously in force and that the Flak was not

* *Häuptling* was an IFF device that operated in conjunction with the *Würzburg* radar.

engaging his planes, as it certainly would have done in normal circumstances.

The approach of the bomber stream to the south of the Ruhr was clearly shown by the searchlights, the bursting flak shells and the explosions in the air and on the ground that marked the end of British bombers whose unhappy fate it had been to be intercepted by Kammhuber's conventional night-fighters, up in strength. When the leading bombers reached the Krefeld area, however, they did not turn north towards Essen, as had been expected, but south towards Düsseldorf and Cologne. Hermann's fighters sped after them. Harris's target for that night was in fact Cologne, which had already undergone the devastating raid just five nights previously, and he had dispatched a further 653 aircraft to the hard-hit city. For Herrmann and his fellow fighters this meant an unforeseen complication: the anti-aircraft guns that defended the cathedral city did not belong to *General* Hintz's *II. Flakkorps* but to the *7. Flakdivision* under *General* Burchardt, and to fly over Cologne meant with certainty that Herrmann's pilots would come under fire from the hundreds of heavy- and medium-calibre guns defending the city.

The first of Herrmann's pilots to shoot down a British bomber in the midst of the Flak over Cologne was Friedrich-Karl Müller, whose large nose had earned him the affectionate nickname '*Nasenmüller*' and when the ten of them who had taken part submitted their reports on landing, their claims amounted to a total of twelve bombers. That twelve bombers were indeed destroyed over Cologne was certain, but the Flak, who had never destroyed more than one or two in any previous night raid, also claimed them all. There followed a period of horse-trading, and it was finally decided that Burchardt's gunners and Herrmann's *Wilde Sau* pilots would be credited with six bombers each.

On completion of the operation Herrmann landed at Bonn/Hangelar airfield, although he did not know exactly where he was until he got out of his aircraft he had put down at the first convenient field that he saw, a practice that was to become normal operating procedure for the *Wilde Sau*. Physically and emotionally exhausted by his experiences, he went to bed, and early the following morning he was woken by an orderly – Hermann Göring was on the telephone.

Major *Friedrich-Karl Müller.*

Göring told Herrmann that he was to report to *Generaloberst* Hans Jeschonnek at Berchtesgaden that morning. He, Göring, wished to speak to him. The outcome of Herrmann's visit was that he was instructed to set up a night-fighter *Geschwader* of single-engined machines, JG 300, of which he was to be *Kommodore*. A first *Gruppe*, with its own aircraft, would be formed immediately at

Bonn/Hangelar, and he was to select pilots both for that *Gruppe* and for two others, which would be stationed at Rheine and Oldenburg but would share aircraft with the day-fighter units there as so-called *Aufsitzgruppen*, or lodger units.

Having thus convinced his superiors of the possibilities a Fw 190A-5 was quickly adapted – and given the affix U2 – by incorporating engine exhaust shrouds, to mask the exhaust flames at night, and anti-glare shields. The Fw 190A-5/U2 *Jabo-Rei* – the abbreviated form of *Jagdbomber mit vergrösserter Reichweite* or fighter/bomber with extended range – was armed with two wing rooted MG 151 cannon and an ETC 250 bomb rack under the fuselage. To extend its range two 66-gal. drop tanks were fitted under the wings and a limited number of aircraft were modified with the *Naxos Z* homing device.

Herrmann's first task, apart from gathering together the necessary pilots with experience of flying at night and the qualities appropriate to the swashbuckling nature of the job they were to do, was to begin devising and practising techniques and tactics. Herrmann said that he estimated that it would be the end of September before JG 300 could engage in operations. He was mistaken.

During the night of 27/28 July, 1943, with the mass bombing of Hamburg – known as 'the night of the fire-storm' – *Major* Hajo Herrmann's Wild Boars were up in such strength as they could muster. Under his command he now had three embryo *Gruppen*, I./JG 300 at Bonn/Hangelar under *Major* Ewald Janssen; II./JG 300 at Rheine led by *Major* Kurt Kettner; and III./JG 300 under *Major* von Buchwaldt at Oldenburg. He had his *Stabsschwarm* (Staff flight) at Hangelar, but his headquarters were in a country house near Bonn, the Schloss Allner, from where he would commute to Hangelar in a Fieseler Storch when leading his *Wilde Sau* men into action. The *Gruppen* at Rheine and Oldenburg were lodger units, II./JG 300 with the day-fighter *Gruppe*, II./JG 1, equipped with the Fw 109; and III./JG 300 flying the Bf 109 day-fighters of III./JG 1. The *Stab* and I./JG 300 at Hangelar had a mixture of both types of machines, including some Bf 109Ts, a version originally designed for operation from the aircraft carrier *Graf Zeppelin*, which was never completed. JG 300 had already experienced fatalities. Its first loss had been that of the twenty-

Major *Ewald Janssen,*
Gruppenkommandeur
I./JG 300.

three-year-old *Leutnant* Heinz Strauss of 4./JG 300, whose Fw 190 had crashed near Staaken, Berlin, during a searchlight practice on the night of 21 July. The *Geschwader* had suffered a heavy blow when the officer whom Herrmann had first appointed to command I./JG 300, *Major* Willy Gutsche, had been killed when his aircraft crashed from unknown causes the following night. Even this early the dangers of flying a single-engined machine, not equipped with blind-flying aids, by night were becoming apparent. Some *Wilde Sau* machines had operated *ad hoc* during the night of the attack on Essen that had come between the first two major attacks on Hamburg, and four machines had been lost, three pilots, *Feldwebel* Gunther Hattendorf, *Leutnant* Hans-Werner Schmidt and *Feldwebel* Heinrich Grill, paying the ultimate price. During the same raid *Feldwebel* Wolfgang Knobloch, severely wounded by machine-gun fire from a British bomber, had crash-landed his damaged Fw 190 at Rheine.

By the time, then, that JG 300, or the *Geschwader Herrmann* as it had come to be colloquially known, flew its first full-scale defensive mission over Hamburg on the night of 27/28 July, 1943, it had already lost six aircraft, the pilots of five of which had been killed. It had not been an auspicious beginning. But that night Herrmann's Wild Boar concept came closer to being vindicated. Twelve machines took off from Hangelar, Rheine and Oldenburg to hunt in the light of the fires from the inferno below, where they were joined by a small number of conventional night-fighters. Herrmann's pilots shot down four bombers over the city out of the total of seventeen that Bomber Command lost that night. Herrmann lost just one of his machines, the Fw 190 of *Leutnant* Fritz Tesch of 5./JG 300, at thirty-two years of age one of the older of the Wild Boar pilots, who had to crash-land, severely injured, after his fighter had been damaged in combat with a British bomber.

Two further raids completed the Battle of Hamburg, the first comparatively successful, the second one a failure. The aiming point for the attack during the night of 29/30 July was the same as that chosen for the previous raid, with the bombers approaching from the north. A total of 777 bombers took part and although the pathfinder's initial markers fell out of the target area a good concentration of bombing was achieved. Fortunately, for the people living in the area, the atmospheric conditions had changed from those of the first raid and they were mercifully spared the fire-storm that caused so much death and destruction during the first raid. Nevertheless, it was estimated that nearly 1,000 people lost their lives as a result of this bombing raid.

What turned out to be the final bombing attack of Hamburg was on the night of 2/3 August, 1943, when 740 RAF bombers were directed to targets to the north of the city. Violent thunderstorms over this region of Germany caused problems for the RAF pathfinders who were unable to pinpoint any targets with the result that damage and casualties on the ground were relatively light. Nevertheless, RAF Bomber Command lost thirty aircraft to Flak, conventional night-fighters and *Wilde Sau* operations.

The rise in Bomber Command losses was certainly due to the concerted effort now being made by the operational units of the *Nachtjagd*. Herrmann's *Wilde Sau* tactics, practised above the target by both his own single-engine fighters and the conventional twin-engine aircraft of the *Nachtjagd*, played a large part in the recovery of Germany's response to the night attacks. Many of the crews of the traditional night-fighter units, now freed from the restrictions of *General* Kammhuber's *Himmelbett* system, took enthusiastically to a new, freelance role. Pilots of Hajo Herrmann's JG 300 claimed approximately twenty kills for the loss of three of their own aircraft and one pilot, while the majority of the rest of the bombers destroyed fell to Kammhuber's men.

There was inevitably a transitional period before the change could be made from the close control of night-fighters by the *Himmelbett* technique to loose control from the Divisional Battle Command posts and until improved intercept radars, less susceptible to 'Window', could be fitted into the fighters. It was during this period that Hajo Herrmann's Wild Boars, boosted by considerable official publicity, achieved fame and hero status among the German population. The conventional night-fighter men were more critical.

In the immediate aftermath of the Hamburg catastrophe. Göring once more demonstrated his inherent capacity for peremptory, impulsive and irrational decision-making and disregard of protocol. Herrmann attended a short series of meetings that Göring convened to discuss the performance of Kammhuber's night fighters and the way ahead, and at one of the meetings it emerged that Kammhuber, who was not himself present, had been less than sympathetic to Herrmann's original proposals for single-engined participation in the night battle against Bomber Command and that he had taken no action following the encounter between Herrmann's pilots and the RAF Mosquito over Berlin in April. Göring thereupon criticised Kammhuber severely, turned to Herrmann and told him, 'I am subordinating the *XII. Fliegerkorps* to you!' The *Reichsmarschall* went on to say that henceforth Herrmann would be responsible for everything that happened in the field of night-fighters, and that he, Herrmann, should issue orders to that effect to Kammhuber. It was as if the Chief of Staff of the RAF was placing a Squadron Leader in a position of authority above an Air Marshal, and it put Herrmann in an impossible position. Herrmann decided to interpret Göring's instruction in his own way: he would co-operate with Kammhuber's officers to his utmost, but not from a position of superiority. He could not blatantly disobey Göring's instruction, and he would not embarrass Kammhuber by demanding from Göring strict terms of reference and a formal statement of the extent of his powers of control and command. In effect he relied on Göring's reputation for not following through his off-the-cuff decisions, a reliance that proved to be justified. It inevitably became accepted that Herrmann was now Göring's protege, and he was able to exercise a degree of authority far above that implicit in his comparatively lowly rank of *Major*. Recalling those days, Herrmann wrote:

'It must appear somewhat surprising that Göring would wish to put me in a position of authority above the Commanding General; I was equally surprised at the time. But such measures on the part of Göring were not all that unprecedented. Drastic measures usually followed drastic statements. Galland, too, was a very young operational commander without command experience when he was made Inspector of Fighters. Dieter Peltz was a highly talented Stuka pilot and was promoted from Captain to Staff Colonel and appointed *Fliegerführer* England (Officer in Charge of Air Operations against England). My case was easier to explain. Göring was up to his neck. I was his last hope in a situation of extreme emergency ... He clearly felt that he was progressively losing Hitler's confidence. And Hitler was his shining example.

'At the time I did not fully appreciate Göring's inner conflict. Of course I was aware, when he spoke to me on the telephone about Hamburg, that he was in a state of agitation. But I also felt that he was well in control of himself, and I formed the opinion that he was motivated by fear and dismay.

'So it is understandable that he should simply leave me with orders to go to the *XII. Korps* in Deelen, take over command and see that my instructions were obeyed, and then himself go home to Emmy. All I could do, flabbergasted as I was, was to look at his Adjutant, *Oberst* von Brauchitsch, and ask him what was going on. I told Brauchitsch that I would not act in such a way towards Kammhuber, even though I considered him a bureaucratic air commander. I said I was prepared to fly to Deelen and call together the whole of the senior command staff and give a presentation of my ideas. Brauchitsch said that I should do that for a start.'

While Herrmann was not prepared to go over Kammhuber's head, he was equally unprepared to allow his Wild Boars to be subordinated to Kammhuber and integrated into the overall air defence system. He therefore asked for, and was granted, independence of control:

'When I later reported personally to Göring he said to Loerzer, his old comrade from World War One and now his Head of Personnel, "Bruno, you'd better think what sort of a job we can find for Hajo Herrmann... *Jagdführer* (Fighter Commander) or something like that." I protested. I said that the correct status of my operational command could only be a *Jagddivision* (Fighter Division) directly subordinate to him, Göring, and not on any account subordinate to Kammhuber or Stumpff, in overall control of air defence. *Generaloberst* Stumpff had just come down from Norway, where he had led a comfortable life.'

Following this meeting Herrmann was notified that he had been awarded (August 2, 1943) the *Eichenlaub* (Oakleaves) to the *Ritterkreuz*. He subsequently received the *Schwertern* (Swords) on January 23, 1944. Herrmann was also instructed to form two new *Wilde Sau Geschwaderen*, JG 301 and JG 302, and, together with JG 300, they would form *30 Jagddivision* that he would command. *Major* Kettner who was *Gruppenkommandeur* of *II Gruppe* took over as *Kommodore* JG 300. *Major* Helmut Weinreich, from Herrmann's old bomber *Geschwader*, KG 30, and already the holder of the *Ritterkreuz*, became *Kommodore* of JG 301 while Ewald Janssen became *Kommodore* of JG 302.

Owing to the demands being made on German fighter resources elsewhere, the three *Geschwaderen* could, at best, provide

serviceable aircraft for only one *Gruppe* in each (mostly Messerschmitt Bf 109G-6s and Focke-Wulf Fw 190A-5/U2s, some equipped with Naxos Z homing equipment). Other *Wilde Sau* pilots were forced to rely on, when available, the aircraft of released day fighter *Staffeln* based on the same airfields. Combat successes at night rose sharply during the second half of 1943 and the pilots of 30 *Jagddivision* attracted considerable public acclaim. Not unnaturally the *Wilde Sau* aircraft soon displayed signs of strain, being flown constantly by day and night. Serviceability rates decreased steadily so that soon both day and night flying efforts declined. Furthermore, justifiable criticism came to be levelled at these freelance tactics by the established night defence organisation, not least by the pilots engaged in conventional night fighter operations. Radar screens were becoming confused by the often unplotted and frequently unauthorized *Wilde Sau* operations, which were never under close control. Also the radio channels were frequently jammed by the chatter of excited day fighter pilots that close control of the broadcast of information to the night fighters became impossible. Inevitably this ingenious expedient died, and the *Wilde Sau* pilots were retrained for return to conventional day fighting tactics.

CHAPTER SEVEN

An Aircraft to fit the Rôle

ALTHOUGH the A-5 series was the principal variant in 1943, many sub-variants of this type soon became available to fill the increasing rôle demands made by the *Luftwaffe* High Command. In fact the A-5, from its very beginnings, was designed to accept a much wider variety of modification – the Umbau *(Umrüst-Bausätze)* – that gave the many variants of this series the 'U' affix.

The Fw 190A-5 was primarily used as a fighter and fighter-bomber, powered by a 1,600-hp BMW 801D-2 engine that was moved approximately six inches forward from its previous location and increased the length of the fuselage to 29 ft 5 in. The span was 34 ft, with a height 12 ft 4 in., and the wing area 189 sq ft. The standard armament comprised two 7.9-mm MG 17 machine-guns, mounted in the nose, two 20-mm MG 151 cannons, mounted in the wing-roots, and two 20-mm MG/FF cannons mounted on the wings. The A-5 also had the FuG 16Z and FuG 25 radio equipment installed. Records show that 723 aircraft of this series were built by Focke-Wulf, Fieseler, AGO, and Arado with a number of the aircraft equipped with tropical modifications and designated Fw 190A-5tp.

To test the Fw 190A-5 as a night ground-attack aircraft three different, and experimental, installations were fitted to *Werk Nr* 783 in an attempt to discover the most effective means of damping the flames emitted from the exhaust outlets. Two designs were developed by the firm of Treiber, and another firm, Klatte, had developed a circular split exhaust pipe.

Two aircraft, Fw 190A-5 *Werk Nr* 1083, with the registration GE+LA, and *Werk Nr* 711, registration TN+ZK, were prepared with these modifications. The side exhaust pipes were fitted with large fairings, code-named '*Ofenschirm*' (Fire-screen), with additional fairings, code-named '*Kohlenkaste*' (Coal-box), fitted beneath the engine .

The tests were flown at the *Luftwaffe* Test Centre at Rechlin on June 22, 1943, by *Oberleutnant* Ziller and *Hauptmann* Schmitz and an observation aircraft, a Junkers Ju 88A, was used to check how effective the flame protectors were. 711 made five night landings but both pilots reported that vision was impaired by reflections from the bright surfaces of the aircraft's skin. To double-check these findings two additional pilots, named Stephan and Mondrig, flew the same aircraft on the nights of June 24 and 25, 1943.

During the observation flights with the Ju 88, the Fw 190A-5, *Werk Nr* 1083, was used with tests being made at altitudes of 3,400 ft, 13,600 ft, and 20,400 ft. Tests were made conducted under varying flight conditions with the engine developing normal, medium and full power. The Fw 190 repeatedly attacked the Ju 88, in level flight, passing it at a distance of between 130-150 ft. From reported observations of the Ju 88's crew it was found that at altitudes of 3,400 and 13,600 ft no trace of exhaust flame could be seen, and that only at full power at an altitude of 20,400 ft could a small flame be seen. Repeated observation

Fw 190A-5/U13 carries two x 66-gals fuel tanks under wings. Ground crew member hands on for dear life.

concluded that the visible flame was coming from the exhaust outlet of cylinder number 8, but after many adjustments it proved impossible to eliminate. Taken over all, the final report showed that the flame-damping equipment was within an acceptable tolerance.

As a result of these tests, five aircraft, Fw 190A-5/U8 *Werk Nr* 1449, 1450, 1482, 1513 and Fw 190A-5/U13, *Werk Nr* 180925, were fitted with the flame-damping equipment and re-designated as Fw 190A-5/U2 *Jabo-Rei* night fighter-bombers. These aircraft were destined for the *Wilde Sau* unit and became the first of JG 300s 'customized' acquisitions. This version was powered by the BMW 801D-2 engine and was armed with two MG 151s located in each wing root. It was also fitted with an ETC 250 bomb rack that could carry either an SC 250 or SC 500 bomb beneath the fuselage. It was the usual practice for the aircraft to be fitted with a 66-gallon external fuel tank under each wing to give an increased range and other special equipment included a modified FuG 16Z radio, and a landing searchlight.

The next modification of the Fw 190A-5, in chronological order, was the A-5/U3, which became the forerunner of the later F-2 series. The Fw 190A-5/U3 *Jabo* and the 'F' series were officially designated as '*Schlachtflugzeug*', or ground support aircraft.

Fw 190A-5 probably with JG 54 in Russia carried an SC 250 lb bomb on fuselage rack.

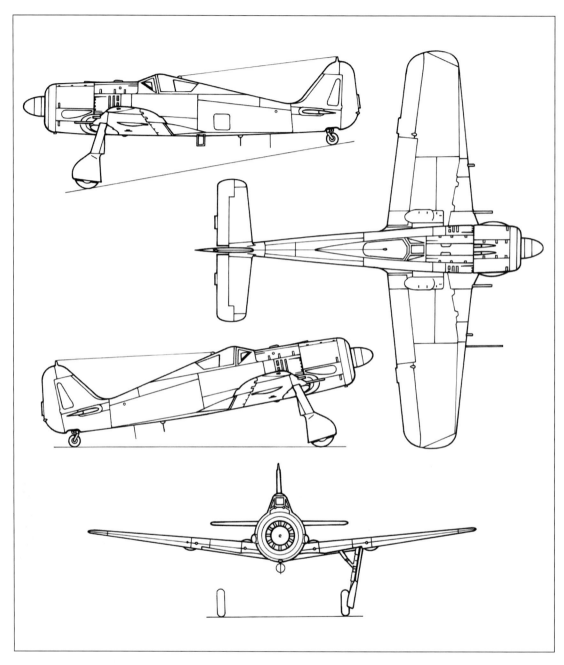

The finished Fw 190A-5/U3 began to be delivered during May   *Fw 190A-5*
1943. With additional defensive armour weighing 893-lbs its
armament was restricted to two MG 17 machine-guns, with 900
rounds each, and located in the nose, forward of the cockpit. The
ETC 250 bomb rack under the fuselage could carry either a

SC 250 or SC 500 bomb, with two external tanks of 66-gallons capacity. Alternatively, combinations of one SC 250, and four SC 50 bombs under the wings could be carried, or eight SC 50s under the fuselage and wings.

The next modification, the Fw 190A-5/U4, was intended as a reconnaissance-fighter, similar to the Fwl90A-3/U4. It was to be fitted with two Rb 12 cameras, however, it is likely that this remained in project form only. The existence of further modified A-5s in numerical order, the Fw 190A-5/U5, /U6 and /U7 is not known but remains doubtful.

The Fw 190A-5/U8 became the prototype for the G-l and G-2 series. Like these it was a *Jabo-Rei*, or a fighter-bomber with extended range, and fixed armament consisted of two MG 151 fitted in the wing roots. Normal bomb load comprised one SC 250 bomb beneath the fuselage and two external fuel tanks, each of

Fw 190A-5/U3 with two SC 50 bombs under each wing and an ETC 250 rack under the fuselage.

66-gallons capacity, were carried beneath each wing.

Fw 190A-5/U8, *Werk Nr* 1286, was used for experiments with heavier bomb loads. In one case it was fitted with a special bomb rack that incorporated additional struts to carry one 2,200-lbs or a SB 1000 mine-bomb. Yet another experiment was made with a bomb rack, moved forward 10 inches to enable it to carry a SC 500 bomb, weighing 1,100-lbs.

*Bomb rack equipped
190A-5s of I./SG 4, Italy
early 1944. Note national
marks partially obscured
by rough painting.*

Fw 190A-5/U8, *Werk Nr* 1288, was modified to carry Methanol in the front fuselage tank for engine injection.

Probably in desperation the *Luftwaffe* High Command had ordered Focke-Wulf to carry out a feasibility study to use an Fw 190A-5/U8 for 'suicide' missions. An A-5, *Werk Nr* 1428, was intended to become a *SV-Flugzeug* (SV stood for *Selbstvernichtung* or Suicide aircraft) but it is not known if it was ever used in this capacity. It was planned that such SV aircraft would dive into the bomber formations or on important targets.

A very late Fw 190A-5/U8, *Werk Nr* 150871, was used to test a guidance device, designated TSA-2, for experiments with Bomb-torpedoes (BT).

Of the Fw 190A-5/U9 *Zerstörer* only two examples were built. These were *Werk Nr* 812 and 816, the latter aircraft later being designated V35. These served as prototypes for the A-7, A-8 and the F-8 series with both being fitted with the new wing designed for the A-6. While *Werk Nr* 812 had an armament of two 13-mm MG 131 machine-guns mounted on the front fuselage and two 30-mm MG 151 cannons in the wing roots, *Werk Nr* 816 had an additional MG 151 cannon mounted under each outer wing. Both prototypes were powered by the BMW 801D-2 engine. *Werk Nr* 812 was transferred to the Test Centre at Tarnewitz on August 14, 1943, with the V-35 following soon after.

Only a single example of the Fw 190A-5/U10 was built, *Werk Nr* 861, which served as prototype for the A-6 series. By now the standard engine for the Fw 190, it was fitted with a BMW 801D-2 and the normal armament of two MG 17 machine-guns and four MG 151 cannons it also featured the new A-6 wing. After intensive testing, which was completely satisfactory, this aircraft was incorporated into the so-called *Werks-Schwarm* on July 28, 1943. The *Werks-* or *Industrie-Schwarm* was a unit of four or five Fw 190s which were flown by works pilots to defend the Focke-Wulf factory in Bremen against Allied air attacks. Beside the company's test pilot Melhorn, who was killed in action, Kurt Tank repeatedly took part in actions against Allied bombers until he was forbidden to do so by the Air Ministry.

Fw 190A-5/U11 *Schlachtflugzeug* became the prototype of the

The Fw 190A-5/U3 carries SC 50 bombs under each wing and a SC 500 bomb under the fuselage.

projected ground-attack versions designated A-8/R3, F-3/R3 and F-8/R3. This was a normal Fw 190A-5, *Werk Nr* 1303, which had the outer wing MG FF cannon removed and replaced by underslung nacelles carrying a 30-mm MK 103 cannon. The 20-mm MG 151 cannons in the wing roots and the MG 17 machine-guns mounted over the engine were retained and this aircraft was transferred for intensive weapons tests to the Test Centre at Tarnewitz on September 18, 1943.

The next modification was the Fw 190A-5/U12 *Zerstörer*, which might have been more accurately designated A-5/R1, since it was the first Fw 190 to have the *Rüstsätzen* R1. Fw 190A-5, *Werk Nr* 813 with the registration BH+CC, was selected, and so become the prototype of the A-7/R1 series. The two nose-mounted MG 17 machine-guns were retained on this aircraft but the two wing-mounted MG FF cannon were removed and replaced by underslung nacelles housing two 20-mm MG 151 cannon in each. The nacelles were officially designated WB 151/20 (WB for *Waffenbehalter* or weapons container). On July 1, 1943, the machine was also transferred to Tarnewitz, carrying the new armament of two MG 17 machine-guns and six MG 151 cannons.

The second prototype, *Werk Nr* 814 with the registration BH+CD, also designated as a Fw 190A-5/U12 was given the same armament as *Werks Nr* 813 and transferred to Tarnewitz on *A WB 151 nacelle.*

August 20, 1943, as a prototype for the A-6/R1 and A-8/R1 series.

Fw 190A-5/U13 represented a further stage in the *Jabo-Rei* development (*Jabo-Rei* or fighter-bomber with extended range), which had begun with the A-5/U2. Fw 190A-5, *Werk Nr* 817 and registration BH+CG, was modified for this purpose. All armament was removed except the wing root-mounted MG 151 cannons. One ETC 501 bomb rack was fitted under the fuselage and external tanks of 66-gallon capacity each were attached to the wings with racks, which, like those of the A5/U8, were developed by Messerschmitt for the Me 109. Night flying equipment was similar to the A-5/U2 and a landing searchlight was installed in the wing. This aircraft in turn was transferred to Rechlin for intensive testing on April 15, 1943.

A torpedo fighter, the Fw 190A-5/U14 carrying a LTF 5b torpedo. The ETC 501 fuselage rack has been adapted for this purpose and the tailwheel lengthened to give the fuselage added clearance.

The Fw 190A-5/U13, *Werk Nr* 825, also served as a prototype for the G-3 *Jabo-Rei* version and this had wing racks developed by Focke-Wulf under each wing to carry one type SC 250 bomb, or one fuel tank of 66-gallon capacity.

A different role was envisaged for the Fw 190A-5/U14, of which two examples were built: *Werk Nr* 871 and 872 with the markings TD+SI and TD+SJ. All armament was removed except for the two MG 151 cannon in the wing-roots and in place of this it carried a torpedo, type LTF 5b, which was attached to an adapted ETC 501 torpedo rack. The gross weight of the aircraft with

torpedo, but without external tanks, was 10,251-lbs, and with two 66-gallon tanks under the wings, 11,464-lbs. The fin was enlarged and the tailwheel leg lengthened to give the torpedo ground clearance on take off. Maximum speed without torpedo and external tankage was 323-mph, while with torpedo only and no external tanks it was reduced to 310-mph. Fw 190A-5/U14, *Werk Nr* 871, was transferred for initial tests to Adelheide, near Delmenhorst (NW Germany) on August 9, 1943, and was demonstrated to the *Kriegsmarine* and *Luftwaffe* at Gotenshafen. However, as no serial production was undertaken and no subsequent combat action was reported, it is presumed that the trials did not prove successful and that the the naval and airforce observers were not overly impressed.

This photograph was taken during unstallation of the necessary electrical equipment for the torpedo-release.

The next version was also a torpedo-fighter, the Fw 190A-5/U15. Only one aircraft of the type was built, armament being removed as with the A-5/U14. Instead of the normal LTF 5b torpedo it was intended to carry the LT 950 guided-torpedo designed by *Blohm u. Voss*, with Askania ALSK 121 guidance equipment. Although intensive tests were carried out at Gotenshafen with the LT 950, carried by an He 111 and a Ju 88, it is not known if the Fw 190A-5/U15 was similarly tested.

Another attempt to strengthen the armament of the Fw 190 for attacks upon the 4-engined bombers was the Fw 190A-5/U16. For this modification Fw 190A-5, *Werk Nr* 1346, was rebuilt, the outer wing MG 151s being removed and replaced by a nacelle beneath each wing which housed a 30-mm. MK 103 cannon. This aircraft was transferred to Tarnewitz on August 24, 1943, for weapons tests.

The last modification of the Fw 190A-5 series was the A-5/U17, which served as a prototype for the Fw 190F-3 series. This *Schlachtflugzeug* (Ground support aircraft) had an armament of two nose-mounted MG 17 machine-guns and two wing root-mounted MG 151 cannons. In addition it incorporated ETC 50 bomb racks beneath each wing to carry SC 50 bombs.

The single version of the Fw 190A-5 series fitted with a *Rüstsätz* was the Fw 190A-5/R6. These were normal Fw 190A-5s already in service, but subsequently fitted with the Wfr Gr. 21, and they played an important role in the fight against the B-17 Flying Fortresses. The Wfr Gr. 21 was a rocket originally used by the Army in the so-called '*Nebelwerfer*', a rocket projector designed by an old rocket specialist, Rudolf Nebel, consisting of five tubes, each housing one Wfr Gr. 21.

Fw 190A-5/U3 with an ETC 250 bomb rack under the fuselage and 66-gal. external fuel tanks under each wing.

On October 14, 1943, the Fw 190A-5/R6s of JG 1 and JG 26 had their first real combat test when 228 four-engined bombers of the US 8th Air Force set out from England for a raid upon Schweinfurt, where over forty per cent of the German ball-bearing industry was concentrated. It was planned that these Fortresses

would be joined over the target by another strong bomber unit
taking off from US 9th Air Force bases in Libya. The raid was a
failure because the close formations of bombers were split up by
the exploding Wfr Gr. 21s, which were discharged into the
formations by Fw 190A-5/R6s from a range at which the American
gunners had no chance of hitting back at their attackers. With the
formations broken up in confusion, single bombers became easy
prey for the fighters. According to Allied reports sixty-two
bombers were shot down, seventeen more crashed before or
during landing, and a further 121 aircraft were damaged so
severely that about thirty per cent of them had to be written-off.
According to these same reports, the Germans lost 186 fighters,
but *Luftwaffe* sources, reporting the same action, claimed 121
Allied bombers destroyed for a loss of thirty-eight fighters with
fifty-one severely damaged.

Another weapon which achieved considerable success against the
bombers was the new Hexogen ammunition, which was first used
by the fighter units in the spring of 1943. These were incendiary
grenades which produced seven searing flames of 12-in. length,
one after another. When one of these projectiles hit its target it
penetrated the outer skin and other plates, sending out its lethal
flames at rapid intervals. A single hit in close proximity to the fuel
tank of a Fortress was sufficient to send it down in flames.

The most difficult problem facing the German pilots in their
combat with the four-engined bombers, was to find a method of
attack which offered the best possible chance of success with
minimum loss to themselves. Orders from the *Luftwaffe* High
Command repeatedly demanded that these aircraft should be
attacked in the traditional manner, from behind, and that pilots
should open fire at the closest possible range. However,
experience showed that this was the shortest way to self-
destruction.

It was decided, therefore, to attack head-on and in closed
formation, at the same altitude as the attacking bombers, waiting
until the very last moment to dive beneath or pull up over them.
This method proved successful only for the more experienced
pilots but not for the younger ones whose ability to judge speed
and distance had not fully developed. Many of these young pilots
lost their lives when they crashed into their target because they

had miscalculated these factors. So the method of attack was changed, the German fighters continuing to attack from the front, but at an angle of ten degrees above the flight path of the bombers. This proved to be the most successful method and was retained for a long time.

In the late Spring of 1943 preparations were made for the production of the new Fw 190A-6 series. Although this had been planned to begin in April, it was not until June that the programme got under way. The A-6 was to be produced only by AGO, Arado and Fieseler and, since it was intended as an assault aircraft (*Schlachtflugzeug*), it was necessary to develop adequate armour for the underside of the aircraft. The armour shield of the engine was already satisfactory, but the oil cooler required additional protection.

Intensive tests of the new installation were undertaken with Fw 190A-6, *Werk Nr* 410258, and with the outer wing armament removed. This left two MG 17 machine-guns mounted in the nose and two MG 151 cannons in the wing roots. In addition it had one ETC 501 bomb rack beneath the fuselage. The prototype of the   A-6 series, as already described, was the Fw 190A-5/U10,

Fw 190A-6 of I./JG 54 Grunherz, Siwerskada, Winter 1943/44.

Werk Nr 861. In its final form the A-6 had an armament of two engine-mounted MG 17s, two MG 151s in the wing roots and two additional MG 151s in the outer part of the wings. Provision was also made for the installation of FuG 16Z-E and FuG 25 radio equipment. With completion of development and testing, the new armour protection was available for installation after August 6, 1943.

After successful tests with Fw 190A-5/U12, *Werk Nr* 813, production of the modified Fw 190A-6/R1 *Zerstörer* was ordered with the final armament now replacing the outer wing MG 151 cannon with under-wing nacelles carrying two MG 151 giving the aircraft a total armament of two machine-guns and six cannons. Although, in its final form, the aircraft was provided with an extremely effective fire-power the additional weight and drag from the nacelles reduced the range by 19-20 miles and the maximum speed by some 25-mph. As this version was urgently required for service on the Eastern front, the first sixty aircraft, which had been delivered to *Luftzeugamt Kupper*, were rebuilt there and were ready for service on November 30, 1943. In January 1944, AGO were ordered to supply ten Fw 190A-6/Rls, and from February the schedule was for fifty every month, athough it is doubtful AGO were ever able to produce on this scale.

Fw 190A-6 of I./JG 54 runs up engine while connected to battery starter. Russia's winter was hard on man and machine. Siwerskaja.

Fw 190A-4/U4, Eastern Front, 1943.

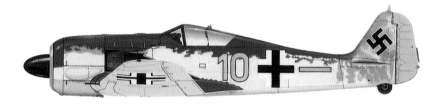

Fw 190A-4 of 6./JG 26 'Schlageter', Northern France, 1943.

Fw 190A-4 of I./JG 51 'Mölders', Siwerskaya, Russia, 1943.

Fw 190A-4 of I./JG 51 'Mölders', Immola, Russia, 1943.

Fw 190A-4 of I./JG 51 'Mölders', Russia, 1944.

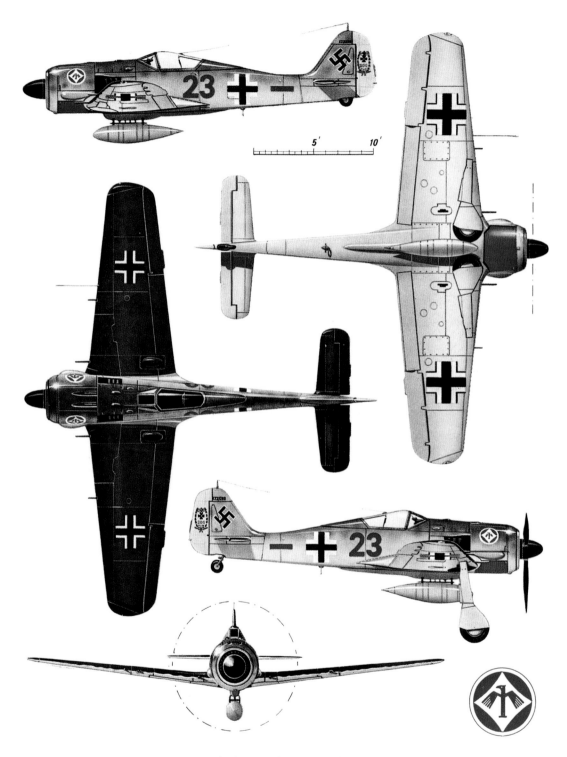

Fw 190A-7 of II./JG 1 'Oesau', of Major *Heinz Bär*

Fw 190A-4 of I./JG 51 'Mölders', Russia, 1944.

Fw 190A-4 flown by Oberleutnant *Erich Rudorffer,* Staffelkapitän *of 6./JG 2 'Richthofen', Tunis, 1943*

Fw 190A-4 of I./JG54 'Grünherz', Siwerskaya, Russia, 1943.

Fw 190A-4 of I./JG54 'Grünherz', Siwerskaya, Russia, 1943.

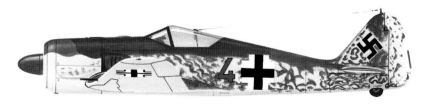

Fw 190A-4 of JG 26 'Schlageter', Northern France, 1943.

Fw 190A-5 of I./JG 51 'Mölders.'

Fw 190A-5 flown by Hauptmann *Heinrich Krafft,*
Gruppenkommandeur *of I./JG 51 'Mölders', Russia, 1942.*

Fw 190A-5/Trop. (Jabo), with an SC 250 bomb, Sicily 1943.

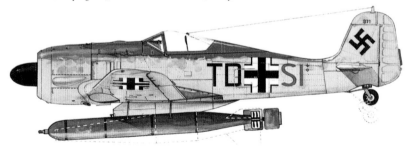

Fw 190A-5/U15 with an LT F5b torpedo.

Fw 190A-5 of JG 300 'Wilde Sau' with a 66-gallon external fuel tank.

Fw 190A-5/U8 of SKG 10 (Schnellkampfgeschwader)
with an SC 250 bomb, France, June 1943.

Fw 190A-6 flown by Major *von Graff of a Training Unit*
(Blindflugschulen) *when shot down July 27, 1943.*

Fw 190A-7 of II./JG 1 'Oesau', of Major *Heinz Bär.*

Fw 190A-7 flown by Oberstleutnant *Josef 'Pips' Priller,*
Kommodore *of JG 26 'Schlageter', June 1944.*

Fw 190A-8 of 5./JG 300 'Defence of the Reich'.

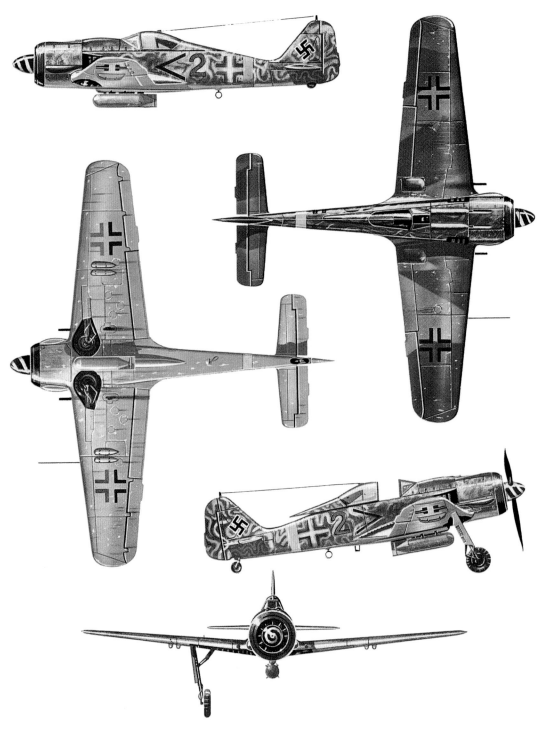

Fw 190F-8 of 2./Schlachtgeschwader 1 flown by the Gruppe Adjutant, *Hungary, winter 1944/45.*

Fw 190A-8/U3 flown by the Gruppenkommandeur *of I./JG 54 'Grünherz', Siwerskaya, Russia, 1944.*

Fw 190A-8/U3 of III./JG 54 'Grünherz', Russia, 1944.

Fw 190A-8 of 5./JG 300 'Defence of the Reich', 1944.

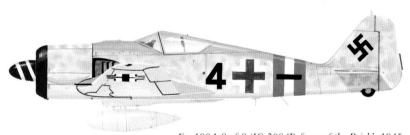

Fw 190A-8 of 8./JG 300 'Defence of the Reich', 1945.

Fw 190A-8 of (Sturmstaffel)./JG 4 'Defence of the Reich', 1944/45.

Fw 190F-8 of 2./Schlachtgeschwader 2 'Immelman' flown by the Gruppe Adjutant, *Hungary, winter 1944/45.*

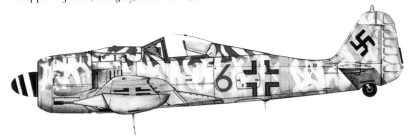

Fw 190F-8/R3 of Schlachtgeschwader 2 'Immelman', *Hungary, winter 1944/45.*

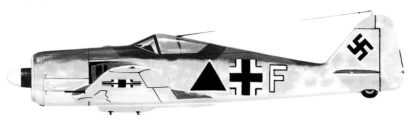

Fw 190G-2 of an unknown Schlachtgeschwader, *Eastern Front, 1943.*

Fw 190A-8 of 8./JG 300 'Defence of the Reich' January 1945.

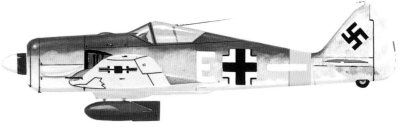

Fw 190G-3 of II./SG 10, Rumania, 1944/45.

Of the projected Fw 190A-6/R2 *Zerstörer* series, only a single prototype, the Fw 190V51 *Werk Nr* 530765, was built. It was completed in March 1944, and became the prototype for the Fw 190A-7/R2. The prototype had a slight modification to the armament when the wing mounted MG 151 cannon were replaced by 30-mm MK 108 cannon beneath each wing.

The Fw 190A-6/R3 was a project only and was never built, while of the Fw 190A-6/R4 only a single prototype was produced. This was Fw 190V45, *Werk Nr* 7347, which, in its final form, was to be powered by a 2,000-hp BMW 801TS engine with a turbo-blower. Since this engine was not available when *Werk Nr* 7347 was first built, the normal 1,700-hp BMW 801D-2, but with a GM-1 booster, was installed. In this form the prototype was completed in mid-September 1943 and transferred to Rechlin for testing of the GM-1 installation on September 18, 1943. Shortly afterwards, it was returned to the manufacturer for installation of the BMW 801TS powerplant, though this did not become available until July 1944. It was later transferred to Langenhagen, near Hanover, but flight testing was not completed before the war ended.

The last version of the Fw 190A-6 was the A-6/R6 *Pulk-Zerstörer*, '*Pulk*' was a *Luftwaffe* 'slang' expression applied to US Air Force close formation bombers. This variant was equipped with the Wfr Gr 21 rocket-projector, and it was intended that Fieseler should

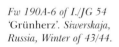

Fw 190A-6 of I./JG 54 'Grünherz'. Siwerskaja, Russia, Winter of 43/44.

produce this version. For its modification, the design team followed what was normal practice and issued modification instructions, called *Änderungs-Anweisung* (ÄA). These consisted of the necessary drawings together with written instructions to enable *Luftwaffe* units to carry out the work should the modification not be incorporated during production. When aircraft had already been delivered to units, *Änderungssätze* (Modification sets) were made up by the manufacturer and delivered to the *Luftzeugamt* responsible for the type, who in turn supplied them to unit workshops. The Fw 190A-6/R6 first came into being by the incorporation of ÄA123, and from November 1943 Fieseler began to produce A-6s with the R6 set incorporated. Altogether, 569 Fw 190A-6s were built from April to September 1943, fifty-five by Arado, 280 by AGO and 234 by Fieseler.

By the end of September 1943 there were 3,223 Fw 190s in the 'A' series produced.

The Fw 190 A-6/U3 was a *Jabo* conversion fitted with wing and fuselage racks similar to the A-5/U3.

In the figures given above the first aircraft of the new A-7 series, production of which began in December 1943, are not included.

Prototypes for the new A-7 series were Fw 190V35, *Werk Nr* 816, and Fw 190A-5/U9, *Werk Nr* 812, the latter aircraft has previously been described. The Fw 190V35 had a new powerplant, the 2,000-hp BMW 801F, which was an improved version of the 801D-2, but reliable supplies of this engine did not appear until the later development of the Fw 190A-9 series.

Only eighty examples of the A-7 were produced and incorporated a number of changes over the previous series. The engine-mounted 9.7-mm MG 17s were replaced by 13-mm MG 131 machine-guns; four 20-mm MG 151 cannon in the wings. The electrical equipment was simplified and a Revi 16b gun-sight was fitted to replace the former C 12d. The FuG 16Z-E and FuG 25 was the standard radio equipment and provisions were also made for a new tail-wheel arrangement.

Athough delivery date for the A-7 series was December 1943, the first aircraft of this series did not become available until January 1944, and were manufactured by Focke-Wulf, AGO and Fieseler, who were responsible for producing at least half of the final total.

Fw 190A-8/R1s were used for gound support as well as interception. Here is seen an aircraft of 9 Staffel of Jagdgeschwader 2 'Richthofen'.

Of the Fw 190A-7/Rl only the prototype, Fw 190A-5/U12, *Werk Nr* 813, was completed, but this was also used as the prototype for the A-6/R1 and has already been described .

The Fw 190A-7/R2 *Zerstörer* was designed to carry two 30-mm MK 108 cannons in the wings and replacing the 20-mm MG 151 cannons. The prototype of this series, and also for the A-6/R2, was Fw 190V51, *Werk Nr* 53 0765.

Production started at the Fieseler factory in December 1943 with ten aircraft coming off the line in January 1944, ten in February and thirty in March.

The reintroduction of the MW 50 water-methanol engine booster gave the Fw 190A-8 additional speed when crucially needed, but the aircraft's principal characteristic was an internal fuel capacity increased by 25-gallons. This feature improved the maximum loaded weight to 9,424-lb and this, in turn, allowed more armament variations. This, the final fully produced 'A' series, was to be built in larger numbers than any other sub-variant. The Fw 190A-8/R1 *Zerstörer* had the two outer-wing cannon were each replaced by flat nacelles each containing two fast-firing 20-mm MG 151 cannon. This, at the time, made the Fw 190 the heaviest armed aircraft with the *Luftwaffe* as it could

now carry six 20-mm cannon and two 13-mm machine-guns. The Fw 190A-8/R2 was similar in all aspects save that the paired MG 151 cannon, housed in the under-wing nacelles, were replaced by pairs of 30-mm MK 108 cannon.

Fw 190A-8 of 2./SG 2, Hungary 1944/45.

The Fw 190A-8/R3 was a ground-attack fighter with two long-barrelled 30-mm MK 108 cannon, which had a lower firing rate but with higher muzzle velocity, mounted on the outer wing.

The Fw 190A-8/R7 *Rammjäger* was intended to be used for ramming attacks against Allied bombers. A small number of this type were operated by special *Sturmstaffeln*, attached to the traditonal *Jagdgeschwaderen*, and although fitted with standard armament it also incorporated additional armour plating.

Designed as a bad-weather interceptor fighter the Fw 190A-8/R11 had standard armament but was equipped with the FuG 16Ze and FuG 25a radio and a PKS 12 automatic pilot. This development was principally to counter Allied bombers which were, by 1944, bombing 'blind' through cloud. The A-8/R12 was a modification with the same purpose and, like the A-8/R11, was powered by the turbo-supercharged 2,000-hp BMW 801TS engine and utilized a heated cockpit. The only difference between the two types was that while the A-8/R11 had standard armament the A-8/R12 used MK 108 cannon as a replacement for the MG 131. There is, however,

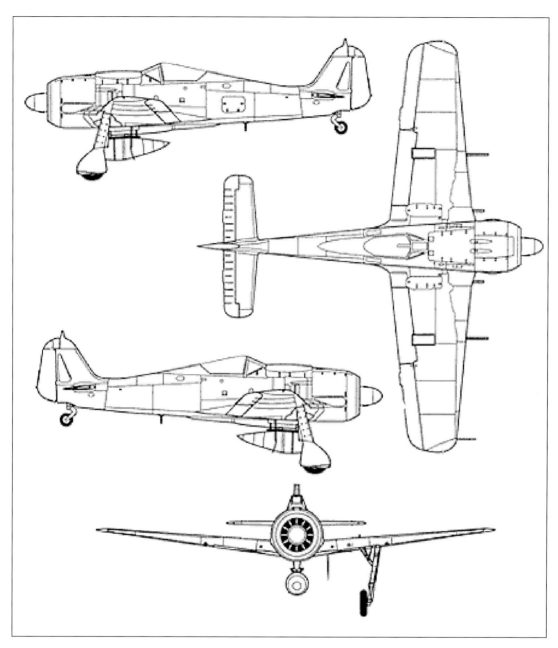

Fw 190A-8

no evidence that either type were ever used operationally.

An 'oddity' in this series was the Fw 190A-8/U1, an *Umbau* modification of which only three examples were completed. A standard Fw 190 was converted to include a tandem cockpit by adding a second seat with duplicate instruments and flying controls aft of the standard cockpit. The top decking of the rear

fuselage was adapted to allow an extended canopy. This variant was brought about by a proposal to convert Junkers Ju 87 pilots on to the Fw 190 in a ground support rôle, and the two prototypes, prepared by Focke-Wulf, were intended to provide patterns for Service establishments to carry out their own conversions. The first prototype Fw 190A-8/U1 flew on January 23, 1944, and the second was delivered to *Jagdgeschwader* 103 in July that year to re-train former Ju 87D pilots. However, only one conversion is known to have been carried out by a Service unit and, given the designation Fw 190S-8, was used primarily for high-speed liaison between the various *Luftwaffe Geschwaderen*. The

Fw 190A-8 loaded with SC 500 lb. bomb awaits take off for ground attack mission, Russia.

Fw 190A-8/U1 dual-seat trainer

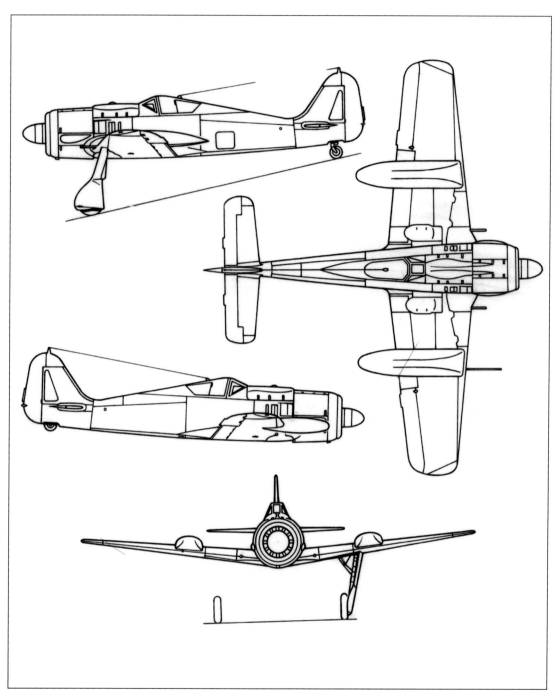

Fw 190A-8 fitted with Doppelreiter.

Fw 190A-8/U11 reverted to the ground-support rôle and operated with the Ju 87D in a mixed *Schlachtgeschwader*. It was armed with a single 550-lb SC 250 bomb fitted under the fuselage and under-wing racks for four 110-lb SC 50 bombs. In addition it was also

fitted with two 13-mm MG 131 machine-guns and two 20-mm
MG 151 cannon.

During this time of development with the A-8 *Major* Hans-
Gunther von Kornatski, a leading, albeit aggressive, pilot with
Jagdgeschwader 4, proposed that special *Staffeln* should be formed
within existing *Jagdgeschwaderen* with the purpose of ramming
British and American bombers that were now making regular
appearances, day and night, over Germany. Kornatski's idea was
that as the bomber formations relied on their 'lead' aircraft to a
large extent its removal would cause confusion for those
remaining and, to be sure of its destruction, it should be rammed.
Generalmajor Adolf Galland, the *General der Jagdfieger* and to whom
the proposal was made, had no hesitation in turning the plan

down. Galland's own views on the morality of such a scheme was
that he believed strongly that even in such a destructive war as was
being experienced there was a certain 'chivalry' applied by fliers
on both sides. His pragmatic response, however, was that the loss
of German pilots would be much greater than could be justified by
this 'kamikaze' action.

An Fw 190S-8, a tandem two-seat conversion of the Fw 190A-8 airframe intended primarily for conversion training.

Subsequently, during the final weeks of the Reich, the
Rammkommando Elbe was formed but had very little success
especially when responsibility for its operations was taken from
the *Luftwaffe* and came under the control of the SS.

Some of Kornatski's suggestions did, however, provide more
viable options and an experimental *Sturmgruppe* was instigated
using heavily armed Fw 190A-8s. With additional plate metal
armour and closely escorted by the more conventional

Hauptmann
Wilhelm Moritz.

interceptors, who were to ensure that these *Sturmflugzeug* would not be hindered by Allied fighters, they would attack bombers that were flying in close formation. They were to press home their attack at all costs and, should there be no alternative, they were to ram the bomber with the pilot baling out. Many of the *Sturmgruppe* pilots, being more realistic than the planners, could see that there would be very little chance of survival, given the combined closing speeds of both aircraft, and preferred to use their heavy armament to achieve their purpose.

The combination of heavily armed *Sturmflugzeug* and the more conventional fighters proved very successful and plans were made to add a *Sturmgruppe* to each of the *Reichsverteidigung* (Reich Defence) *Geschwaderen*. The urgent requirement for fighter aircraft and pilots to support the German armies in France following the Normandy invasion made the scheme less viable although, in the latter months of the war, several *Sturmgruppen* were attached to a number of *Geschwaderen*. Those formed included IV.(*Sturm*)/JG 3 '*Udet*', which was the first to be established in April 1944 and was commanded by *Hauptmann* (later *Major*) Wilhelm Moritz. Moritz was awarded the *Ritterkreuz* on July 18, 1944, after forty-one victories and went on to add three more. *Major* Hans-Günther von Kornatski, from whose original proposal the units were formed, commanded II.(*Sturm*)/JG 4 and within JG 1 '*Oesau*' there was also a *Sturmgruppen* established.

It was intended to continue the 'A' series with the Fw 190A-9 as a continuation of the *Rammjäger*. A prototype Fw 190V34, *Werk Nr* 410230, was allocated (a second prototype Fw 190V36 was recorded but as no *Werk Nummer* was given it is unlikely that any construction was carried out). The prototype V34 was initially fitted with the 2,000-hp BMW 801F engine (subsequently replaced with a BMW 801TS of similar horsepower) but did not go further than the design stage.

The Fw 190A-10 was the last design of the 'A' series and although scheduled for service in March 1945 remained on the drawing board. It was again to be powered by the BMW 801F engine and to accommodate a robust armament. In addition to two nose-mounted 13-mm MG 131 machine-guns the design made provision for 20-mm MG 151 cannon in each wing root and, on each outer wing, additional MG 151 cannon or 30-mm MK 108 cannon. An ETC 501 bomb-rack was to be attached beneath the fuselage to carry one SC 500 bomb or an external fuel tank of 66-gallon capacity.

CHAPTER EIGHT

The Battle for Germany

THE BATTLE for Germany, from its very beginning, had to be fought from the air, although RAF Bomber Command's initial efforts were only moderate in size and results. However, when Air Marshal Arthur Harris took over command he made his presence felt from the very beginning and built the force into a war machine that finally, with the USAAF, tore the heart out of Germany.

During the last week of July 1943 both RAF Bomber Command and the US 8th Air Force undertook a sustained attack on German 'war effort' industry. The intensive Allied bombing activity during this period became known as the '*Blitz* Week'.

On the night of July 24/25, 1943, aircraft of RAF Bomber Command conducted an extremely devastating bombing raid on Hamburg's shipyards and diesel engine works.

In the early afternoon of July 25, Flying Fortresses from the 1st and 4th Bomb Wings of the US 8th Air Force took off from their bases in East Anglia and headed out over the North Sea *en route* for North-West Germany. Aircraft of the 4th together with a number of 1st BW squadrons headed for Kiel. The 1st BW aircraft were to bomb the docks while the 4th BW aircraft would go on beyond Kiel to bomb the Heinkel aircraft manufacturing plant at Warnemünde. The remaining 1st BW aircraft headed for Hamburg to continue that which the RAF had started the night before. While the Kiel detachment were able to fulfil their mission the bombers headed for Warnemünde had little success. The B-17s, headed for Hamburg, encountered a 15,000 feet pall of smoke hanging over the city caused by the RAF's nocturnal exploits. Only the first formation of US bombers were able to line-up on their targets before the smoke covered the ground and obliterated any chance of visual recognition. The bombing raid resulted in a high attrition rate as nineteen B-17s were lost, five by anti-aircraft barrage.

The time had come for the Allied bomber force to make

Fw 190A-2 with engine running. Note stock of bombs in foreground.

concerted attacks on Germany and on July 28 the chosen target was a factory producing components for the Fw 190, the Fieseler works at Kassel, where B-17s from 1st Bomb Wing were to attack. In addition the AGO factory at Oschersleben, where the production of the Fw 190 was in full swing, was to be targeted by B-17s of the 4th Bomb Wing.

182 B-17F Flying Fortresses from the 1st Bomb Wing and 120 from the 4th Bomb Wing started their engines at dawn of the 28th preparatory to take off. They headed over the North Sea and climbed to 30,000 feet but, due to a number of aircraft having to

abort through engine problems or other difficulties, the original force was very much reduced and, as soon as this smaller force entered German air space they were attacked by a large number of Fw 190s, Bf 109s and Ju 88s. The raid on Kassel was of limited success as a low cloud base prevented bombing accuracy On their return flight the bombers, still being attacked by over 100 *Luftwaffe* fighters, were met by 123 American fighters waiting on the German border to escort them back to their bases. A number of the German aircraft were flying out of the range of the bomber's guns and firing the Wfr Gr. 21 rockets from under-wing

Fw 190 stands awaiting service.

tubes but the fighter escort managed to shoot down nine enemy aircraft.

The B-17 Flying Fortresses of the 4th Bomb Wing followed, initially, the course followed by their compatriots and flew towards the Hamburg/Kiel vacinity before changing course in a south-east direction that would take them to Ochersleben.

The 4th Bomb Wing's 120 bombers, led by the 94th Bomb Group, soon encountered bad weather conditions which caused

the formations to break-up and disperse. Further, as some of the bomber formations were about to cross the German coast line Fw 190s from JG 1 'Oesau' pounced on them causing heavy casualties. The lead formation, the 94th, had somehow escaped this debacle and had continued on their journey to the target. Fifteen B-17s of the 94th managed, through cloud breaks, to unleash their bomb loads as did the thirteen aircraft of the

Ground crew swarm over this Fw 190. Note the dappled, upper scheme.

Fw 190 A-8. Flown by the Komandeur of I./JG 26, France, July 1944.

Fw 190 of II./SG 1. Note Green Dragon emblem on cowling,

following formation, the 388th Bomb Group. Subsequent photo-reconnaissance of the target showed considerable damage to the AGO factory and this halted their production of the Fw 190 for many weeks.

Surprisingly all fifteen Flying Fortresses of 94th Bomb Group managed to return to their base at Bury St Edmunds later that day.

The following day, July 29, the 4th Bomber Wing had another chance to fulfil their mission on the Heinkel factory at Warnemünde and this time were able to destroy most of the plant that was, at that time, mass producing the Fw 190.

The Heinkel factory was attacked while a diversionary raid flew to St Omer to distract the German fighters. One hundred and eighteen P-47s from three Fighter Groups protected the bombers but no enemy fighters appeared.

An analysis of German key industrial areas concluded that all were situated within a 600 mile range of England and the decision was made to concentrate the major attacks on them. The meeting took place in Casablanca and a statement was issued that the aim of the American and RAF bomber forces would be the total destruction of the German military, industrial and economic system by means of 'round-the-clock' bombing. It was a sombre statement. RAF Bomber Command would target cities with known military and other 'war-effort' industries with bombing attacks during the night, which would also have a demoralizing effect on the civilian population. The US 8th Air Force would continue the mayhem by bombing specific targets during the day.

From July 1943, therefore, the Battle for Germany could be said to be the starting date of the sustained bombing campaign which was to claim the lives of thousands of aircrew of bother sides, high civilian casualties and horrendous damage to German cities. The British Prime Minister's statement that the bomber would always get through was horribly correct.

Fw 190 flies overhead revealing ventral load.

On August 12, 1943, 143 B-17 Flying Fortresses took off to carry out a concerted attack on Germany's industrial heart, the Ruhr Valley. The Ruhr was the centre for Germany's steel and heavy industry production, vital to the ever growing armament requirement now being made by the *Wehrmacht*. For the Allies this would remain a prime target and one that would continually be on the receiving end of the joint efforts made by Britain and the United States.   On the outward journey the bombers were escorted by 131 fighters, that were to provide a defensive shuttle service, while the return journey was to be covered by the 4th Fighter Group, the oldest fighter group in the 8th Air Force having been established in September 1942 with the take over of

Ground crew load bomb under this Fw 190. Note 66-gallon drop tank.

the RAF 'Eagle' squadrons. This group and the bombers had to face a force of waiting Fw 190s at 29,000 feet. They attacked from the front to be met by the 334th Squadron. When the bombers arrived at their target it was covered with dense smoke generated by the defences. Intense flak made the bomber's task harder as they were forced to circle the target. The second target was next, Cologne.

The Ball Bearing Factory Attacks   *Fw 190, France.*

Four days later the Flying Fortress flew to bomb a Paris airfield
and were attacked as they crossed the coast of France. The 334th
Squadron was heavily engaged. On the same date preparations
were being made for an attack on a German target that was to put
a strain on the US 8th Air Forces bombers and men. Planners
began work on details of the raid against the ball bearing factories
at Schweinfurt. The five factories and railway were the selected
targets as they were responsible for two thirds of Germany's
bearing production.

  On August 17, one of the greatest and fiercest air battles of the
air war was fought when a force of 8th Air Force bombers attacked
the ballbearing factories at Schweinfurt and the Messerschmitt
works at Regensburg.

  The planners had to take one thing into consideration.
Germany had successfully expanded fighter production and two,
major factories produced forty-eight percent of German fighter
production.

Fw 190A-4 of
I./JG 3 'Udet'. Note
twin bomb/fuel tank
racks under wings.

These factories were prime targets and as such were suitably defended, any force that attacked would have to pay a heavy price. To make the bomber's task harder the decision was taken to attack both targets on the same day. Schweinfurt and Regensburg were to be targetted by the 8th Air Force from England and the Fw 190 plants by the 9th Air Force based in North Africa.

The attacks were codenamed '*Alabama*' for Schweinfurt and '*Haymaker*' for Regensburg.

The force was split into two sections, one to leave England at 8.30am for Regensburg and the Schweinfurt group fifteen minutes later. The Regensburg bombers would be used as a decoy and attract the main opposition. After the bombers had flown past Frankfurt the Schweinfurt bombers would swing towards their target with the object of bombing both targets at the same time. The Schweinfurt force would then be required to make the return journey to England and the Regensburg bombers turn south and fly to North Africa. There, they would refuel and on the flight back to England attack another German target. It was complicated and its success depended upon a number of known factors.

It was a severe test for the American Air Force as it was their
biggest bomber operation and deepest penetration into German
air space since the 8th Air Force had began operations from
England. The bombers were loaded with 787 tons of bombs split
between the two forces (307 and 480 tons). To again complicate
matters further a diversionary force of thirty-six B-26s and ninety
fighters would bomb the German airfield at Bryas in France
escorted by ninety RAF Spitfires. Two other attacks were carried
out by Hawker Typhoons which bombed airfields near Lille and

Poix followed by attacks on railway yards at Dunkirk and Calais.
All appeared set for the American Air Force's greatest challenge.

Armament crew load large bomb (500-lbs) on this Fw 190.

On the day of the attacks August 17, 1943, the force of 230
bombers attacking Regensburg took off in the morning and
crossed over the English coast at 09.30 hours. The bombers made
a stream fifteen miles long. On reaching the French coast twenty-
four P-47 Thunderbolts caught up with the bombers to ward of
German fighters, which stayed their distance. A second group
took over and escorted the bombers to the German border, where

they had to turn back due to lack of fuel. Once over the Low countries the bomber formation into a mass of German fighters.

The *Luftwaffe* had been deploying fighter units from outside the *Reich* and they were deployed along a 150 miles corridor containing 300 fighters. As the B-17s crossed the border the conflict began and a shuttle service of German fighters kept the pressure up. During the first hour twenty-four bombers were shot down.

Unfortunately the second wave of bombers destined to attack Schweinfurt was delayed on their English bases for more than six vital hours. Eventually 146 B-17s crossed the English Channel and set course for the Scheldt Estuary. The formations were met

Pair of Fw 190 fighter-bombers during take-off for sortie.

ninety-six RAF Spitfires, which escorted them for fifteen minutes to Antwerp, during which time no enemy fighter appeared. The next escort fighters, the P-47 Thunderbolts, took over, albeit late, and flew as far as the German border. However, the whole German defence system had been aroused by the Regensburg attack and the defending fighters had been refuelled, rearmed and were waiting.

The last group of bombers, the 100th Squadron, reached their IP point where they started their run and heavily bombed the target. They turned and headed for North Africa. There was no sign of the Schweinfurt force as this had been fatally delayed in

England due to bad weather, and it took off for Germany several hours late.

The bombers had not long to wait before the German fighters appeared, sweeping down on the squadrons and instead of the normal two prong attack the unit went in packs of twelve Messerschmitt Bf 110s attacked with rockets, to be followed by

four more as the others drew away. At 2.15pm the bombers still had 190 miles to travel, or just over one hour's flight time, before reaching the target, Schweinfurt. A total of 300 fighters swarmed around the bombers which had dropped 435 tons with the result that output was reduced by thirty-four percent. The raid had lasted just eleven minutes and it was time to go home. Initially, twenty-two B-17s were destroyed in the run-up to Schweinfurt where no more than 140 tons of bombs were dropped. At around 15.00 hours. Thirteen more fell during the return flight to England.

Flaps fully down on this JG 54 'Grünherz' Fw 190 as it makes final approach.

They were met by escorting P-47s who covered them to Antwerp where RAF Spitfires took over. A tally of losses for the day's fighting was thirty-six B-17s and twenty-seven badly damaged, plus a total of 790 aircrew, a toal of sixteen percent of the forces despatched. Obviously this rate of attrition could not be sustained if the daylight campaign was to be increased.

Over the next few days bombers were despatched to targets in France while the 8th and 9th Air Forces recovered. Despite frantic

Fw 190 fighter and Dornier bomber on well equipped airfield.

View of Fw 190 in French, Armée de L' Air *national markings.*

efforts to improve the armament of the B-17G it was decided to attack Schweinfurt again as the first results were disappointing, and on October 14, 291 Flying Fortresses were despatched to bomb that vital target. Sixty bombers failed to return from that raid and of the survivors seventeen were destroyed in crash landings in England,

and no fewer than 121 required fairly extensive repairs. Only a small percentage despatched for the raid returned undamaged. A total of 649 airmen were killed, wounded or posted missing. The *Luftwaffe* also suffered and they, too, knew that their fighters could not withstand such a sustained assault on a day to day basis. Viewed dispassionately the 8th Air Force and other American Bomb Groups could withstand the losses and, like Fighter Command, the loss of highly trained crews would be replaced.

These, and other horrific attacks provided a measure of the huge task facing the American daylight bombing planners. As the intelligence picture of German fighter tactics and deployment was improved from 1943, effective diversionary attacks could be launched, and by the end of 1943 American fighters could accompany the bombers to targets over 500 miles deep into Europe, and that included Berlin. This was due mainly to the magnificent North American P-51 Mustang equipped with long range tanks and the Merlin engines, and the P-47 Thunderbolt,

Ground crewman fits a cowling cover on this Fw 190.

which also carried similar tanks. It was the beginning of the end of the reign of the Fw 190 fighter.

It was at this period that the Americans decided to adopt the British radar system of H2S which scanned the ground below on reaching the target. The RAF also used this in addition to 'Oboe',

A Fw 190 moves on to the runway as groundcrew work on a second machine parked nearby.

This device guided the British night bombers to the target on a fixed beam called 'Cat'. As the bomber reached the target the second station, also using a beam called 'Mouse' calculated where the bomber was along the 'Cat' beam and on reaching the target sent a signal to the bomber to bomb. With that and H2S the British bombers had an excellent idea of where they were. The 'Cat' beam when the aircraft was flying along it gave off a steady signal. When the aircraft strayed to either side it received either the Morse signal of dots or dashes.

With H2S equipped B-17s (four) the Americans attacked Emden and bombed the target through an overcast sky. The bombers were accompanied by 262 P-47s and entered German air space for the first time with the aid of a new 108-gallon drop fuel tank. They were met by Fw 190s and Bf 109s and they, themselves, were attacked by the P-47s who flew the whole mission. One P-47 and seven B-17s were lost.

'Big Week'

March 1944 was a busy time for the USAAF as it stepped up it attacks and, on the 3rd of that month, the planners were instructed to prepare for a concentrated period of mass attacks on the German homeland which was to include a number of raids upon Berlin. These would be supported by a night bombing campaign by Bomber Command. It was a carefully planned strategy and the attacks were to bring home to the 4,300,000 citizens of Berlin the realisation that Germany could not possibly win the war as in addition to the bombing attacks Allied ground forces had entered German territory from the west and the

Basic Luftwaffe *camouflage scheme is carried by this Fw 190.*

Russian Red Army from the East.

The fear in the *Reich* was the opening of a third front from the south from where bombers of the 15th Air Force were now flying over Germany and both that force and the 8th were conducting shuttle raids. It was now necessary that the German tactics had to alter fast and their overall plan was to meet mass with mass. Unfortunately, the *Luftwaffe* was not the force that it had been and was gradually dwindling in strength.

Fw 190 of JG 3 awaits engine removal for service.

Seven hundred and forty-eight bombers were dispatched on the first day for the raid on Berlin and the USAAF generals were aware that according to intelligence not only would the bombers meet the *Luftwaffe* in force with all the fighters they could put up, but the anti-aircraft barrier was massive. The flight to Berlin and back extended over ten hours with the bombers being escorted by eighty-nine P-38s, 484 P-47s and 130 P-51s.

The report of an 8th Air Force fighter pilot tells of the German reaction in the following words.

'It looked like there were millions of enemy aircraft, Bf 109 and 110s, 410s and Ju 88s and, of course, a mass of Fw 190s. I rolled to starboard and dived on fifty Do 217 fighters hoping to break them up so the bombers could hit the target before the German fighters could organize another attack. I flashed ahead through the 217s causing them break off in all directions.

During the retreat from France in 1944 German pilots often carried crew member in the radio compartment. Second view shows passenger in his cramped position.

I skidded to port and began firing at 'tail-end-Charlie' who turned away smoking. By now my canopy had frosted up and I had little vision. In this state I was bounced by three Fw 190s and I turned head-on into them. Two flashed past and all three then kept on going.

By now all the American and German fighters had dropped their fuel tanks and the sky was full of whirling aircraft through which the bombers droned. At 23,000 feet about sixty to eighty Fw 190s diving upon the Americans, and above then there appeared to be another section of 100.'

The American pilot thought there was no way he was going to survive as his force was outnumbered as they were trapped.

'A gaggle of enemy fighters approached head-on, firing as they came and at the last moment did a split 'S' which was followed by the us and we ran into another trap. The fighter was obviously being controlled by a master aircraft.

The fighter was obviously being controlled by a master aircraft. I saw tracers like glowing balls passing by my cockpit and I jerked the throttle, giving my prop fine pitch. One German overshot and I got on to his tail firing two second burst of armour piercing incendiary bullets that struck the enemy fighter in the right wing.

Fw 190, early 1944. Note spinner marking and matching cowling and wing tip colours. Ground crew aid pilot adjust his flight harness

Black smoke billowed from the 190 and a stream of Glycol from his engine, slowly increasing in size and volume util it poured out.'

It was possibly a Bf 109 the pilot saw. The final part of this report is gruesome to say the least and it does give a vivid impression of what the pilots on both sides faced.

'I managed to get on to the tail of another brightly coloured Fw 190 and I followed it down to the deck, dropping just above the tree-tops, twisting and turning making it impossible to get a clear shot. For some reason the German started flying straight and level and I closed to within 100 yards. I squeezed the trigger of my guns and the Fw 190 burst into flames, small fingers of fire streaming back from the engine. They multiplied and eventually engulfed the fuselage beyond the cockpit, which filled with smoke.

'The German writhed in his seat, moving his head erratically from side to side. Fire burst out of the cockpit and a burning gloved hand clawed at the side of the cockpit release hatch, fists banging on it in an attempt to dislodge it. The canopy blew off, the aircraft inverted, and a figure shrouded in flames stood up, the fire slowly eating away his clothing and the flesh underneath.

Now the burning thing was trying to clamber out of the cockpit but the slipstream kept him pinned. He seemed to turn towards me, extending an outstretched hand and trying to speak. I was only fifty yards away viewing this agonising scene from the security of my own cockpit. It took a long time for that *Luftwaffe* pilot to die and I positioned my aircraft to help end the agony of my opponent when the burning mass slumped back into his seat. The sky was filled with swirling pieces of metal, dismembered limbs and pieces of flesh.'

More Fw 190s flews towards the P-51 and the pilot, who was now running short of ammunition turned to face them to fire and break away. Finally he reached the coast of England and of the group of nine Mustangs five did not return.

It is a graphic picture of what the pilots of both sides experienced, the bombers and fighters, and it was not all one way as the next experience related by a Fw 190 pilot reveals.

View shows details of Fw 190.

'I led a formation of about seven aircraft to meet with a bunch of Martin B-26 Marauders and opened fore about 300 yards with a salvo of rockets into the close formation. There were two certain hits and one bomber immediately

caught fire and exploded, while a second lost large parts of it right tail unit and began to spiral earthwards.

In the meantime three other fighters that had taken off with me had also successfully. My partner waded into the Marauders with all his rockets. One pilot had crash landed and managed to free himself from the burning wreckage with very severe burns. We were now flying in the opposite direction to the Marauders and I led my formation back, firing my four 20-mm cannon as I did.

The engagement had lasted for a few seconds and another Marauder of the last string was on fire and then exploded. I attacked another bomber in the van of the formation and saw it was heavily damaged and I wanted to know what was happening to it. Then it happened. A hail of fire enveloped me. A Mustang had caught me napping. A sharp rap hit my right knee, the instrument panel with its indispensable instruments was shattered and the engine hit, its metal covering working loose and partly carried away.

I had only one way to get out of this crate which now as apparently only good for dying in. After a dive I saw an autobahn below but in a few seconds I was over my airfield and started banking to come in. It was remarkably quiet below me and I cut my engine, a long trail of smoke drifted behind me. It was

Fw 190 being manhandled by groundcrew. The aircraft is guided by the man controlling the tailwheel.

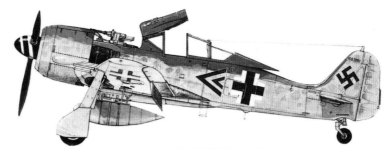

*Fw 190A-8/R7 'Rammjäger' of
1./JG 26 'Schlageter' September 1944,*

Fw 190F-7 of 2./SG 4. Sardinia/Italy, 1944.

Fw 190F-8 of II./SG 4.

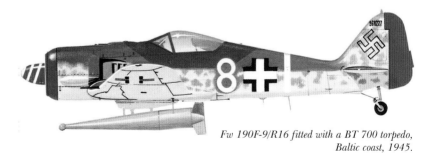

*Fw 190F-9/R16 fitted with a BT 700 torpedo,
Baltic coast, 1945.*

Fw 190F-8 of 2./SG 2 'Immelman', Hungary, winter 1944/45.

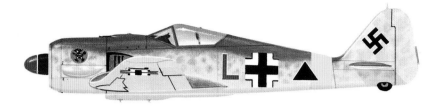

Fw 190G-3 of I5./SG 1, Deblin area, 1943.

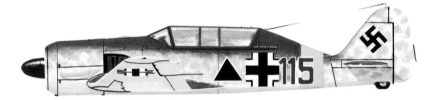

Fw 190S-5 of an unidentified unit, 1944.

Fw 190V13, the first prototype of the Fw 190C-1, with a DB 603 engine.

Fw 190V18 prototype with the Hirth supercharger.

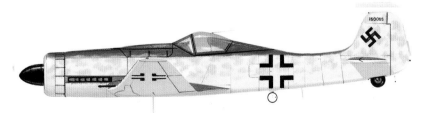

A first production Fw 190D 'Dora', in standard camouflage.

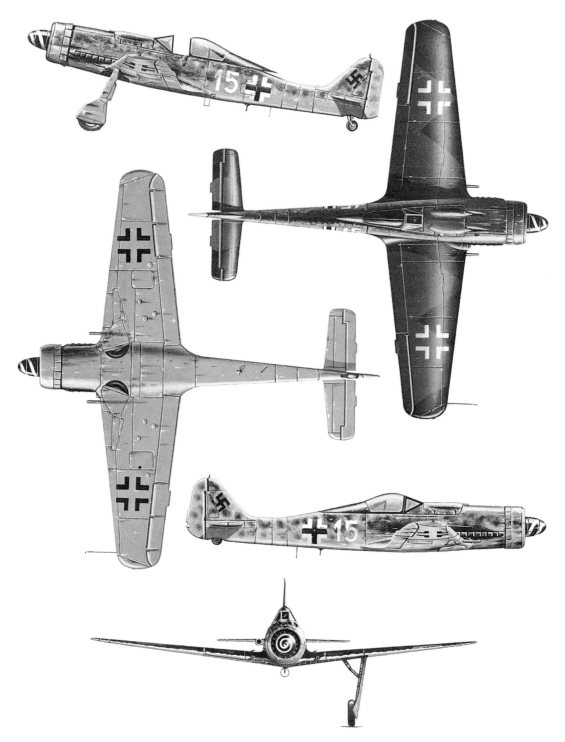

Fw 190D-9 of 1./JG 26 'Schlageter', November 1944 .

Fw 190D-9 of 15./JG 3 'Udet', early 1945.

Fw 190D-9 of 10./JG 54 'Grünherz', Wemmel, Belgium, 1945.

Fw 190D-9 in standard camouflage, 1944-45.

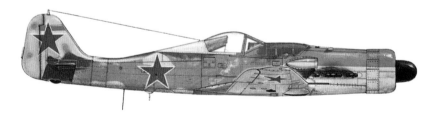

A captured Fw 190D-9 used by the Soviet Baltic Fleet, Finland, June 1945.

Fw 190D-9 flown by a Major beim Stab *during the Defence of the Reich. 1945.*

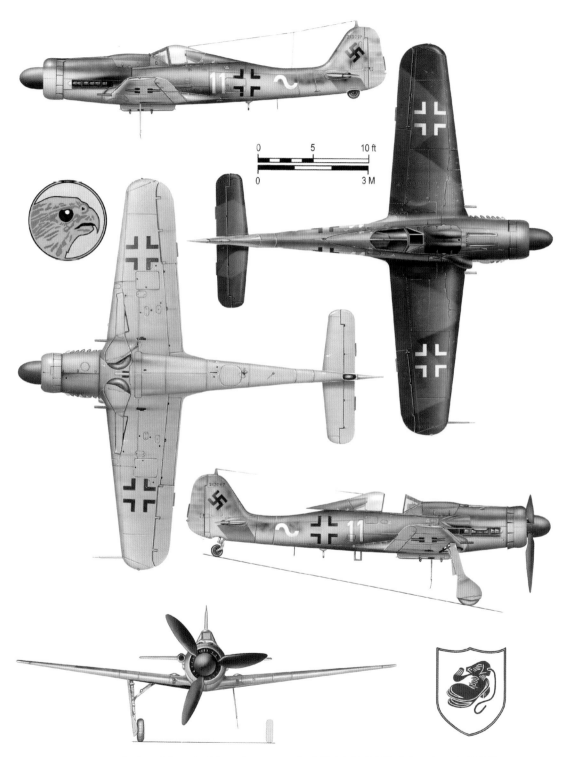

Fw 190D-9 'Weiss 11' flown by Ofw. Heinz Marquardt of 13./JG 51 'Mölders', Prenzlau, April 1945.

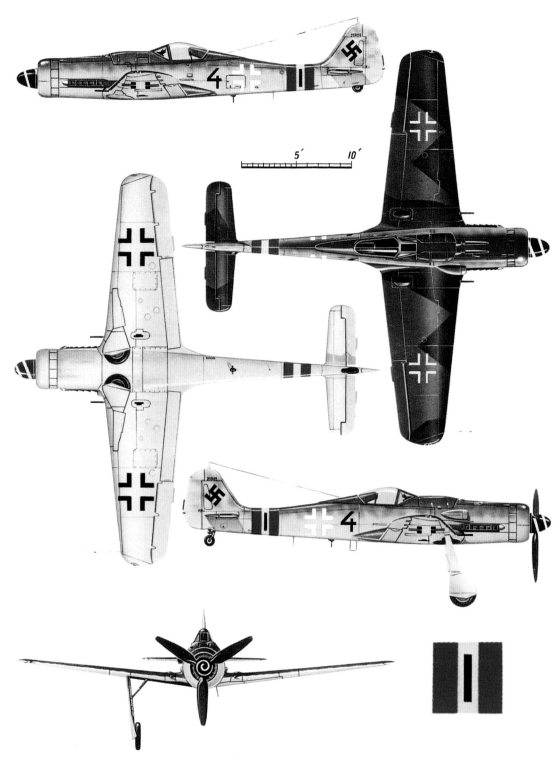

Fw 190D-9 of III./JG 54 'Grünherz' in 'Defence of the Reich' colours, Germany 1944/45.

*Ta 152H-1 (Werk Nr 15 0168) after capture by
advancing Allied forces, May 1945.*

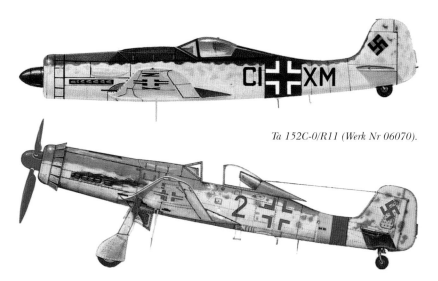

Ta 152C-0/R11 (Werk Nr 06070).

Ta 152H-1 of Geschw. Stab, JG 301, April 1945.

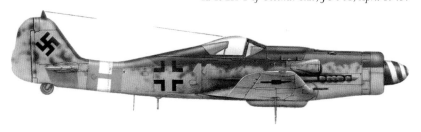

Fw 190D-9 of II./JG 2 'Richthofen', May, 1945.

Fw 190D-9 (Werk Nr 21 3240) of JV 44, flown by
Oberleutnant *Klaus Faber, Germany,May 1943.*

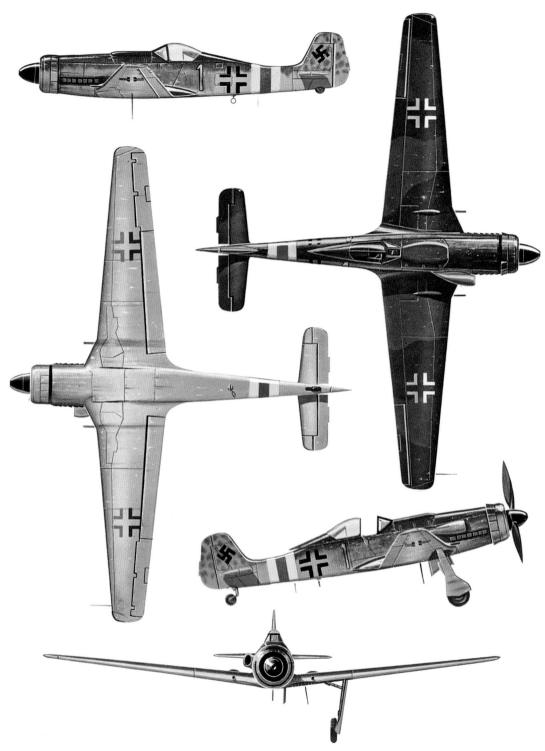

Ta 152H-0 in 'Defence of the Reich' colours, Germany 1945.

The result of a bad landing.

only then I noticed that Thunderbolts in a low-level attack were giving our airfield the works. Touching down I realised my wheel was flat and I touched down at 150-mph. I got out of the fighter and ran for the nearest bomb-crater.

On the morning of March 24, the bombers returned once again to Schweinfurt to finish the job they had started and 403 bombers and 540 fighters from ten groups almost totally eliminated the target, putting it out of action for months. The *Luftwaffe* did its best to protect the plant but it had neither the pilots or fuel with which to do so. On March 28th, attention was turned to enemy airfield in France and a sweep was carried out by 453 fighters protecting 364 bombers. The bombers had inflicted great damage to German installations but very little activity was seen in the air. The German fighters never appeared. A force of 233 B-17s and 428 fighters made their way to Brunswick for the second time in one month and the *Luftwaffe* was waiting. The bounced the formations without any warning from above, the front and rear squadrons and then harried the force to the target and back to France.

The last great battle staged by the Luftwaffe was Operation *Thunderbolt* and the *Luftwaffe* planned to put into operation the 'Great Blow' for which it had hoarded hundreds of fighters. It was planned for the morning of 1st January, 1945, and just as dawn was breaking hoards of German fighters attacked Allied airfield in the hope of destroying its strength if only to take the pressure off the fighters face with persistent attacks defending the German cities.

Initially the attacks were a great success as airfield after airfield was strafed. But the airfields to the rear escaped the carnage and soon allied fighters and intense ground flak drove the German fighters off. Although a large number of allied bombers and fighters had been destroyed, there was plenty more in reserve and they were rushed to fill the gaps. The 'Great Blow' had turned into the great disaster as hundreds of low flying German fighters used up their ammunition and were sitting ducks for the opposition which chased them for miles as they tried to get back to base. *Luftwaffe General* Adolf Galland was firmly opposed to Operation *Thunderbolt*, preferring to hoard the fighters to defend Germany until sufficient numbers of the new Me 262 jet fighter was in general service.

CHAPTER NINE

In Search of High Performance

ALTHOUGH the Fw 190A had proved itself a first-class fighter, its powerplant remained the weak point. The official altitude at which the BMW 801 developed its full power was 23,000 feet but, in fact, at altitudes exceeding 20,000 feet the Fw 190A was not an effective fighter. Accordingly, the Focke-Wulf team was forced to seek ways and means of developing a high-altitude version: the result of their efforts were the B and C series.

To test the viability of the projected B series, which was officially called the '*Hochleistungsjager*' (high-performance fighter), prototypes, *Werk Nr 0046, 0047, 0048* and *0049* of the Fw 190A series were selected, and were officially designated the pre-production series Fw 190B-0. As a real prototype of the projected B-l series the Fw 190V12 was planned, but there is no evidence in the Focke-Wulf files that the V12 was ever built. One B-l, *Werk Nr 811*, was tested, but this was a rebuilt Fw 190A.

The first prototype, *Werk Nr 0046*, was modified with a larger wing, the area of which become 218½ sq. ft as compared with the standard 197 sq. ft. All armament was removed and the BMW 801C-1 engine was replaced by the BMW 801D-2 with a GM-1 booster. For high-altitude flight a pressurised cabin was designed in which the sliding cockpit hood had double windows and the side windows were heated. Modification was completed at the beginning of January 1943 and the aircraft was transferred to Rechlin on January 9th. Earlier publications have stated repeatedly that later machines of the B series were powered by Daimler Benz engines, but this is not correct; all Fw 190Bs had the BMW 801D-2 as standard. *Werk Nr 0047* retained the normal wing

The pressurised cockpit of a Fw 190B-0. The numbers denote cracks in the canopy after tests.

of 197 sq. ft and the BMW 801D-2 with GM-1 booster was installed.

Armament consisted of two MG 17s mounted over the engine and two MG 151/20s in the wing roots. The pressurised cockpit, heated windows and double sliding hood were the same as installed on *Werk Nr* 0046. This aircraft was transferred to Rechlin on May 4th, 1943, and was followed on August 10th, 1943, by *Werk Nr* 0048 which was of the same configuration and similarly equipped. There is no evidence that *Werk Nr* 0046 to 0049 were ever used in front line service. Testing of the pressurised cockpits was carried out with aircraft *Werk Nr* 0046, 0047 and 0048 together with another rebuilt Fw 190A-1, *Werk Nr* 0055, but before the aircraft were transferred to Rechlin, intensive testing was undertaken at Hanover-Langenhagen, which was then the main airfield used for flight testing the Fw 190, and is today the civil airport of Hanover and an important stage for Berlin air traffic.

Although the three aircraft mentioned, *Werk Nr* 0046, 0047 and 0048, commenced test flying immediately upon transfer to Rechlin, these tests were continually delayed due to shortage of components and materials, and it was not possible to bring the development to a satisfactory conclusion until December 1943. Chief Test Pilot Sander complained repeatedly that different parts of the equipment were not functioning satisfactorily: frame

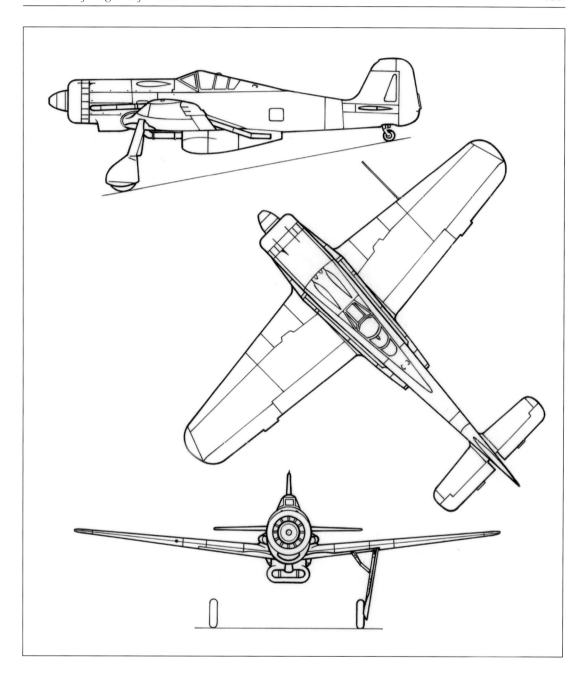

Fw 190B-0 with the new engine and ventral radiator scoops.

members of the pressurised cockpit were made too sharp and cut the sealing packings; valves failed to seat properly; and the windows failed under pressure. Additionally, the crews at Langen-hagen were forced to undertake other tests with the same aircraft, including experiments with larger wings, turbo-blowers and other

equipment. As a result, development work on the pressurised cabins was delayed more and more, and a long time elapsed before all the problems could be considered as solved.

The single Fw 190B-1, *Werk Nr* 811, had the same equipment as the Fw 190B-0s, differing only in its armament, as it retained the MG/FFs in the outer wings. In the original design the B-1 was to have four MG 17s and two MG/FFs, but *Werk Nr* 811 had two MG 17s, two MG 151s and two MG/FFs.

The results of the tests of these five Fw 190Bs must have been unsatisfactory as no series production was ordered.

The projected C series had a similar fate; only prototypes were built and no series production was undertaken.

The first prototype was the Fw 190V13, *Werk Nr* 0036, registration SK+JS. This, and the second prototype. *Werk Nr* 0037, were also taken from the A-1 series and rebuilt to the C-0 design. Main difference of the C series, compared with the A and B, was the installation of the Daimler-Benz DB 603A engine of 1,750-hp instead of the BMW 801.

The ring radiator in front, and the step of the oil radiator under the engine cowling gave the Fw 190C-0 quite a new profile. All other features of the A-0 series were retained except for the armament; on the V13 the outer wing guns were removed, so that only the engine-mounted MG 17s and the two MG 151s in the wing roots remained. But the V13 was only the first step in the

The First C-series prototype, the Fw 190V13, which was modified from an Fw 190A-0 and had the DB 603A-0 engine installed.

The Fw 190V16 was the second B-series prototype.

development of the Fw 190C high-altitude fighter, which was dependent on the Daimler-Benz DB 603G engine with Hirth turbo-blower; and great difficulties were experienced with the development of this latter item of the powerplant.

The first experimental aircraft with the turbo-blower fitted was the Fw 190A-1, *Werk Nr* 0040, registration CF+OY. Due to the increased power developed by the engine it was necessary to enlarge the tail surfaces, the new tail being manufactured of wood. Installation of the turboblower also required a large fairing beneath the fuselage, and a four-blade VDM propeller was fitted, resulting in the V18 looking very different from the V13. In its experimental form the V18 had no armament. When it was found that the DB 603G engine with turbo-blower was insufficiently developed to put the Fw 190C into service, the V18 was rebuilt again, having some minor modifications incorporated and the series produced DB 603A-1 engine installed, also with Hirth turbo-blower. This modified version was designated Fw 190V18/U1 and was re-registered GH+KO. Tests of this aircraft were

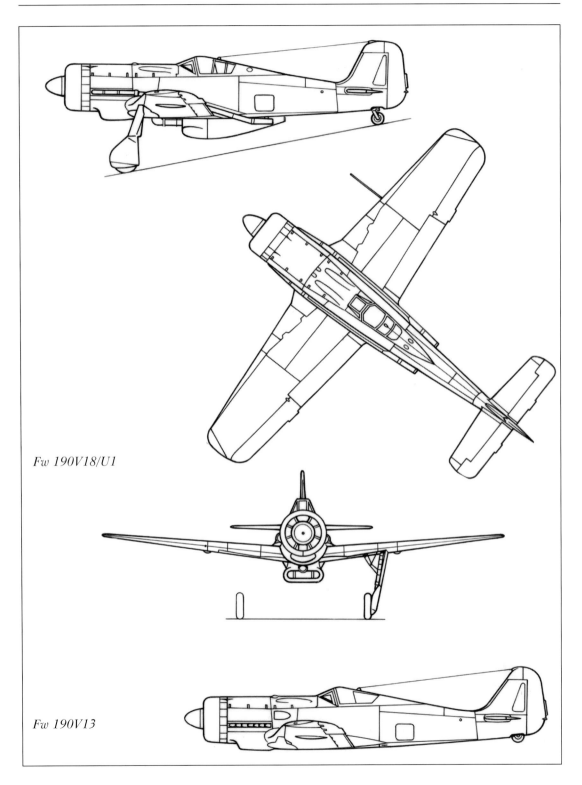

Fw 190V18/U1

Fw 190V13

The first genuine C-series prototype was the Fw 190V18. It is shown here with a ventrally mounted TK11 turbo-supercharger.

A profile of the Fw 190BV18 with the civil registration CF+OY.

unsatisfactory, however, and it was later rebuilt as the Fw 190V18/U2, being thus the prototype of the Ta 152H.

The second prototype was the Fw 190V29, registration CF+KS, which was originally Fw 190A, *Werk Nr* 0054. During rebuilding it was given a pressurised cockpit and the same enlarged tail as its forerunner, but retained the normal A-series wing with an area of 197 sq. ft, and was powered by a DB 603G engine. This aircraft was transferred to the Hirth Motor Works in Stuttgart on June 27th, 1943, for installation of the Hirth turbo-blower, but this did not operate satisfactorily and it was later sent back to the Focke-Wulf factory and rebuilt, for a second time, also as a prototype of the Ta 152H.

Fw 190A *Werk Nr* 0055 became the Fw 190V30, undergoing the same modifications as the V29, and was registered GH+KT. Whilst the other DB 6030-powered Fw 190C-ls were equipped with VDM metal propellers, the V30 had a four-bladed wooden propeller manufactured by Schwarz. This version suffered the same fate as the others, ultimately becoming a prototype for the Ta 152H.

Fw 190V30 converted from the Fw 190A-1, Werk Nr 0055. Civil registration GH+KT.

Fw 190A-1 *Werk Nr* 0056, registered GH+KU, was singularly different from the others modified as Fw 190C-1, for it was the only one to end its life with this latter designation. Completed with the enlarged tail, wings of 197 sq. ft area, pressurised cockpit and DB 603G powerplant it was transferred to the Hirth factory at Stuttgart for installation of the turbo-blower. It was later flown to Rechlin for test purposes and there it was totally destroyed in a crash on April 29th, 1943.

Fw 190A, *Werk Nr* 0057, registered GH+KV, was modified like the other Fw 190C-ls and designated Fw 190V32. It, too, was later rebuilt as a prototype Ta 152H.

The last aircraft of the Fw 190C-1 experimental versions was the Fw 190A, *Werk Nr* 0058, registered GH+KW and designated Fw 190V33. The only difference between it and the other Fw 190C-l's lay in its armament, which consisted of two engine-mounted MG 131's and two MG 151s in the wing-roots, and it was later rebuilt as yet another Ta 152H.

It seems likely that the Fw 190C-1 series might have become a very effective high-altitude fighting aircraft if the Hirth turbo-blower installation had proved satisfactory. Its failure can only be blamed on the desperate shortage of high-performance steel, and was but one of many powerplant projects which broke down from this cause. The Hirth Motor Company of Stuttgart-Zuffenhausen, abbreviated HMZ, developed three types of turbo-blowers driven by the engine exhaust gases. Type 9-2281, as used on the Fw 190, was also installed on six other types of aircraft as follows:

> Heinkel He 111H-21 with Jumo 21 IF (Type 9-2281B-22), Dornier Do 217V13 and V14 with DB 603A (Type 9-2281A), Junkers Ju 88A-4 with Jumo 211Q (Type 9-2881D-2), Henschel Hs 130A-0/U6 with DB 605 (Type 9-2281A-2) and Henschel Hs 128 with DB 605 (Type 9-288 ID). In addition, two Heinkel He 274 aircraft built in France and fitted with DB 603A engines were also to have Type 9-2281C blowers installed.

The turbo-blowers themselves worked quite satisfactorily; failure occurred in the tubes used to conduct the exhaust gases from the engine to the turbo-blower assembly, the material used in their construction being unable to withstand the high temperature of the exhaust gases. The whole installation was constructed at the Eberspaecher factory, using Sicromal 8, but in the first report on the equipment, issued by HMZ on May 23rd, 1944, they stated quite openly that the Sicromal was unable to stand up to the temperatures involved and that the exhaust tubes were damaged after as little as

Fw 190V32 with the civil registration GH+KV and converted from the Fw 190A-0, Werk Nr 0057.

ten hours operation.

Their second report, issued on October 26th, 1944, told the same sad story, this additional five months of development having only raised the operational life to approximately 20 hours.

Altogether, eighty-one turbo-blowers were installed, mostly of experimental construction. Series-built models were first delivered in June 1944 and supplied mainly for He 111s and Ju 88s, a few being installed in Do 217s and Ta 152s. For the record, the Hirth-blown DB 603A and C which equipped the Fw 190C-ls developed 1,740-hp for take-off and the normal combat power at an altitude of 40,000 ft was 1,390-hp. Because of the lack of a suitable powerplant the decision was taken to end development of the C series; a decision made easier, however, by the promise shown by the long-nosed Fw 190D and Ta 152 developments. The failure of the German aero-engine industry to produce a first-class high-performance engine was a continual and limiting factor to the performance of their aircraft during both the 1914-1918 and 1939-1945 Wars.

The failure within the German aircraft industry, brought about an unhappy situation as it was, indirectly, responsible for the death of *General-Luftzeugmeister* Ernst Udet. A number of men who, at the time, were serving *Luftwaffe* officers of senior rank, have subsequently given fresh evidence regarding th circumstances surrounding Udet's death and, as a result it is now possible to throw more light on the events leading up to the event.

Udet, it has been said, was pushed into high position by the Nazis by virtue of his undoubted standing as second only to Manfred von Richthofen in the list of German air aces of the 1914-1918 War. In spite of a post-war reputation as a playboy, he was appointed Inspector of Fighters and Dive-Bombers in February 1936 and later became Director General of Air Force Equipment. He was inclined to regard his position as that of chief test pilot to the *Luftwaffe*, and while he certainly had the ability to test aircraft for himself, in his position it was the assessment of an aircraft's operational capabilities that was required and in this respect Udet may well have had his limitations.

It would appear that, about four weeks before Udet's death, Hitler took Göring to task for the failure of the *Luftwaffe* in gaining mastery over the Allied air forces. It was the usual tirade of reproaches and complaints and Göring was quick to shift the responsibility. Following Görings dressing-down by Hitler he summoned Udet to his headquarters and, in the presence of State Secretary Milch, he proceeded to pass on Hitler's comments in vitriolic form, every aspect of his complaints being enlarged out of all proportion.

General-
Luftzeugminister
Ernst Udet

Udet was so overwhelmed by this totally unexpected attack from Göring that he was rendered speechless; like any first-class officer he was prepared to accept the blame for any of his own failings, but that he should accept responsibility for the inadequacy of the whole of the *Luftwaffe* was more than unjust. He left Göring's HQ, still without saying a word, all that he had heard buried deeply in his mind. He knew then that Göring, who at that stage of the war was more interested in his own comfort and safety than matters military, would not hesitate to sacrifice anyone to save his own skin.

When Udet returned to his own headquarters it was apparent immediately to all who knew him that something serious had occurred, for his whole manner was changed.

A few days before his death he received in his office *Major* Brauer, former pilot of the giant Junkers G38, whose aircraft had been destroyed on the ground by Allied aircraft during the Balkan campaign. Brauer, who was very skilled in handling large aircraft, had requested a new command and Udet, who was a very close friend, had appointed him supervisor and chief pilot of the Large-Transporter development (*Grossraum-Transportflugzeug*) programme at Junkers which included the Ju 290 and Ju 390.

When Brauer saw Udet he immediately noticed the change in his manner, and his mind was filled with unasked questions, all wanting to know what had happened to his friend Ernst.

He asked Angermund, Udet's adjutant and adviser, but he merely shrugged his shoulders.

On the evening before Udet's death some senior officers from his Technical Office, including Raidenbach, Angermund, Bloch and some others, were guests in his home. There was plenty to drink, and even more to talk about, but about midnight something happened which must have seemed strange to those who knew Udet well: he suddenly said that it was very late, there was a lot to do the following day, and that they must leave. This had never happened before.

Normally when Udet held a party time ceased to exist. He threw himself wholeheartedly into the fun, finding much-needed relaxation from the stresses and strains of his command, drink flowing freely from night till morning.

And now this!

Perhaps Angermund had a presentiment, but even he could not

foresee the tragedy that was to be enacted after they had all gone. And so, at a moment when Ernst Udet most needed the companionship of a real friend to help him see the situation in its true perspective, he was quite alone. The silence of the house was shattered by the bark of a pistol – and Udet was no more.

At this time, November 17th, 1941, before the United States had entered the conflict, Udet could hardly have foreseen the final collapse.

Today, when one can look back on the development of events in Germany, it is apparent that Udet had been unduly apprehensive. It is possible, however, that Göring's remarks had, for Udet, some grains of truth and that he felt himself partially guilty for the failure of the *Luftwaffe*.

Some weeks later *Generaloberst* Hans Jeschonnek, Chief of the German Air Staff, was to end his life in a similar manner. With his death, the two men who had done their utmost to bring about a powerful German air force, in accordance with the wishes of Hitler and Göring, had ended their lives.

Both had learned that Göring's loyalties were to himself alone.

During 1943, yet another experimental Fw 190 was built, which belongs to no special series. This was the Fw 190V19, designated in the Focke-Wulf files as Fw 190Wb-1 and a compromise between the Fw 190C and D. Its most conspicuous feature was an entirely new wing.

Originally Fw 190A-0, *Werk Nr* 0041 and registered GH+KP, it was given a wing with a straight leading edge from tip to tip, which was placed 4¹/₂ inches forward of the normal position.

Since this aircraft was powered by a Jumo 213 engine, it was necessary to give it the enlarged tail unit of the C series. Tests showed that the new wing offered no improvement in performance, and the electric and hydraulically operated undercarriage caused considerable trouble; and finally the V19 was written-off after a crash on February 16th, 1944. It is presumed that the Fw 190V19 was to have become the prototype of the projected Ta 153.

Meanwhile, two more main branches had grown on the Fw 190 family tree. These were the F series or *Schlachtflugzeug* (battle-planes) and had been developed from the Fw 190A-4/U3 and A-5/U3; and the G series which was a development for *Jagdbomber mit vergrosserter Reichweite* (fighter-bombers with increased range) and abbreviated to '*Jabo-Rei*' utilizing previous refinements of the Fw 190A-4/U8 and A-5/U8.

The first of the F series was the Fw 190F-1, which corresponded to the Fw 190A-4/U3. thirty aircraft of this series were built during the second half of 1942, differing from the A-4/U3 in its armament, the Fw 190F-1 having MG 151s in the wing instead of MG/FFs.

The F-l was soon followed by the F-2, production of which began at the end of 1942 and ran until the Spring of 1943, 271 aircraft of the series being built. In contrast to the Fw 190A-5/U3, this aircraft had increased armament consisting of two engine-mounted MG 17s and two MG 151s in the wing roots, and carried beneath the fuselage an ETC 501 bomb rack, which in turn carried an ER 4 rack, to which four SC 50 bombs were attached.

A considerable number of these aircraft were completed with tropical equipment and were used in Italy and Tunisia.

The Fw 190F-3 was the series version of the earlier Fw 190A-5/U17, of which type 247 aircraft were built in 1943, carrying identical armament to the F-2. It differed from the A-5/U17 in two main respects, however, for it was given the wing of the A-6 and beneath the fuselage was mounted an ETC 250 bomb rack, which could carry either a SC 250 bomb or a fuel tank of 66-gallons capacity.

This series were also equipped with two ETC 50 bomb racks under each wing, which were so arranged that SC 50 bombs could be dropped in pairs. By this installation, the Fw 190F-3 became redesignated Fw 190F-3/Rl, again a considerable number being fitted with tropical equipment for use in Italy and Tunisia.

Only one other version of this series was built: the Fw 190F-3/R3, in which the four ETC 50 bomb racks were replaced by one 30-mm. MK 103 under each wing.

Production of the Fw 190F-3 was carried out only by Arado, ending in May 1943. Of the F-3/R3 series only twenty aircraft were built, including the single Fw 190A-5/U11 which served as prototype.

This latter aircraft and the first three Fw 190F-3/R3s, which were delivered on December 28th, 1943, served only for the test programme at Rechlin and Tarnewitz. The next five, delivered in January 1944, and the remaining eleven which followed shortly after, came into action with *Schlachtgeschwader* 1.

Further development of the F series, as ground attackers, and

Fw 190F-3 of II./JG2 'Richthofen' provides close up view of leading edge markings.

the G series, as fighter bombers, was carried out. The Fw 190F-4, planned to be built in 1944, and again, only by the Arado factory and later re-designated an Fw 109F-8 had an armament of two 13-mm MG 131 machine-guns and two 20-mm MG 151 cannons, and carried under each wing two ETC 50 racks with SC 50 bombs. Beneath the fuselage it had either one ETC 501/ER 4, carrying four SC 50 bombs, or one SC 250, or a fuel tank of 66-gallon capacity. The Fw 190F-5, later re-designated as Fw 190F-9, was

similar,to be manufactured by Arado and Fieseler.

The Fw 190F-6, later re-designated as Fw 190F-10, and F-7 remained projects only.

The Fw 190F-8 was an equivalent of the A-7/8, and 385 aircraft of this series were built. Armament consisted of two MG 131s and two MG 151s and four SC 50 bombs could be carried on ETC 50 racks beneath the wings. Compared with the F-3 series, the F-8 had quite a number of modifications:

Extensive release mechanism for four wing and four fuselage bombs, which could be dropped singly, simplified electrical equipment, fittings for installation of standard tail wheel, modification in fuselage for installation of 25-gallon cruising fuel tank, radio FuG 16Z-Y (without Y arrangement), to be followed by FuG 16Z-S in April 1944, installation of variometer, and C-3 injection for all aircraft.

Production started at the Arado factory in March 1944, and at *Norddeutsche Dornier-Werke* in April 1944, some of the aircraft being delivered with tropical equipment as Fw 190F-8tp.

It was required by the Air Ministry that fifteen aircraft each month of the F-8 series were to be delivered as F-8/U1 trainers. Modification was to be effected by *Änderungs-material* (modification set) *Nummer* 137, but there is no evidence that these trainers were actually built.

Fw 190F-8/U2 and F-8/U3 were intended to be equipped with the newly developed BT's. The BT, full name *Bomben-Torpedo*, was a weapon which had been proposed by *Dr* Benecke of the Office for Technical Armament at the Air Ministry, and was developed by the Research Group '*Graf* Zeppelin' in Stuttgart. The BT would have become a very devastating weapon and consisted of a torpedo which could be manufactured very easily and cheaply. In contrast to the normal LT torpedo of the *Luftwaffe*, production of which took some 2,000 man hours, a BT 400 could be manufactured in only sixty man hours. At a total weight of 959 Ibs. it contained 440 Ibs. of explosives. The main body of the BT 200, 400 and 700 was of cast-iron, whilst those in the larger categories, the BT 1000, 1400 and 1850 were constructed from welded steel plates.

For BT actions, the Fw 190F-8/U2 and F-8/U3 were equipped with the TS IIA gunsight device, the former to carry the BT 700, the latter the BT 1400. Initial experiments with the Fw 190F-8/U3, in which the BT 1400 was dropped on soft ground, were so successful that it was planned to use the weapon against pillboxes or similar targets. All of the experiments with the BT's ran successfully, but the course of the war was such that there was not time to bring them into front-line service, and the experiments came to an end in February 1945.

The Fw 190F-8/U2 and F-8/U3 were modified from the normal F-8s by Menibum. They were to be equipped for field service with

Mechanics working on a Fw 190F-8. The armament of this aircraft includes two wing-root mounted MG 151 cannon and two engine-mounted MG 131 machine-guns.

ETC 503 racks under the wings to carry two 66-gallon fuel tanks and were also the prototypes of the projected F-8/R15 and F-8/R16 series.

Fw 190F-8/U14 was a torpedo fighter corresponding to the Fw 190A-5/U14. The next version was the Fw 190F-8/R1, delivery of which began in March 1944. The normal bombing equipment of two ETC 50s under each wing later replaced by ETC 71s. It is not certain if the Fw 190F-8/R2, which was to have two MK 108 guns under the wings, was ever built.

Of the Fw 190F-8/R3 only two experimental examples were produced by *Norddeutsche Dornier-Werke* in November 1944. In addition to the normal armament of two MG 131s and two MG 151s they carried two MK 103s. It was planned to modify this version for long-range service, in which case an external fuel tank of 66 gallons would have been installed beneath the fuselage and ETC 503 bomb racks were to be fitted beneath the wings.

The Fw 190F-8/R5 was to have an additional fuel tank of 25-gallon capacity in the rear fuselage, but was cancelled by the Air Ministry at the end of 1944. Fw 190F-8/R8 and the all-weather fighter Fw 190F-8/R11 remained projects.

Fw 190F-8/R13 was to become a night assault aircraft as successor of the Fw 190A-5/U2, with BMW 801 TU, TS or TH as powerplant, carrying two engine-mounted MG 131s. Two

This photograph was taken during installation of the necessary electrical equipment for the torpedo-release.

external 66-gallon tanks were to be carried under the wings on ETC 503 racks, with FuG25 and FuG 15 ZS radio equipment installed. Drawings and construction details were ready in December 1944 and it was the intention that production of this version should be carried out by Klemm Aircraft Company. This plan was later changed, with Blohm & Voss chosen as the manufacturers with production to begin in January 1945, but this was prevented by the course of the war.

The Fw 190F-8/R14 was to be a torpedo aircraft successor of the Fw 190A-5/U14. In general appearance it was similar to the F-8/R13, but had the following modifications:

ETC 502 instead of ETC 501 under the fuselage, fuselage support on frame 4, raised tail wheel and PKS 12 directional control. The construction data was available with production to begin at Weserflug, Berlin (the former Rohrbach factory) in February 1945, but this, too, failed to materialise.

The Fw 190F-8/R15 was intended as the production version of the Fw 190F-8/U3, with ETC 502 rack, MG 131's removed and with PKS 12 directional control. Production was to have been carried out by Blohm & Voss from February 1945 but, war being in its final stages, it was yet another shelved project.

The Fw 190F-8/R16 corresponded to the Fw 190F-8/U2 and it was to have carried the BT 700, but was only tested with the BT 400. From such information as is available it would appear that only one aircraft of this version was built, by Blohm & Voss. Both the Fw 190F-8/R15 and F-8/R16 were equipped with the TSA IIA gunsight device with bomb release mechanism. It is very probable that the Fw 190F-8/R16 used for the experiments with the BT 400, was the same aircraft which tested the Blohm & Voss BV 246 glide-bomb, although the weapon was intended to be delivered by bombers such as the Heinkel He 111 and Junkers Ju 188. First aircraft to carry the BV 246 had been the Fw 190A-4 registration VL+FG, the tests being carried out at Karlshagen.

In July 1944, four of the glide-bombs were to be dropped by a Fw 190 at Karlshagen, but on July 6th, all tests were stopped and orders issued for all available BV 246Bs to be assembled there. In all, twenty-nine BV 246Bs came together and these were destroyed by an air raid on July 17th. The tests were later continued with new glide-bombs, of which almost 600 were produced by the end of 1944, but even by the end of the war field service tests had not been completed.

The Fw 190F-8 was also used for experiments with other special armament; five being used for tests with the air-to-air missile X-4 'Rührstahl' which had the official GL/C number 8-344. In addition to the Fw 190, Ju 88G-1 and Ju 388J night fighters were to be equipped with the X-4, but early tests showed that high-speed aircraft were better suited for this weapon. In the autumn of 1944 tests with the new weapon began, Fw 190V69, *Werk Nr 582072*

Fw 190G-2, Werk Nr 41 0258 and civil registration GL+MY.

being the first to carry the X-4. It was a normal Fw 190F-8 with PKS 12 directional control and ETC 715 racks beneath each wing to carry the missile. The experimental nights were carried out at Gütersloh from August 11th, 1944. Fw 190V69 was soon followed by Fw 190V70, *Werk Nr* 580029, but this aircraft crashed on August 25th, 1944. The Fw 109F-8s, *Werk Nr* 583431, 583438 and 584221 were then fitted with the X-4 equipment and testing continued until the end of January 1945. On February 6th, 1945, further development was stopped in favour of weapons which could be produced more simply.

Another Fw 190F-8 was fitted experimentally with frames under each wing to carry rocket projectiles of the type Wfr Gr. 28/32, two of these weapons being carried on each frame. These missiles were used experimentally in field service, but no further development was undertaken.

Fw 190F-8 pilot aircraft mounted on an eplosive packed Ju88G1 as part of the 'Mistel' programme.

Yet another improvisation was the '*Mistel*' combined aircraft project. Originally intended against the Oder bridges following the retreat of the *Wehrmacht* from the Eastern Front, unmanned Junkers Ju 88s were filled with explosives and guided over the target by the 'piggyback' fighter. The fighter would then release the 'bomb' and return to its base. Ninety-five '*Mistel*' aircraft were built using Me Bf 109s, Fw 190A-5s. A-8s and F-8s.

When, in 1944, aircraft such as the Junkers Ju 87 and Henschel
Hs 123 – which were used to attack tanks – became obsolete, it was
decided to equip the Henschel Hs 129B ground assault aircraft
with the '*Sondergerat 113A*' (special device 113A), a vertical-firing
recoilless 77-mm mortar, which fired grenades of 45-mm calibre.
Shortly after Focke-Wulf were ordered to prepare the Fw 190F-8
to use this device, firing of the guns to be effected by electrostatic
or magnetic devices, the whole installation having the designation
SG 113A '*Förstersonde*'. The two different methods of firing the
device were undergoing separate development: the electrostatic
system by the Research Institute at Braunschweig, and the
magnetic system by Professor Feldtkeller at the Research Institute

*Fw 190V75 converted
from Fw 190F-8 (Werk
Nr 58 2071) with a
SG 113A Förstersonde
device installed that set up
a magnetic field, created by
a tank on the ground, and
triggered two 77-mm guns
that fired vertically down.*

Fw 190F-8 converted from a Fw 190A-5 to carry MG 13 machine-guns in the forward fuselage and eight SC 50 bombs.

in Stuttgart. Eventually, Fw 190F-8, *Werk Nr* 582071 was transferred to Stuttgart for the installation of the better of the two systems. In the event, the magnetic device was fitted and the aircraft was then flown to Langenhagen for installation of the weapon itself. On October 17th, 1944, now re-designated Fw 190V75, the aircraft was flown to Stuttgart for final tests. Meanwhile, the Air Ministry had ordered the modification of two more Fw 109F-8s, one being *Werk Nr* 933425, which was transferred to the Weapons Test Centre at Tarnewitz on December 6th, 1944. Nothing further is known of the fate of these two aircraft. It was also planned to equip other aircraft with a similar arrangement for attacks against bomber formations, in which case six 30-mm cannon were to be employed, firing vertically upwards.

Three further experimental Fw 190F-8s – Fw 190V78, *Werk Nr* 551103, Fw 190V79, *Werk Nr* 581304 and Fw 190V80, *Werk Nr* 586600, were to be fitted with the new AG 140 (AG = *Abschussgerät* = discharging device), which were, in fact, rocket racks for different air-to-air missiles.

The F-8 series was followed by the F-9; the difference between the two versions was the same as between the A-8 and A-9 and the powerplant was the BMW 801TS/TH with modified oil cooler. Armour plating for the radiator and oil tank was reinforced and they had only single exhaust ejectors. Production began at Arado and *Norddeutsche Dornier-Werke* in the middle of 1944. Modified versions of the F-9 were the same as those projected for the F-8, namely R13, R14, R15 and R16, but there is no evidence that any of these were built.

Production of the Fw 190F-10 series was scheduled for March 1945. Armament comprised two MG 131s, two MG 151s and two MK 103s and four SC 50 bombs could be carried on ETC racks beneath the wings, and the aircraft was powered by the BMW 801F. At best, a few may have been completed before the end of the war, but it is unlikely that they saw operational service.

Nothing is known of the Fw 190F-11, -12, -13 and –14 and of the Fw 190F-15 only a single prototype – Fw 190V66, *Werk Nr* 584002 – was completed. This was powered by the BMW 801TS/TH, the fuselage and wing being taken from the A-8 series. The undercarriage was modified by a larger wheel and FuG 16 radio equipment was installed. Armament comprised two MG 131s and two MG 151s and an ETC 504 bomb-rack.

Compared with the F-8/F-9 series, the Fw 190F-16 was to embody the following modifications:

Larger wheels (740 x 210-mm.), wings as for the F-8, with larger undercarriage doors, to accommodate new under-carriage, ETC 504 bomb-racks, FuG 16 replacing FuG 15, BMW 801TS/TH powerplant, electrical operating mechanism for undercarriage and ailerons and TSA IID gunsight device for aiming of missiles.

Fw 190V67, *Werk Nr* 930516, was selected as prototype and should have been ready for testing by May 1945, but it is unlikely that it was completed.

An Fw 190F-16/R5 was also projected, and this was to have two additional 24-gallon fuel tanks in the wings, but it did not progress beyond the drawing board, and the Fw 190F-17 also remained a project only.

The Fw 190G family commenced with the G-l, forerunner of which was the Fw 190A-4/U8, and altogether forty-nine Fw 190G-1s were built by Focke-Wulf, Arado and Fieseler.

Like all the G series aircraft, the G-l had only two MG 151s, but an ETC 500 rack to carry one SC 500 bomb was mounted beneath the fuselage. Two external fuel tanks were carried under the wings on racks which were originally designed by

Weserflug for the Ju 87, only the fairing of the racks being manufactured by Focke-Wulf.

Performance of the G-l varied according to the fuel carried: with a maximum range of 932 miles or an endurance of 3 hours 56 minutes, top speed was 258-mph. With a reduced range of 646 miles or an endurance of 2 hours 25 minutes, the maximum speed became 289-mph.

Two Fw 190G-3s of II./SG 10.

The Fw 190G-2 was a versatile version developed from the Fw 190A-5/U8, of which series 468 aircraft were built during 1942-1943, the AGO factory in Oschersleben alone producing 128 of this

batch. Armament was two MG 151's as usual with the G series.

The prototype of the Fw 190G-3 series – the Fw 190A-5/U2 – has already been mentioned, and this aircraft was used for a variety of rôles.

Originally Fw 190A-1 *Werk Nr* 1083 it was destined to become the prototype of the A-5/U13 series, which was to be forerunner of the projected G-3 series. In this capacity it had the official designation Fw 190V42. After successful test flights it was rebuilt and modified to a Fw 190A-5/2 night-fighter/bomber, which has already been described. *Werk Nr* 1083 ended its career on a ferry-flight from Adelheide to Langenhagen in the autumn of 1943, when it was so seriously damaged that it had to be written off.

The following variations of bomb-load and external fuel tankage were possible:

One SC 500 bomb beneath the fuselage and two 66-gallon tanks under the wings, the latter being attached to jettisonable racks designed by Messerschmitt, or:

One SC 500 bomb beneath the fuselage and two 66-gallon tanks under the wings, the latter being attached to fixed Focke-Wulf racks, or:

One SC 250 bomb beneath the fuselage and two SC 250 bombs under the wings, but no external tanks.

At a speed of 267-mph the first two versions had a duration of 3 hours 6 minutes and a range of 960 miles.

At about this time it was considered desirable to carry out landing tests with the Fw 190 to prove the undercarriage strength for operation in forward areas, and these were undertaken by the *Deutsche Versuchsanstalt für Luftfahrt* (German Experimental Establishment for Aviation) in Berlin-Adlershof. A Fw 190G-2, registration SS+GJ, was transferred to Adlershof and special measuring devices were fitted to the undercarriage. *Dipl. Ing*

Fw 190G-3 with an SB 1000 bomb. (The lower fin of the bomb has been cut away to allow clearance for take-off)

Friedrichs piloted the aircraft for the tests and altogether nine different landings were made, of which only four were evaluated. The first was a normal approach with low sinking speed at a landing speed of 115-mph on a smooth grass surface. The fifth had a high sinking speed at a landing speed of 109-mph on a dry concrete runway. Landing number six was carried out with a sinking speed of 6½ feet/sec, at an approach speed of 107-mph, but was only a touch landing, the pilot opening up again immediately for another circuit. The ninth landing became the last, because the aircraft came down with a sinking speed of 33 to 40 feet/sec, at an approach speed of 108-mph. The pilot checked too late and the aircraft hit hard, and while the undercarriage survived, he fuselage was fractured. The subsequent report commented, somewhat dryly, that the behaviour of the undercarriage-leg was satisfactory!

In contrast to the Fw 190A-5, the G-3 had the following modifications as standard: PKS 11 directional control, Focke-Wulf designed bomb-racks and external tanks, mounting for installation of a robot camera in the wing.

During later production the Fw 190A-6 type wing was fitted. 150 aircraft of this series were to be built by Focke-Wulf by August 1943. Installation of the robot camera was effected by modification set ÄA. S5.

Further development of the G-3 series was carried out during production, the following modifications being incorporated:

Installation of variometer, on aircraft produced from October 15th, 1943.

Increase in performance, increase in manifold pressure and C-3 injection by ÄA. 104.

Night flying equipment: Dimmers installed as ÄA. 116, Zeiss searchlight as ÄA. 128.

Directional control PKS 11: Directional gyro and high-speed base caster installed extra in the field. From January 1944, PKS 11 was no longer installed on a production basis.

Wing-racks: From January 1944 production aircraft were delivered without wing-racks. If necessary, Messerschmitt bolt mechanism could be installed at units.

Armament changes to four ETC 50 under wings (G-3/R5) in the field, to produce a 'Schlachtfluzeug' similar to the Fw 190F-3.

Some batches of the G-2 and G-3 series were delivered with tropical equipment as Fw 190G-2tp and G-3tp. It is not known if the Fw 190G-3/R5 was ever built and in the Focke-Wulf files no evidence can be found of any modifications of the Fw 190G-1, G-2 or G-3.

In the fighter-bomber categories of the Fw 190, the existence of the G-4, G-5, G-6 and G-7 series is doubtful, and there is no evidence of their construction to be found in the Focke-Wulf files.

The Fw 190G-8 was a counterpart of the A-8 and F-8 H series, and compared with its forerunner – the Fw 190G-3 – it had the following modifications:

Fuselage modifications for installation, as required, of 25-gallon cruising fuel tank, or GM-1 fuel injection, FuG 16 Z-Y radio equipment moved forward, ETC 501 fuselage bomb-rack moved forward eight inches, and fitted as non-jettisonable, balloon cable-cutting device in wing deleted, preparations for standard tail wheel (380 x 150-mm.), PKS 11 directional control not installed after January 1944, aircraft delivered without under-wing racks after January 1944, and additional oil tank installed only as modification set ÄA. 105.

With two 66-gallon fuel tanks beneath the wings and one SC 500 bomb under the fuselage the Fw 190G-8 had a cruising speed of 264-mph and a range of 1,052 miles; when the tanks were replaced by SC 250 bombs and the under-fuselage SC 500 by one SC 250, cruising speed was 268-mph but its range was reduced to only 510 miles. Production of the G-8 series ended in February 1944, and the following modified versions of the series were constructed:

Fw 190G-8/R4, which had GM-1 fuel injection, and Fw 190G-8/R5, which carried two ETC 50 racks under each wing instead of the ETC 250s and had a 25-gallon cruising fuel tank in the rear of the fuselage.

The Fw 190G-9 and G-10, as counterparts of the A-9 J and A-10 existed only as projects. Finally, mention should be made of the Fw 190S-8, a two-seat trainer version which did not reach the production stage. It would, in fact, have only been a replacement for the Fw 190A-8/U1.

The Fw 190 had proved itself to be an outstanding fighter aircraft, but in spite of all development efforts it still retained one great weakness – it was an inadequate fighter at those altitudes at which the Allied bomber fleets made their attacks. The situation was a repetition of that which had arisen in the 1914-1918 War when, due to the inability of the German aero-engine industry to provide powerplants offering adequate high-altitude performance, German fighter aircraft had to wait until Allied fighters and bombers came down to an altitude at which they could make an interception.

CHAPTER TEN

The Long-Nosed 'Dora'

ALTHOUGH *the General-Luftzeugmeister Amt* had allocated priority to develope Focke-Wulf's designs for their Fw 190D, colloquially known in the *Luftwaffe* as the *Langnasen-Dora* (long-nosed Dora) a problem over a suitable engine was encountered. While the company believed the turbo-charged Daimler-Benz DB 603 would offer more development potential for their new design the difficulties incurred with the turbo-blower, as already related, had made the availability very limited. The engine chosen, therefore, was the Jumo 213 of 1,750-hp, and since this was a liquid-cooled in-line engine, other modifications to the airframe became necessary. Accordingly, the projected Fw 190D-9 retained the wing of the A-8, with an area of 218½ sq. ft, but the fuselage became 4-7 feet longer and the vertical surfaces were also enlarged.

It was planned originally to build six prototypes of the new D-9 using A-series airframes. The A-0 airframe *Werk Nr* 0039, which became the Fw 190V17 (civil registration CF+OX), flew in March 1942 powered by a Jumo 213A engine. It was modified and armed with two engine-mounted 7.9-mm MG 17 machine-guns and two 20-mm MG 151 cannons in the wing-roots. Later, in the summer of 1942 the remaining five airframes, powered by similar engines, were ready for testing. *Werk Nr* 0042 became Fw 190V20, *Werk Nr* 0043, the V21, 0044 became the V22, 0045 the V23 and 0055 the V25.

The next stage in the development of the Fw 190D involved another aircraft of the A-series; *Werk Nr* 0043, civil registration GH+KR. It incorporated a new wing with larger span, having a wing area of 211 sq. ft, and was powered by one of the first

Jumo 213A's developing 1,750-hp. Curiously enough, it had no pressurised cockpit, although it was projected as a high-altitude version. It was armed with two engine-mounted MG 151s with a further two MG 151s in the wing roots. When ready for testing it was designated Fw 190V21, and transferred to Rechlin. Considerable trouble was experienced with its hydraulically-operated undercarriage and electrical equipment. It was rebuilt at a later date and served as a prototype of the Ta 152C-0, with a DB 603E engine, together with the V18/U2, V29, V30, V32 and V33.

The armament for the remaining D-series protoypes was similar as that for the V17.

The Fw 190V53 Werk Nr 17 0003, seen from the rear and showing the alteration to the fuselage with the installation of the Jumo 213 engine.

The Fw 190V53

The Fw 190V53

Late the following year, 1943, a number of Fw 190A-7 airframes were adapted to take the Jumo 213A-1 engine and were designated for *Luftwaffe* evaluation as Fw 190D-0.

The first, *Werk Nr* 17 0003, civil registration DU+UC, was given the prototype designation Fw 190V53 and retained its A-7 armament of two nose-mounted 7.9-mm MG 17 machine-guns and four 20-mm MG 151 cannons (two in the wing-roots and two mid-wing) although it was later intended to replace the MG 151s with 30-mm MK 108 cannons.

The Fw 190V53
Werk Nr 17 0003

The original Fw 190A-0 *Werk Nr* 0039, which had already served as an experimental aircraft under the designation Fw 190V17, now became the Fw 190V17/U1, first prototype of the D-9 series. It was completed in May 1944 and test flying at Langenhagen began in the same month. It was followed only four weeks later by Fw 190V53. It featured the same modifications' as the Fw 190V17/U1 but with the additional armament as specified above although the nose-mounted MG 17 machine-guns were subsequently replaced by two 13-mm MG 131 machine-guns. Test flying of the V53 showed excellent results, the only serious adverse comment being that installation of the engine-mounted MG 131s impaired forward vision.

The next prototype of the D-9 series was Fw 190V54, *Werk Nr* 17 0024 which was completed in July 1944. This was the same as the V17/U1 and identically armed with two MG 131s and two MG 151s.

Production of the Fw 190D-9 series was carried out at two plants, the Focke-Wulf plant at Cottbus and Fieseler's plant at Kassel-Waldau. The first finished aircraft started to come off the line by August 1944 with the first two from Cottbus, *Werk Nr* 21 0001 and 21 0002, being completed with a Jumo 213C engine – which although similar to the Jumo 213A engine that was being installed in the A-9 series, differed in that it allowed for a cannon to fire through the airscrew shaft. Because of this the standard VS 111 airscrew could not be used and was replaced by the VS 19 model. These two sole examples of the Fw 190D-10 were armed with a single 30-mm MK 108 cannon, firing through the airscrew hub, ans a single 20-mm MG 151 in the port wing. *Werk Nr* 21 0009 was delivered to Junkers Motor Works for intensive studies. In addition to the modifications mentioned above, fuselage construction was strengthened and the design of the engine mounting was changed. Armament consisted of two MG 131s and two MG 151s and provision was made for installation of one ETC 504 rack under the fuselage which was to carry either one 66-gallon fuel tank or, occasionally, one SC 250 bomb. Commencement of production was delayed because during testing of the prototypes Fw 190V53 was slightly damaged in an Allied bombing raid, and V54 was almost destroyed.

An all-weather version was projected under the designation

Fw 190D-9/R11, but in December 1944 the RLM revoked its orders for the production of this series. Within a month there was a change of heart and it was again ordered into production. Owing to the extreme shortage of PKS 12 directional controls, FuG 125 radio equipment and heated windows, it seems probable that not more than a few aircraft of this version were delivered to the fighter units. Equipment of the D-9 with a special MW 50 booster was also delayed, but from January it was at least possible to supply simple MW boosters, built by the firm of Oldenburg.

So far as is known, the *Jagdgeschwader* which had to share in the desperate fight against the Allied forces on the Western Front (JG 2, JG 26 and III./JG 54) were the first to be equipped with the long-nosed Fw 190D-9. At first, the old fighter pilots had little faith in this new bird. The main reason for this seems curious to the author, who was conversant with the BMW 801 in its, then,

Fw 190D-9 of Jagdverband 44, February 1944.

latest form. It is known that it normally had a power output of 1,600-hp, although it was possible, as the mechanics put it, to 'tickle' it up to 1.800-hp for a short time. But the pilots believed that its normal power output was 1,850-hp and were bitterly

Major *Robert Weiss*.
Kommandeur *III./JG 54*

disappointed to learn that the Jumo 213, which had been fitted to the Fw 190D-9, developed only 1,750-hp. They also disliked the long nose which, in their opinion, would make it less manoeuvrable.

The intensity of their dislike was heightened, if anything, after Kurt Tank came to visit III./JG 54 at their base in Oldenburg in the autumn of 1944, to tell them something of this new version. 'The Fw 190D-9,' he said, 'is an emergency solution until the Ta 152 comes into series production. The main plant of BMW has been totally destroyed by bombing, so that we had no engines available for the airframes standing ready in the factories in quantity. On the other hand, there were available a large number of Jumo 213s, because the bomber programme had been cancelled. It was, therefore, decided to utilise these in-line engines, and I am sure you will soon reconcile yourselves to this new version, since you are all well experienced pilots. I may remark that we are now producing 4,000 fighter aircraft monthly. In the spring we will overtake Allied production figures.'

These more than optimistic remarks were accepted with the greatest distrust by the pilots. The *Kommandeur* of III./JG 54 remarked laconically: 'Provided by that date we have not been destroyed,' but added 'but if you like, let's fly your "Dora-9"'. It seems that *Major* Robert Weiss, the *Kommandeur*, could already judge the trend of the war.

But the pilots were soon to revise their hasty judgement, for they found the new aircraft excellent. They admitted, with enthusiasm, that the D-9 had a wonderful rate of climb, much better acceleration in the dive and also better cruising and maximum speeds. They proved, too, that when a pilot had gained some experience of handling this new version, one could pull a tighter turn in the D-9 than with the BMW-powered Fw 190, or even with the Bf 109. The general opinion of pilots who flew the Fw 190D-9 confirmed that it was the best propeller driven fighter available to the *Luftwaffe* during the 1939-1945 War.

During familiarisation training with the new fighter, two *Staffeln* of III./JG 54 were transferred to Achmer and Hesepe, near Osnabruck. It was here that the jet-fighter group, commanded by *Major* Walter Nowotny, who scored 258 victories during the 1939-1945 War, was stationed. This *Geschwader*, JG 7, was equipped with

the Me 262A-l jet-fighter, which had come as a great surprise to Allied bomber units. But this outstanding aircraft had one very weak point – it was extremely vulnerable during take-off and

A captured Fw 190D-9 under evaluation by American pilots.

landing. The Jumo 004B-1 jet engines could not be given full thrust until the aircraft had gained some altitude, and during landing the pilot had to stop the engines and glide down. Time and time again during their landing glide, the jets were attacked by low-flying Mustangs or Thunderbolts. When the Me 262 pilots tried to re-start their engines they were usually unlucky. Sometimes they were even more unfortunate when only one engine caught, the unbalanced thrust immediately pulling one wing over resulting in a fatal accident.

So, the long-nosed Fw 190s were chosen to protect the jets during take-off and landing, and when the Ta 152s came into service in limited numbers, they, too, were used for this purpose.

It was in these dark days, in the autumn of 1944, that another leading ace lost his life. This was *Hauptmann* Emil Lang, who had become commander of II./JG 26 at the end of June 1944. Flying with JG 54 he had already scored a total of 159 victories and had been awarded the *Ritterkreuz mit Eichenlaub* (Knights Cross with Oakleaves). Although he was already thirty-five years of age, he started his career with JG 26 in fine style, destroying three Spitfires in five minutes on July 9th, 1944. On August 26th, he shot down three more Spitfires, which brought his total score to 173 victories, the final figure. Flying an Fw 190A-8, *Hauptmann*

Fw 190D-9 crash-landed over Britail.

Lang took off from Melsbroeck for Düsseldorf on September 3rd, accompanied by *Leutnant* Gross and *Gefreiter* Borreck. Flying at an altitude of 650 feet, the three Fw 190s were jumped by eight Thunderbolts over St Trond, and in the short battle which followed *Hauptmann* Lang was fatally hit, crashing vertically to the ground. The other two aircraft escaped without damage.

The D-11 series which followed had a similar fate, only a small batch of prototypes being constructed. These were powered by the Jumo 213F with MW 50 booster. Engine-mounted guns were omitted, there being only two MG 151s in the wing-roots and two MK 108s in the outer wings. It was intended to instal the Jumo 213EB engine as powerplant at a later date but this was not realised.

Only seven prototypes of the D-11 series were built:

Fw 190V55, *Werk Nr* 17 0923. Powered by the Jumo 213F-1 with MW booster, test flights proved the gear ratio of the third stage of the compressor was too low.

Fw 190V56, *Werk Nr* 17 0924. Equipped the same as the V55, it was first flown successfully on August 31st, 1944, with a water/Methanol booster.

Fw 190V57, *Werk Nr* 17 0926. Rebuilt from a normal A-8 to D-11 specification and similarly equipped to the V55.

Fw 190V58, *Werk Nr* 170933. Another rebuilt A-8, identical to the V57 above.

Fw 190V59, *Werk Nr* 35 0156. Also a rebuilt A-8, was the same as the V57 and V58 experimental D-11s. It crashed on October 9th, 1944.

Fw 190V60, *Werk Nr* 35 0157. The only D-11 without any

Only seven prototypes of the Fw 190D-11 were built. the aircraft pictured is the Fw 190V56, Werk Nr 17 0924, which first flew on August 31, 1944.

armament, otherwise identical.

Fw 190-61, *Werk Nr* 35 0158. Another former A-8, identical to the V57, V58 and V59, it served as a flying testbed for the Junkers Motor Works.

Of the following projected developments of the D-11 series none were realised:

Fw 190D-11/R20. Generally similar to the D-l Is mentioned above, but fitted additionally with MW high-pressure device in the fuselage and PKS 12 directional control.

Fw 190D-11/R21. As the D-11/R20 but equipped in addition with FuG 125 radio. Of the next series, the Fw 190D-12, four different versions were projected, but only two were completed before the end of the war:

Fw 190V65, *Werk Nr* 35 0167, a rebuilt A-8, was to become prototype of the D-12/R5 series. Its powerplant was the Jumo 213F-1, which was to have been replaced later in 1945 by the Jumo 213EB, and this version was equipped with the MW high-pressure device. Armament comprised one engine-mounted MK 108 and two MG 151s in the wing-roots, and four additional fuel tanks were accommodated in the wings with a total capacity of 69-gallons. The D-12/R5 did not, however, go into series production.

Fw 190D-12/R11, the all-weather version of the D-l2, was the only version of the series to go into production. Prototypes were the Fw 190V63, *Werk Nr* 35 0165, and V64, *Werk Nr* 35 0166, both rebuilt A-8s. They were completed in November and December

1944 respectively. Powerplant was the Jumo 213F with MW 50 booster and the fuselage was modified slightly for installation of an engine-mounted MK 108 gun and armament was completed by two MG 151s in the wing-roots. Equipment fitted included PKS 12 directional control, FuG 125 radio and heated windows. Production commenced in March 1945 at the Arado and Fieseler plants, but only a few were delivered.

The following two versions remained projects only:

Fw 190D-12/R21, similar to the D-12/R11 without all-weather equipment, being fitted instead with the MW high-pressure device in the fuselage.

Fw 190D-12/R25, similar to the D-12/R5, but was to have had the Jumo 213EB engine as powerplant, MW high-pressure device accommodated in one wing and an additional tank of 28½-gallons capacity in the fuselage.

Intended successor of the D-12 series was the Fw 190D-13, but only two experimental aircraft of the version were built, and these were generally similar to the D-12, the main difference being the provision of an engine-mounted MG 151 instead of the MK 108. The Fw 190D-13/R5 corresponded to the D-12/R5 except for armament, and remained a project only. The Fw 190D-13/R11 was identically similar to the D-12/R11 except for armament, the engine-mounted MK 108 being replaced by a similarly-mounted MG 151. Two prototypes were built, Fw 190V62 *Werk Nr* 73 2053, and Fw 190V71 *Werk Nr* 73 2054, both rebuilt from Fw 190A-8s.

Another crash-landed Fw 190D-9. The markings indicate it was the aircraft of a Major beim Stab.

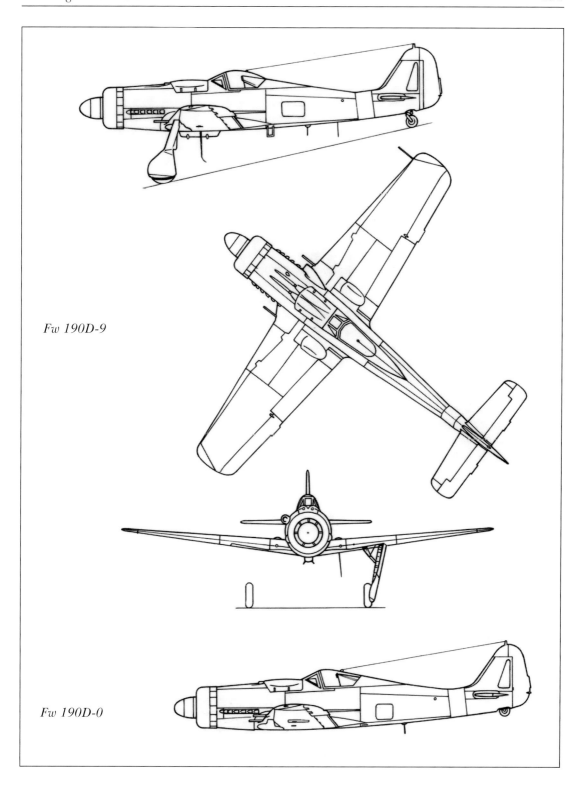

Fw 190D-9

Fw 190D-0

These two aircraft were completed in November and December 1944 respectively.

The Fw 190D-13/R21 was a counterpart to the D-12/R21, but remained a project only. The last D-series version to achieve production status – at least two aircraft of the series being built – was the Fw 190D-14. As prototypes of this series were selected the Fw 190D-9 *Werk Nr* 21 0040, which became re-designated Fw 190V76, and the Fw 190D-12 *Werk Nr* 21 0043, re-designated Fw 190V77. In comparison with the D-12 and D-13, the Fw 190 D-14 series had the following modifications:

Daimler Benz DB 603E powerplant, which was later to be replaced by the DB 603LA. Armament was the same as for the Fw 190D-12 with only minor changes of the engine-gun mounting necessitated by the change of engine. The MW booster installation required modification for the same reason, and provision of a new oil tank was necessary, together with different engine instruments. Both of these experimental Fw 190D-14s were completed before the end of hostilities, but test flying was not finished.

The last version of the D-series – the Fw 190D-15 – remained a project only. It was intended to produce it from A-8/F-8 airframes, powered by the DB 603E engine, and the booster for the DB 603 was to be replaced later by the MW high-pressure device.

An all-weather version, the Fw 190D-15/R11 was also projected, with the equipment necessary for this role consisting of PKS 12 directional control, FuG 125 radio and heated windows. This version, too, was to be rebuilt from A-8/F-8 airframes, but its production was prevented by the collapse of armed resistance in 1945. Of the Fw 190D series, altogether 674 aircraft were built.

The Fw 190D series were the last to bear the Focke-Wulf Fw prefix, although they no longer had any real connection with the old factory of Henrich Focke and Georg Wulf. Further developments were to get the prefix Ta, indicating the real creator of this outstanding aircraft.

How quickly the breakdown of the German forces, and especially of the *Luftwaffe*, proceeded in the latter stages of the 1939-1945 War may be seen from a review of the strength of the fighter units which were equipped with Fw 190 or Ta 152 aircraft in mid-January 1945:

Fw 190D-9

Luftflotte 3 (WESTERN EUROPE)		
JG 1	*Stab*	5
	I *Gruppe*	27
	II *Gruppe*	40
	III *Gruppe*	40
JG 2	*Stab*	4
	I *Gruppe*	28
	II *Gruppe*	3
	III *Gruppe*	19
JG 3	IV (*Sturm*) *Gruppe*	35
JG 4	*Stab*	2
	II (*Sturm*) *Gruppe*	25
JG 11	*Stab*	7
	I *Gruppe*	23
	III *Gruppe*	42
JG 26	*Stab*	3
	I *Gruppe*	60
	II *Gruppe*	64
	III *Gruppe*	56
JG 27	*Stab*	2
JG 54	III *Gruppe*	47
	IV *Gruppe*	50
SG 4	*Stab*	49
	I *Gruppe*	29
	II *Gruppe*	40
	III *Gruppe*	34
NS Gr. 20		28

Fw 190D-9

Luftflotte 5 (NORWAY)

JG 5	IV *Gruppe*	25

Luftflotte 6 (RUSSIA)

JG 5	III *Gruppe*	25
JG 51	*Stab*	18
JG 52	*Stab*	5
JG 54	*Stab*	1
	I *Gruppe*	35
	II *Gruppe*	44
SG 1	*Stab*	5
	II *Gruppe*	39
	III *Gruppe*	38
SG 2	I *Gruppe*	32
	II *Gruppe*	29
SG 3	*Stab*	9
	I *Gruppe*	47
	II *Gruppe*	34
	III *Gruppe*	39
SG 10	*Stab*	3
	I *Gruppe*	22
	II *Gruppe*	23
	III *Gruppe*	21

SG 77	*Stab*		6
	I *Gruppe*		40
	II *Gruppe*		38
	III *Gruppe*		38
Luftflotte Reich (GERMANY)			
JG 300	*Stab*		6
	II (*Sturm*) *Gruppe*		41
JG 301	*Stab*		5
	I *Gruppe*		38
	II *Gruppe*		40
	III *Gruppe*		26

A total of 1,534 Fw 190 aircraft that were still in action as interceptors, ground-attackers and ramming-fighters (Assault Groups). This may appear to be a considerable number of aircraft, but it must be appreciated that at least one third of this number was not available for operations due to servicing or repair and that only too often complete units were unable to take-off due to a total deficiency of petrol supplies.

Kurt Tank, 'father' of the Fw 190, compiled his ideas of the main causes responsible for the breakdown of the *Luftwaffe* as follows:

1. Lack of a combined Supreme Staff of the German Forces, in which not only military personnel shared, but also leaders of industry together with scientists.

2. Failure of the General Quartermaster from 1943 to make adequate preparations for future military operations.

3. Influence of the *General-Luftzeugmeister* was only a hinderance, because it tended to direct policy, instead of mediating between military command and industry.

4. Lack of a technically-trained officer corps. The foundation of the corps of engineers was a failure since the engineers were only advisers. The *Luftwaffe* officers had no technical knowledge.

5. Failure of the personnel policy due to:

a Non-elimination of inconvenient and critical officers in medium and high positions leading to increased changes of command, which had a bad effect on the leadershipof individual units; and

b Verification in combat being the deciding factor for promotion to high rank. The qualities essential for command – integrity, stability, leadership, knowledge oftactics, technicalities and administration were disregarded entirely.

6. Superiority of the Allied developments of radar techniques.

7. Supreme Command, and Command of the *Luftwaffe* failed completely in their estimation of the weight of the Allied bombing programme. Although intelligence – and intelligent estimates – provided extremely accurate assessment, little was done to step-up fighter production in time.

8. Cancellation of the Me 262 fighter programme and production of this aircraft in the bomber role.

9. Lack of Technical General Staff for War Production without allegiance to the Nazi Party, or without personal interests.

Kurt Tank, who played such a leading role in the German aircraft industry throughout the whole of the 1939-1945 War, must have had a fairly intimate knowledge of all the above factors, and consequently some importance may be attached to his conclusions.

CHAPTER ELEVEN

Notable Fw 190 Pilots

I T HAS BEEN demonstrated that the superlative Fw 190 aircraft was capable of satisfying almost every conceivable demand made of it throughout four of the most difficult years of the War for Germany. Despite frequent bombing attacks on its factories, the flow of aircraft to the *Luftwaffe* continued with apparently little disruption, while new and improved versions appeared in profusion. To the numerous variants already described should be added countless others in other Series, so that by the end of the war with Germany in 1945 over 20,000 Focke-Wulf Fw 190 fighters and fighter-bombers were completed.

As would be expected, such an excellent and widely used aircraft as the Focke-Wulf Fw 190 was flown and fought by numerous outstanding pilots in the *Luftwaffe*, although, it must be said, that those with many of the highest scores were predominantly from Messerschmitt Bf 109 units (in particular JG 52 on the Russian front, although as had already been shown this unit also equipped with Fw 190s in 1943), However, a number of Fw 190 exponents featured high in the victory lists with, perhaps, the most prominent among these being *Major* Heinz Bär, many of whose 220 victories were scored whilst with II *Gruppe*, JG I '*Oesau*'. A Saxon from Leipzig, he was awarded the *Schwertern* (Swords) to the *Ritterkreuz* on February 16, 1942, when his score had reached ninety. Included in his final score were sixteen Allied aircraft destroyed while flying jet aircraft. ninety-six of his victories were claimed on the Russian front, seventy-nine in Western Europe, and forty-five in North Africa. He had fought in the Battle of Britain (having as an NCO won his first victory back in September 1939), over

Oberstleutnant
Heinz Bär

France, North Africa, Italy, Russia and in defence of Germany, and
rose to the rank of *Oberstleutnant* and *Kommodore* of a *Geschwader*.
During the final weeks of the war he was a member of Adolf
Galland's JV 44 flying Me 262 jets in defence of the *Reich*. He
survived the war, but died on April 28, 1957, when the light plane
he was flying in crashed.

Oberstleutnant
Egon Mayer

Another pilot worthy of mention is Egon Mayer, also a Battle of Britain veteran, who was promoted through the commands of JG 2 'Richthofen', eventually becoming the *Kommodore* of the *Geschwader* with the rank of *Oberstleutnant*. His score of 102 victories, including twenty-five four-engine bombers, was almost entirely achieved while flying Fw 190s in the West. He was, in fact, the first *Luftwaffe* pilot to be credited with 100 victories during operations over the English Channel. During the summer of 1942 he downed sixteen aircraft within twenty-one days. This dedicated

Oberleutnant
Otto Kittel

but unassuming pilot, born inBodensee in southern Germany, was killed on March 2, 1944, in aerial combat with P-47 Thunderbolts over France. His award of the Swords was announced on March 2, 1944, the day on which he was killed.

Mayer's score of 102 was equalled by that of *Major* Josef 'Sepp' Wurmheller (see frontis.), who was a member of I./JG 53 '*Pikas*' on the Eastern front and rose to command III *Gruppe* of JG 2 '*Richthofen*' in the West. His high score included at least thirteen four-engine bombers but was killed on June 22, 1944, when he collided with his wing-man during a dogfight over France. His posthumous award of the Swords was announced on October 24, of that year.

Oberleutnant Otto Kittel, who flew the Fw 190 almost exclusively in the East with III./JG 54 '*Grünherz*', opened his score in 1943 as a *Gefreiter*; he rose to *Oberleutnant* in less than two years, reaching the astonishing score of 267 confirmed victories in only 583 combat sorties. On one occasion he was shot down and spent fourteen days in a Russian prison camp before escaping to rejoin his unit. His award of the Swords was made on November 25, 1944, but he was shot down and killed three months later.

Major Erich Rudorffer perhaps enjoyed one of the most varied and eventful careers of any *Luftwaffe* pilot. Also a Saxon from

Major
Erich Rudorffer

Leipzig, he fought with JG 2 '*Richthofen*' during the Battle of Britain, scored eighty-six victories in the West, and 136 on the Russian front, destroying fourteen Russian aircraft in one day. Of his score in the West, twelve victories were gained while flying the Messerschmitt Me 262 jet fighter, and he also flew Fw 190s and bf 109s. He was shot down sixteen times and baled out nine times, was awarded the Swords to the Knight's Cross on January 25, 1945, and survived the War.

Another high-scoring Fw 190 pilots (who also flew a Messerschmitt bf 109s) was *Major* Theodor Weißenberger (of

Major
Theodor Weißenberger

whose 208 victories more than thirty were scored on Fw 190s in the West). His 200th victory was on July 25, 1944, when he was *Kommandeur* of I./JG 7. He finished the war as *Kommodore* of this *Geschwader* but was killed in a motor race at the Nürburgring on June 6, 1950.

One of the most successful and outstanding Fw 190 pilots was Heinz Marquardt who finished the war with 121 confirmed victories flying his beloved long-nosed 'Dora'. As a *Fahnenjunker-*

Fahnenjunker-
Oberfedwebel
Heinz Marquardt

Oberfeldwebel with IV./JG 51 '*Mölders*', Heinz achieved twelve victories in one day but, during the course of obtaining this score, he was himself shot down on nine occasions. He was awarded the *Ritterkreuz* on November 18, 1944, when his score had reached eighty-nine.

Oberstleutnant Hans Philipp achieved his first victory over Poland and reached 200 victories by March 17, 1943. During the Battle of Britain, Philipp was a member of JG 54 '*Grünherz*', becoming *Staffelkapitän* of 4./JG 54 in August 1940. When the '*Grünherz*' *Geschwader* wre sent to fight on the Russian Front Philip went with

Oberstleutnant
Hans Philipp

them and, in February 1942, became *Kommandeur* of I. *Gruppe*.

The following month he became the fourth *Luftwaffe* pilot to reach 100 victories, having received the *Schwertern* (Swords) to his *Ritterkreuz* in the same month on March 12, 1942. On April 1, 1943 he returned to the Western Front when he became *Kommodore* of JG 1 'Oesau'. Hans Philip was killed on October 8, 1943 in combat with P-47 Thunderbolts and with his final score standing at 206.

Oberleutnant Anton Hafner achieved 204 victories. He received the *Eichenlaub* (Oakleaves) on April 11, 1944, when *Staffelkapitän* of 8./JG 51 'Mölders'. Hafner was killed on June 17, 1944, when in combat with a Yak-9.

Oberstleutnant
Anton Hafner

Oberleutnant
Willi Unger

Oberleutnant Willi Unger became a pilot in 1942 after he had served in the ranks as an aircraft technician. Before the war he had been a keen glider pilot and set a number of records in this field. After training he joined IV./JG 5 *'Udet'* in January 1944 and, in a short period, became one of the most successful Fw 190 *Sturmjäger* (ram-fighters). With only a total of thirty-four missions before the war ended he amassed a victory score of twenty-two, nineteen of which were British and American four-engine bombers. he was awarded the *Ritterkreuz* on October 23, 1944.

Oberst Hermann Graf *(Opposite top left)*
Swords (May 19, 1942), Diamonds to *Ritterkreuz* (September 16, 1942). Mainly with JG 52 and became *Kommodore* of this *Geschwader* on October 1, 1944. 212 victories.

Oberst Walter Oesau*(Opposite top right)*
Swords to *Ritterkreuz* (July 15, 1941), *Kommodore* JG 1. 123 victories.

Major Hans 'Assi' Hahn *(Opposite lower left)*
Oakleaves to *Ritterkreuz* (August 14, 1941), *Kommandeur* II./JG 54. 108 victories.

Oberstleutnant Kurt Buhligen *(Opposite lower right)*
Oakleaves to *Ritterkreuz* (August 14, 1944), *Kommodore* JG 2. 112 victories.

(Top left) Major
*Wilhelm-Ferdinand
Galland.*
Ritterkreuz *(May 18,
1943)* Kommandeur *of
II./JG 26* 'Schlageter'.
*Killed August 17, 1943.
55 victories.*

Oberst *Herbert Ihlefeld
(below right)
Swords to* Ritterkreuz
*(April 24, 1942).
130 victories.*

Oberst *Josef 'Pips' Priller
(below second left)
Swords to* Ritterkreuz
*(July 2, 1944).
101 victories.*

CHAPTER TWELVE

Kurt Tank's Focke-Wulf Ta 152

THE SPECIFICATION for this interceptor was issued in late summer 1942 when the Anglo-American bomber forces began the final stages of attacking the German War Machine by day and night. The Allied bombers were now viewed as an extreme danger to German industrial production as they gradually imposed air superiority over the Continent with the aid of large concentrations of protective escort fighters to, and from, targets. What was worse was that German intelligence also knew of the American USAAF's heavy bomber replacement, the B-29, which had been photographed in England, and that the RAF would also, shortly, be replacing its Lancasters and Halifaxs.

It was as early as 1941 that the threat took its first tentative steps when squadrons of RAF fighters were launched against German bases in France. The Fw 190 was to thwart that campaign in the initial stages, but British industry was soon to produce engines, airframes and armament that was equal to, or better than, the 'Butcher Bird'.

As operations were beginning to take place at the higher altitudes the USAAF and RAF were fast becoming equipped with suitable bombers. Superior Allied fighters followed quickly but Germany appeared content to concentrate on defence, rather than attack, when the *Technische Amt* (Technical office) of the RLM (*Reichsluftfahrtministerium* or State Ministry of Aviation) issued a new specification

The specification called for a High Performance Fighter (*Hochleistungsjäger*) in a two-stage, high priority programme. The first stage was named the *Sofort-Programm* (initial programme) and produced the D-series designs with airframe based upon existing fighters then being produce.

Both Focke-Wulf and Messerschmitt submitted proposals, with the latter company submitting designs for the Me 155B, an ultra-wide span high-altitude interceptor, based upon the basic Bf 109 fuselage but with a new wing. For the first stage the Focke-Wulf design was designated as the Fw 190 Ra-2 with a second as the Ra-3. Both designs were initiated with the Ra-2 having a Jumo 213 engine installed and a standard area Fw 190D wing configuration. The second design, the Ra-3, had extended outer wing panels. The Jumo 213E engine, which was used for both prototypes, featured a two stage, three speed supercharger and induction cooler, plus a pressure cabin and provision for a nitrous-oxide GM-1 booster and a methanol-water MW50 injection. The fin/rudder assembly was enlarged and a standard armament of one, 30-mm MK 108 cannon mounted over the Jumo engine and fired through the propeller drive-shaft, and two 20-mm MG 151 cannons in each wing root. The Ra-2 had two additional 20-mm MG 151 cannons in the upper nose section.

The prefix of Ta 152 was applied to both designs to differentiate the new type from the Fw 190F and G designs. This change of prefix, TA, was the result of a decision taken by the RLM as part of a policy to name the aircraft designer, Kurt Tank, in recognition of his contribution to the *Luftwaffe* fighter programme, in addition to the company. Thus, the designs became the Ta 152H and Ta 152K (the suffix 'I' and 'J' not being employed). Despite all this tremendous design and development effort, the RLM's policy of not allowing Tank to concentrate all his efforts upon the new

Ta 152C-0/R11 with civil registration CI+XM.
This aircraft retained the Fw 190A-8 wing but had the DB 603L engine installed.

interceptor early enough, it was far too late for the aircraft to exert much influence on the defence of German air space.

However, what emerged from this design effort was a much larger high-altitude aircraft which incorporated a long fuselage that allowed for additional, internal, fuel to be carried and the cockpit moved rearwards by 1 ft 4in. The fin/rudder had increased area but the tailplane was a standard Fw 190 item.

The programme was considerably slowed by the current demands for supplies of the Fw 190 series by the *Luftwaffe*, and it was not until April 1944, when the Allied invasion of Europe was an acceptable fact, did a priority status be awarded to the Ta designs. Tank was insistant that the Daimler Benz DB 603 engines would be the most suitable powerplant for the 152 and eventually a designation was applied to such an aircraft, the Ta 152C.

The Ta 152H Series.

Prototypes of the Ta 152H design were the H V1 (*Werk Nr* 11 0001) and V2 (*Werk Nr* 11 0002) were completed in July and July 1944. The Allied invasion forces had now landed in Normandy, and the Fw 190C prototypes were being extensively modified to continue with a Ta 152 development programme. The Fw 190V33/U1 (*Werk Nr* 11 0058) had a Jumo 213E-1 engine with a three blade propeller, and a wing spanning 47ft 4in with fuel tanks in the inner section.

The Fw 190V30/U1 (Werk Nr 0055) the prototype for the Ta 152H-0. This aircraft crashed at Langenhagen on August 13, 1944.

The Jumo could be boosted to provide 2,050-hp at take-off, decreasing to 1,800-hp at altitude. The prototype crashed on the day after it made a first flight on July 12, 1944. The second prototype was, therefore, rushed through the factory and

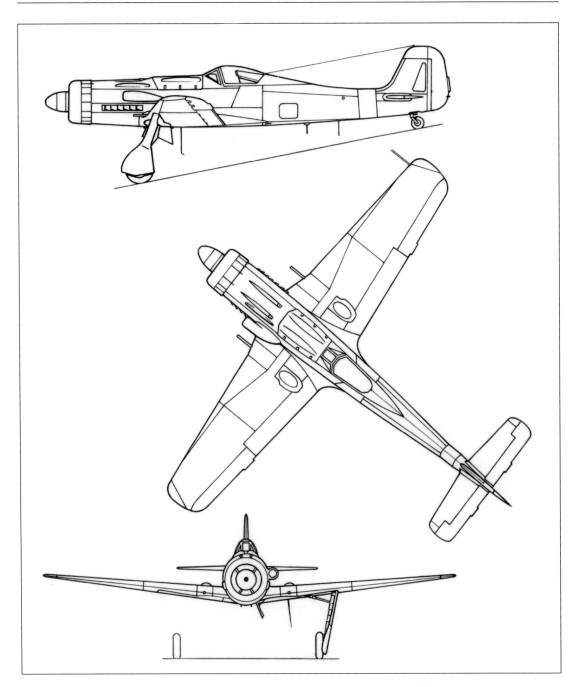

managed to make its maiden flight in August 1944, only to suffer   *Ta 152C-0*
the same fate as the first within days of this event.

The Allied forces had broken out from the Cherbourg Peninsula
and speed was of the essence, although it could have been

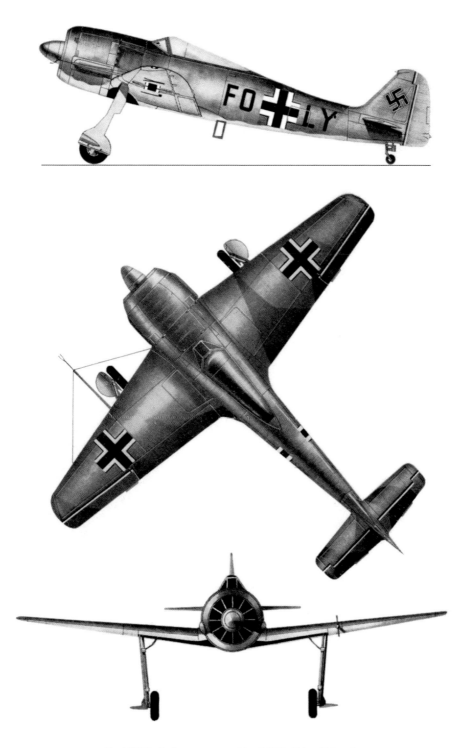

Fw 190V1, the first prototype with a BMW 139 radial engine.

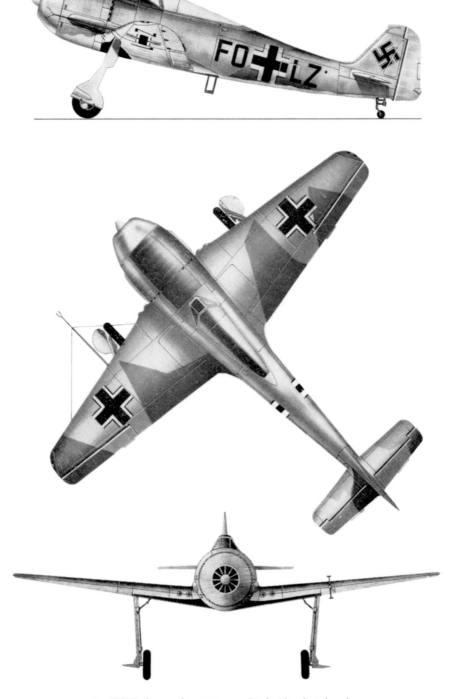

Fw 190V2, the second prototype now fitted with a ducted cowling.

The first production Fw 190A-1, powered by a BMW 801C-1 engine.

Fw 190A-5/U8 'Jabo-Rei' (Fighter/Bomber).

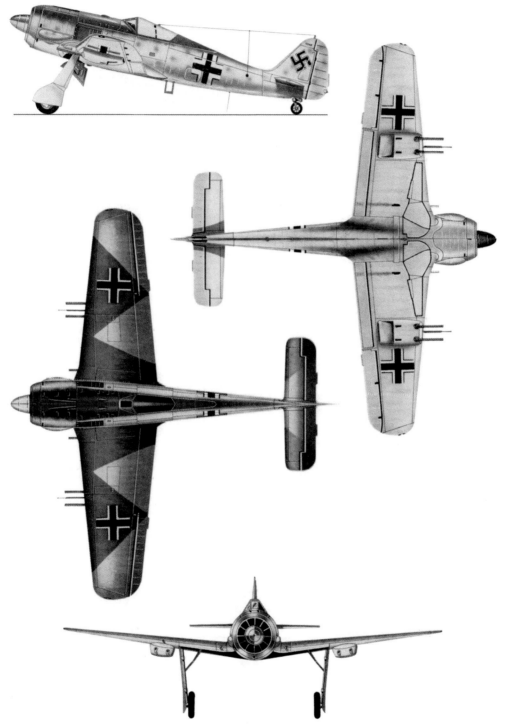

Fw 190A-6/R1.

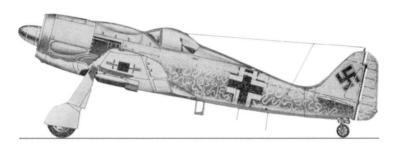

Fw 190F-8.

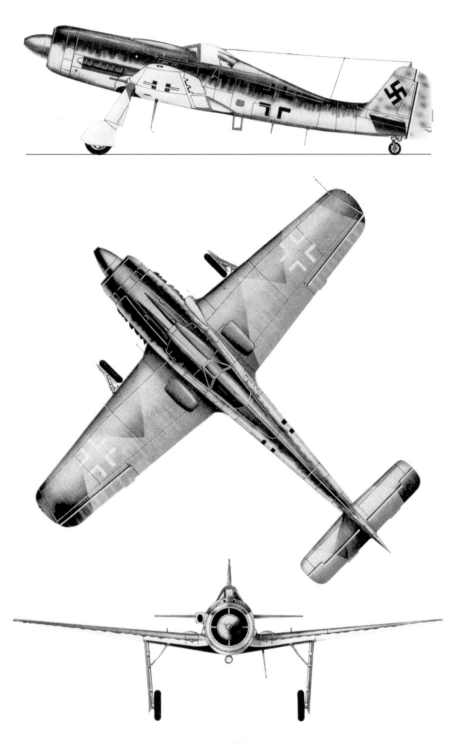

Fw 190D-9.

Ta 152C-1.

The intrument panel of a
Ta 152H-2

considered that priority on all new aircraft development be switched to the new Messerschmitt fighters, the jet-propelled Me 262 or Me 163 rocket fighter.

However, the programme was vigorously pursued with the use of two more prototypes, Fw 190V18/U2 (*Werk Nr.* 0040) and Fw 190V32/U1 (*Werk Nr.* 0057). They were tested with both types of short and wide span wings, with the former being fully armed.

Ta 152H-1
(Werk Nr 15 0005)

Eventually the first twenty, pre-production Ta 152H-0s (wide
span) wings were delivered in October 1944, and were followed by
thirty-four Ta 152H-1 by the following December. More than 150
examples of the 152H-1 were delivered before the factories were   *Ta 152C-1*

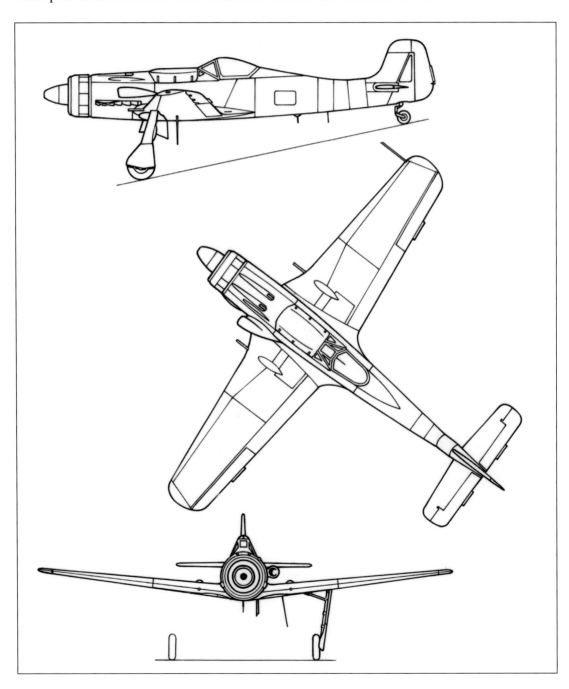

overrun, but rarely took part in the fighting for the homeland as lack of fuel, and trained pilots left them grounded. The complete listing of Ta 152 variants appears below.

Ta 152H-1 wide span wing specifications

Wing span 47ft.4.5in, area 250.8sq.ft. Length 35ft.1.5in. Height 11 feet. Weights, tare 8642-lb, gross 10,472-lb, max permissible 11,502-lb. Max speed 322-mph @ S/L, 465-mph @ 29,500 ft with MW 50, 472-mph @ 41,000 ft using nitrous oxide boost GM-1. Cruise 311-mph @ 23,000 ft. Range 755 miles @ 370-mph, 1,250-hp with long range tanks. Ceiling (N/O (GM-1), 48,500 ft. Climb (initial) (methanol-water injection) 3,445 ft/min. Engine Junkers Jumo 213E-1 of 1,750-hp at take-off, 1,749-hp @ 32,800 ft. Armament one 30-mm engine mounted 30-mm MK 108 cannon (90-rpg) and two 20-mm MG 151 cannon at 175-rpg mounted in the wing roots.

Ta 152B-5/R11.

Wing span 36 ft.1in, area 209.89 sq. ft. Length 35 ft 1.5. Height 11ft.0-in. Weights, tare 9,480-lb, gross 10,750-lb, max permissible 11,900-lb. Max speed 342-mph @ S/L, 428-mph @ 35,270 ft. With GM 1 injection 443-mph @ 44,200 ft. Cruise 315-mph @ 24,600 ft. Range, internal fuel, 775 miles @ 385-mph @ 29,500 ft. With 66-gal drop tank 1,180 miles @ 300-mph @ 21,300 ft. Engine Junkers Jumo 213E-1 of 1,750-hp at take-off, 1,320-hp @ 32,800 ft. Armament Three 30-mm MK 103 cannon (80-rpg). Ventral rack for 1,100-lb bomb load.

Ta 152 variants.

Ta 152A-1. Proposal similar to Fw 190D-9. Never built.

Ta 152A-2. Second unbuilt project similar to above with four 20-mm cannon.

Ta 152C. Three prototypes with DB 603L in-line engines. All weather fighters. Bubble Hood.

Ta 152C-0/C-1. Designation applied to three prototypes with DB 603L engine. Variety of armament.

Ta 152E-1. Photo-recon type of which two prototypes were built.

Ta 152E-2. High altitude interceptor. One prototype, Ta 152V26, completed.

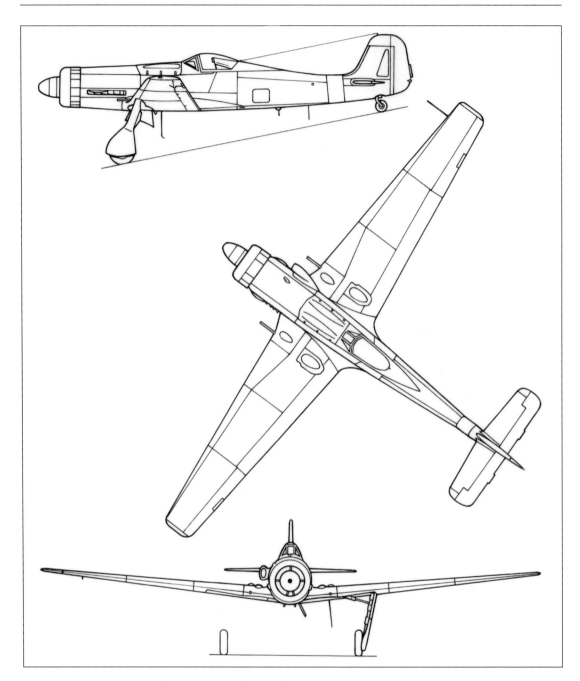

Ta 152H. High altitude variant with Junkers Jumo 213E engine.   *Ta 152H-0*
the prototype Fw 190V29, V30 and V32 built.

TA 152H-0. Batch of twenty pre-production aircraft built
during 1944. Jumo 213 EB engines. Three sub-variants as R11,
R21 and R31.

Ta 152V20 (Werk Nr 11 0020) the prototype of the Ta 152B.

Fw 190V53 (Werk Nr 17 0003) the prototype of the Ta 152B-5and redesignated Fw 190V68

Ta 152H-1. Prototype Ta 152E-2, plus small batch of production aircraft.

Ta 152H-10. FR (fighter recon) variant not completed.

Ta 153. Prototype Fw 190V32 modified from Ta 152H with new, wide, high aspect ratio wing.

The Ta 152B Series.

An examination of the short span 152B, which was considered to be a Heavy Fighter with increased armament, reveals the following variant details.

Ta 152B-4. Project with one MK 103, 33-mm engine mount cannon, plus a further two in wings and two 20-mm cannon or, four wing mounted MG 151 machine-guns.

Ta 152B-5. Based upon the prototype 190V68, or modified 190D-0. New wing and wider track undercarriage. Jumo 213E1 engine, three MK 103 33-mm cannon.

Ta 152B V19 all-weather fighter.

Ta 152B V20/21. As above.

Ta 152B-5/R11. As V19 with addition of two fuselage fuel tanks, making a total of 234-gals. No production.

Ta 152B-7. Project with Jumo 213J engine, two-stage, three speed supercharger with boost to 2240-hp for take off.

Ta 152E. Reconnaissance Fighter.

Ta 152E V9 prototype of above, also-

Ta 152E V14. No production.

Ta 152E-2 with cannon (MK 103 or 108) armament and vertical camera in rear fuselage.

Ta 152B specification

Wing span 36 ft 1in, area 209.89 sq. ft Length 35 ft ½ inch. Height 11ft. Weights, tare 10,750-lb, gross 10,750-lb, max permissible 11,900-lb. Max speed 342-mph @ S/L, 443 @ 44,250 ft. Cruise 383-mph. Range 775 miles @ 385-mph @ 29,550 ft. Max 1,180 @ 300-mph. Engine Junkers Jumo 213E-1 of 1750-hp at take-off, 1,320 @ 32,800 ft. Armament as above, plus an optional ETC 503 bomb rack with up to 1,100-lb bombs.

The RLM had been a firm supporter of the DB 603 engine, and when the decision was taken in November 1944 not to proceed with a development of the Bf 109, the Daimler Benz DB 603LA engine be adapted for installation of the Ta 152. Yet another Fw 190D prototype, the V21 (*Werk Nr.* 0043) was fitted with a DB 603B engine, and with the designation of Fw 190V21/U1 with an armament consisting of four 20-mm MG 151 cannon in fuselage and wings.

Following upon a first flight the DB 603B engine was discarded and the DB 603LA installed in its place and the armament modified to a MK 108, 30-mm cannon engine mounted to become the Ta 152V21/U2. Three Ta 152C-0 prototypes flew as the V6 (*Werk Nr.* 11 0006), V7 (*Werk Nr.* 11 0007) and V8 (*Werk Nr.* 11 0008), all weather variant, as the Ta 152C-0/R11.

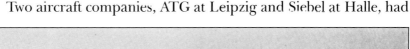

Fw 190V68 with two MK 103 cannons in each wing root.

Two aircraft companies, ATG at Leipzig and Siebel at Halle, had

been selected to produce this Ta 152C-1 variant and making first deliveries in April 1945, with Fiesler starting production in May. Ta 152C-V13 (*Werk Nr.* 11 0013) and Ta 152C-V15 (*Werk Nr.* 11 0015) were abandoned as Ta 152C-1 prototypes and work commenced on the Ta 152C-V16 (*Werk Nr.* 11 0016) and Ta 152C-V17 (*Werk Nr.* 11 0017), Ta 152C-2 prototypes. They flew in April 1945.

The Ta 152C-1/R11 and C-3/R11 were all-weather proposals. Also the C-11/R11 with vertical cameras in rear fuselage abandoned in February 1945. The Ta 152H-10 was accepted as the standard production variant, and the final modification was the proposed Ta 152S-1 tandem two seat fighter-trainer. But, VE Day was days away and the plants overrun bringing to an end the interceptor/ fighter with to meet the threat of the ever encroaching Allied armies. There is little doubt that German Aviation Technology was as, if not further, advanced than the Allies, but they had the immense numerical advantage and that decided the outcome of World War Two.

Ta 152C specifications

Wing span, 36 ft 1in, area, 209.89 sq. ft. Length, 35 ft 6½ in. Height, 11 ft 1in. Weights, tare, 8,849-lb, gross, 10,658-lb, max permissible, 11,733-lb. Max speed, 337-mph @ S/L 460-mph @ 32,800 ft. Ceiling, 40,350 ft. Initial climb rate, 3,050 ft/min. Engine Daimler-Benz DB 603LA of 2,100-hp at take-off, 1,750-hp @ 29,500 ft Armament. One 30-mm MK 108 cannon engine mounted, 90-rpg. Two fuselage 20-mm MG 151, and two wing MG 151s, 175-rpg.

The Ta 152C-0/R11 fitted with the bad weather Rüstsatz.

APPENDIX A

Service Markings & Colour Schemes

IN COMMON with almost all *Luftwaffe* fighters of the first three years of the Second World War, the Focke-Wulf Fw 190 was invariably delivered to operational units painted in pale blue (*hellblau*) on the undersides and in dark green (*dunkelgrun*) with overpainted 'black-green' (*schwarzgrun*). The manner of overpainting the darker colour commenced in the familiar 'splinter' pattern with sharply-defined angular demarcation, but this usually gave way, by 1942, to a softer, irregular demarcation similar to that of RAF practice. Interpretation of the official camouflage patterns was considerably more flexible for most Focke-Wulf units than on others, and it is, therefore, impossible to define a specific camouflage pattern.

Likewise the demarcation between under surface and upper surface colour was variously interpreted. Generally the pale blue was carried up the side of the fuselage where it merged into a pale grey shade which in most cases extended over the rear fuselage. However, on top of this was applied blotches of dark green with many aircraft displaying a 'solid' green area on top of the rear fuselage. What varied greatly was the level at which the dark blotching commenced, and some aircraft displayed blotching on the fin while others did not.

Strictly speaking the shade of pale blue used on the undersides should have been universal on all German fighters, but the relatively rare colour photographs which survive of the Fw 190 taken in 1942, distinctly show that the shade of blue apparently adopted by the Focke-Wulf factories was significantly darker than that used on contemporary Messerschmitt Bf 109Fs

(76 rather than 65 (*hellblau*) 0f the *Farbenkarte* LDv 521/2). Indeed, some Fw 190s appear to be finished in a light shade of blue-grey. This is to some extent was confirmed in Allied combat reports which mention that Fw 190s were painted 'blue-grey' underneath. Later in the war the undersides were more frequently painted in the lighter shade of 'sky blue' although in late 1944 and 1945 some aircraft were painted in a brighter tone (i.e., less grey than in 1942.)

Of course there were numerous *ad hoc* variations of camouflage schemes. In the winter environment of the Eastern Front, fighter units of the *Luftwaffe* applied predominantly white patches and stripes over the dark surfaces to break up the outline of the Focke-Wulf Fw 190 against the snow. Such schemes varied from aircraft to aircraft. In the desert warfare of North Africa the Fw 190 arrived too late to adopt the current sand-brown and green scheme on Bf 109s as they were normally thrown into battle upon arrival. They were usually simply painted in sand-brown all over the upper surfaces with blotches, in this colour, applied to the sides of the fuselage, and usually to the fin.

Markings denoting the theatre of operations were usually confined to prominent stripes around the rear fuselage, although this practice was not widespread until early 1944. In some instances the colour of these stripes coincided with coloured wing tips. No attempt can be made to define an association between colours used and the theatre of operations as any list would be confused by combinations of *Staffel* colours, and the colour of the bands was often chosen simply to define aircraft of specific *Staffel*. It was, however, fairly common practice to paint a single white band round the rear fuselage of Focke-Wulf Fw 190s serving in the Mediterranean theatre.

Aircraft of the *Jagddivision 30* sported a variety of colour schemes, ranging from conventional day camouflage to a combination of greens on the upper surfaces and black under surfaces. During 1941 and 1942 the standard *Balkankreuz*, outlined in black and white margins, appeared on upper and lower surfaces of the wings, and on the sides of the fuselage; in numerous instances later on, over-painting by front-line units tended to obliterate the formal insignia, and the *Balkankreuz* would be over sprayed, denoted in outline only, or omitting the white margin.

(Top) Fw 190 of JG 3 in 'Leopard Spot' camouflage.

(Middle) Hastily applied white 'wavy' winter camouflage in Russia.

(Lower) Fw 190A-1 of 2./JG 2 'Richthofen', France, 1941.

Oberst *Hannes Trautloft*, Kommodore *of JG 54* 'Grünherz', *with the* Geschwader *'Green Heart' emblem enclosing the three* Gruppen *unit badges*

Many night flying units obliterated the crosses under the wings. The *Hakenkreuz* (Swastika) was almost invariably painted on the fin, outlined in white. In most cases the cross was itself painted in black, but later appeared in white outline only.

Unit insignia (in common with almost all German fighters) was displayed as variations of formally adopted badges, such badges being authorized for *Geschwader*, *Gruppen* and *Staffeln*, and others being permitted for use by individual pilots. In the great majority of cases these badges were applied to one or both sides of the engine cowling on the Focke-Wulf Fw 190, although individual pilots' insignia tended

(Top) Fw 190A-4 of II./JG 2 with an unfinished exhaust 'eagle' displayed.

(Lower) Fw 190A-3 of III./JG 2 with a stylized eagle's head added to complete the design.

to be applied to the left side (port) of the cockpit. The Focke-Wulf Fw 190 suffered blistering of the surface paint and discoloration from fumes immediately behind the engine exhaust stacks. This was dramatically disguised on many Fw 190s and *Major* 'Assi' Hahn's *Gruppe*, III./JG 2, achieved the stylish portrayal of a prominent eagle which extended forward over most of the fuselage side.

Other individual pilots markings were associated with their personal victory scores which appeared as small yellow or white 'pennants' painted on the aircraft rudder (which in turn was frequently painted in *Staffel* or other colours). When the pilot in question was awarded the *Ritterkreuz* (Knight's Cross) or a higher grade of this decoration, a representation of the award was displayed together with the number denoting his score at the time of award (as can be seen from the Frontis illustration of Josef Wurmheller); further pennants were then added for subsequent victories.

Staffel Colours & Aircraft Numbers.

Squadron code letters were seldom applied to aircraft of *Jagdgeschwader*, but numbers for individual aircraft within a *Gruppe* or *Staffel* figured prominently on the fuselage. Focke-Wulf Fw 190s displayed coloured numerals forward of the fuselage *Balkankreuz*, the colour denoting the *Gruppe* and *Staffel* and the numeral the aircraft within the *Staffel*. Thus a white numeral denoted the first *Staffel* in each *Gruppe*, i.e., 1, 4, 7 or 10 *Staffel*, black or red for the second *Staffel*, and yellow for the third. The *Gruppe* itself was further denoted by the presence or absence of a further symbol, aft of the *Balkankreuz*; *I Gruppe* aircraft displayed no such symbol, *II Gruppe* aircraft a horizontal bar, *III Gruppe* a wavy line or vertical line, and *IV Gruppe* a vertical cross or a disc. These symbols could be applied in the *Staffel* colour. Further symbol codes were applied to staff members aircraft, *Staffelkapitän*, *Gruppenkommandeur*, *Geschwader Ia* (the Operations Officer), Technical Officer and Adjutant Codes adopted by the *Geschwader Kommodore* varied unit by unit (see diagram opposite).

The unit markings of a Major beim Stab.

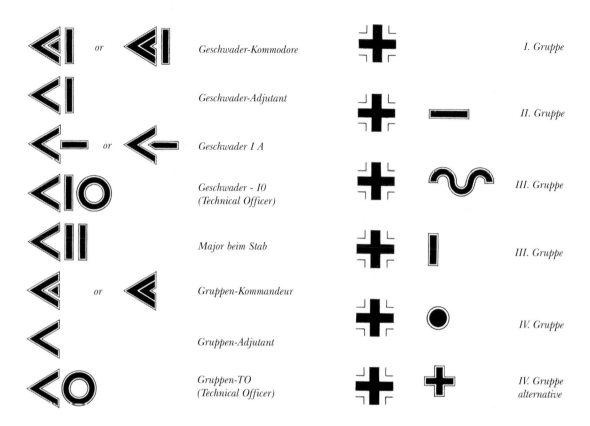

Other sections of the Focke-Wulf Fw 190 were also frequently painted in the *Staffel* colour, though this practice was applied, and dropped, from time to time during the last three years of the war. The under-cowling, spinner (in part or overall), wing tips and base of the rudder, were often painted in such colours, although in some cases the reason for the choice of a particular colour was often remote.

Excepting those *Jagdgeschwader* which remained deployed in the West for long periods, it was common practice to redeploy German *Luftwaffe* units from front to front according to strategic priorities, and this constant movement of aircraft undoubtedly accounted for the numerous, often obscure and possibly confusing, colour schemes and insignia appearing on German fighters. That they conformed to an often short lived practice is undoubted but, seen in retrospect, such schemes appear highly confusing.

A word should also be included about radio codes, as these were frequently seen on German fighters, particularly Fw 190s, and might

(Top) This illustrates the aircraft of the Operations officer (IA) of II Gruppe.

(Lower) Many Fw 190s carried motifs purely for decoration as can be seen with this example where an eye and teeth are added.

*Fw 190A-6 of
Oberstleutnant
Josef 'Pips' Priller,
Kommodore of JG 26
'Schlageter'.
The playing card has the
name of his wife, 'Jutta',
added.*

otherwise be confused with *Geschwader* codes (which seldom, if ever, appeared on fighters). These code letters were invariably painted forward and aft of the fuselage *Balkankreuz*, and also under the wings. They were normally used during flight trial by the manufacturers or during delivery flights to operational units. Occasionally they were used during development flying at Rechlin and other Service trials establishments. Normally they were painted in black, but occasionally, as in the Mediterranean theatre, in white. No pattern of such codes has even been listed, and it is believed that the only criterion that existed was that pairs of letters should not coincide with those adopted as established *Geschwader* codes.

Appendix B   Armament carried by the Fw 190 and the Ta 152

Guns and Cannon

Type of Weapon	Purpose of Weapon	Length ft ins.		Height ft ins.		Weight lbs	Calibre mm	Rate (RPM) of fire	Muzzle (ft.sec) Velocity	Length (ft ins) of Barrel	
MG 17	Machine-gun	3	10.25		6.25	22.50	7.9	1,200	2477		–
MG 131	Machine-gun	3	10.00		4.75	43.50	13.1	930	2461		–
MG 151	Machine-gun	6	3.50		7.75	91.50	15.1	700	3131	4	1.25
MG 151/20	Machine-gun	5	9.50		7.75	91.50	20.0	720	1920	3	7.25
MG/FF	Machine-gun	4	4.75		5.25	78.75	20.0	540	–	2	8.25
MK 103	Mach-cannon	7	7.25	1	1.75	319.75	30.0	420	2820	4	4.75
MK 108	Mach-cannon	3	5.50		8.50	127.75	30.0	650	1705	1	9.50
MK 213	Mach-cannon	5	1.50		7.50	114.75	20.0	1100	3527	3	11.75
MK 213C	Mach-cannon	6	4.00		9.00	165.25	20.0	1300	3492	5	3.00
SG 113A	Anti-tank	5	5.00		–	48.00	77.0	–	650	4	0.00
SG 116	Anti-bomber		–		–	–	30.0	–	–		–
SG 117	Anti-bomber	1	11.75		–	61.75	30.0	18,000	1575	1	9.50

Missiles

Type of Weapon	Purpose of Weapon	Length ft ins.		Weight lbs	Calibre mm	Speed ft/sec.	Weight (lbs) of Explosive
Wfr Gr 21	Rocket Projectile	3	10.25	244.25	210.0	1033	–
Wfr Gr 28/32	Rocket Projectile		–	–	280.0	–	–
RBS B/F21	Rocket Bomb	6	2.50	220.50	210.0	1935	101.00
R100/BS	Incendiary Rocket	6	0.50	242.50	210.0	1476	88.00
R4/M	Air-to-Air Missile	2	8.00	8.50	55.0	1722	1.25
PB.1	Air-to-Ground Missile	2	3.75	14.50	78.0	1227	1.50
PB.2	Air-to-Ground Missile	2	8.00	11.75	130.0	1212	4.50
PB.3	Air-to-Ground Missile	3	2.25	–	55.0	1869	13.90
X4	Guided Missile	6	6.75	133.75	216.0	723	44.00
BV 246	Glider Bomb	11	7.50	1615	542.0	–	958.00

Bombs and Torpedoes

Type of Weapon	Purpose of Weapon	Length ft ins.		Diameter ft ins.		Weight lbs	Weight (lbs) of Explosive
BT 200	Bomb-Torpedo	7	10.25	0	11.75	485.00	220.50
BT 400	Bomb-Torpedo	9	8.00	1	2.50	959.00	441.00
BT 700A	Bomb-Torpedo	11	5.75	1	4.50	1719.50	727.50
BT 700B	Bomb-Torpedo	11	0.25	1	5.50	1664.50	705.50
BT 1000	Bomb-Torpedo	12	10.00	1	6.75	2601.50	1565.25
BT 1400	Bomb-Torpedo	14	11.50	2	7.50	3329.00	2028.25
BT 1850	Bomb-Torpedo	15	4.50	2	7.50	4239.50	2314.75
SC 50	Bomb	3	6.75	0	7.75	110.20	55.00
SC 250	Bomb	5	5.00	1	2.50	551.00	297.50
SC 500	Bomb	6	7.50	1	6.50	1102.00	595.00
SC 1000	Bomb	9	2.25	2	1.75	2204.00	1168.50
SB 1000	Bomb	9	2.25	2	1.75	2204.00	1874.00
SC 1800	Bomb	11	5.00	2	2.00	3968.30	2204.00
LT F5b	Torpedo	17	7.00	1	5.75	1686.50	–
LT 1A	Torpedo	17	7.00	1	5.75	1763.00	–
LT 1B	Torpedo	17	7.00	1	5.75	1686.50	–
LT 2	Torpedo	16	4.50	1	5.75	–	–
LT 850	Torpedo	18	8.50	1	5.75	1785.75	441.00
LT 950	Torpedo	18	8.50	1	5.75	–	441.00

Remarks

Developed by *Rheinmetall Borsig* from T6-200(MG 15): Belt of 500 rounds weight 32$\frac{1}{2}$-lbs.
First used in A-5/U9. Weight of Electrical Equip.: 1$\frac{3}{4}$-lbs; Belt length 7 ft 10 ins./100 rounds: weight 17$\frac{1}{2}$-lbs.
MV. Quoted for Explosive projectiles: for Anti-tank: 3,363 ft/sec. Elec. Equip. Weight: 1$\frac{3}{4}$-lbs; 100 rounds/37-lbs.
MV. Quoted for Explosive projectiles: for Anti-tank: 2,313 ft/sec. Elec. Equip. Weight. 1$\frac{3}{4}$-lbs; 100 rounds/43$\frac{3}{4}$-lbs.
Swiss designed; produced under licence: Drum weights: 100 rounds/73-lbs; 60/44$\frac{3}{4}$-lbs; 45/36$\frac{1}{4}$-lbs.
Rheinmetall Borsig; due vertical size, generally mounted in pods, under-wing. Weight of projectile; 11.6-oz.
Required protective tubing over barrel to prevent damage to aircraft wing; nicknamed 'Pneumatic Hammer'.
Developed by *Mauser*, in co-operation with *Krieghoff Co.*—1942. Weight of projectile; 12-oz.
Later version of above, after solution of barrel difficulties. Used in late Fw 190/Ta 152 variants.
SG = *Sondergerät* = special device; '*Förstersonde*' = downward firing anti-tank weapon; set of 5 weighed 330-kgs.
'*Zellendusche*' = 'Airframe douche'; 3 versions: 3, 4, or 6 MK 103 upward firing group weapon; little known.
'*Rohrblock*' = 'Tube block.' 7 MK 108 barrels bound together; 1st fired the others; tests on V74. *Werk Nr* 733713.

Remarks

Range 2406 yards, originally used only for Army '*Nebelwefer*' = 'rocket projector.' Tested Dept. E.7 at Rechlin.
Carried underwing in frames on Fw 190F-8s, developed from Wfr Gr. 21 = '*Werfer-granate*' = rocket projectile.
Rocket powered missile, with explosive head, fitted with folding stabilisers.
Incendiary rocket; later also (identical dimensions) R100/MS with explosive warhead: range 2187 yards.
'*Orkan*', Range 1640 yards. Air to Air Missile: 12,000 produced, but only used experimentally on Fw 190's.
Modified 78-mm. Army Rocket projectile. Disadvantage was low aircraft speed, 304-mph, required for launching.
Modified R4/M missile with hollow charge. Used on Fw 190F-9; Eastern Front, 1944.
Also Modified R4/M Missile with enlarged warhead. Tested experimentally; few details known.
'*Ruhrstahl*', range 5,468 yards; length quoted 'with fuse'; span 2 ft 4$\frac{1}{2}$ ins., powered by BMW 109-548 rocket engine.
'*Hagelhorn*' = hailstone. Originally BV226. Intended for use with bombers; Fw 190's used as test carriers.

Remarks

The Bomb-Torpedo was developed on an experimental basis only, and in small numbers only.
The series suffered aiming and release difficulties, though advantages were lower cost,
due to method of construction, and raw-material economies.

SC = '*Splitterbombe*' = splinter bomb: Radius of destruction 20 feet; radius of damage 213 feet.
Radius of destruction 27 feet, radius of damage 426 feet.
Radius of destruction 37 feet, radius of damage 623 feet.
Radius of destruction 57 feet, circle of damage 1,118 feet.
SB = '*Sprengbombe*' = demolition bomb. No detailed information available on destructive powers.
Largest bomb to be carried by Fw 190 aircraft.
Length without fuse 16 ft. 3$\frac{1}{2}$ in. Modified Several times, involving weight increases up to 1,763 Ib.
Originally LT F5b; suffixed LT 1A/1, or -/2, or -/3 according to water running speed.
This torpedo possessed electrical equipment for adjustment of range.
Possessing a range of 8 miles, and a water running speed of 45-mph, only 50 examples were constructed.

Both these torpedo types were very similar, and were manufactured experimentally only.

(Top left) The SG 116 which
included three, four or six
upward firing 30-mm
MK 103 machine-cannon
carried by an Fw 190A-8.

(Top right) 30-mm Mk 108
machine-cannon mounted
beneath the wing of an Fw
190A-5/U16.

(Left) A WB 151 weapons
nacelle.. Seen here attached
to an Fw 190A-5/U12

(Below) A 30-mm MK 103
machine-cannon fitted to an
Fw 190A-5/Ull.

(Top left) The Wfr Gr. 28/32 carried beneath the wing of an Fw 190F-8.

(Top right) The tube that carries the Wfr Gr. 21 rocket projectile. Here fitted to an Fw 190A-4/R6.

(Right) Four SC 50 (110-lbs) bombs on an ER 4 rack which is again fitted to an ETC 501.

(Below) An Fw 190A-4/U8 carrying a SC 250 (551-lbs) fitted to an ETC 501 rack. It also carries two 66-gal. (300-litres) under each wing.

Appendix C   Fw 190 and Ta 152 Projects and Variants

AIRCRAFT		ENGINE		SPAN		LENGTH		WING	PURPOSE
Type	Year	Type	h.p	ft.	ins.	ft.	ins.	AREA (Sq. Ft)	
Fw 190V1	1939	BMW 139	1550	31	2.5	29	0.0	160.4	Experimental
V2	1939	BMW 139	1550	31	2.5	29	0.0	160.4	Experimental
V3	1940	–	–	31	2.5	29	0.0	160.4	Experimental
V5k	1940	BMW 801 C-0	1600	31	3.5	28	10.5	160.4	Experimental
V5g	1940	BMW801C-0	1600	33	10	28	10.5	196.5	Experimental
V7	1941	BMW 801C-1	1600	33	10	28	10.5	196.5	Experimental
V9	1941	BMW 801C-1	1600	33	10	28	10.5	196.5	Experimental
V12	1943	BMW 801C-1	1600	34	5.5	28	10.5	196.5	Experimental
V13	1943	DB 603A-1	1750	34	5.5	31	1.0	196.5	Experimental
V14	1941	BMW 801C-1	1600	34	5.5	28	10.5	196.5	Experimental
V15	1941	BMW 801C-1	1600	34	5.5	28	10.5	196.5	Experimental
V17	1943	Jumo 213-1001-S	1750	40	4.0	31	1.0	218.5	Experimental
V17/U1	1944	Jumo 213A	1750	34	5.5	33	5.5	196.5	Experimental
V18	1942	DB 603G	2000	34	5.5	3	11.0	196.5	Experimental
V18/U1	1943	DB 603A-1	1750	34	5.5	3	11.0	196.5	Experimental
V18/U2	1944	Jumo 213E	1750	47	4.5	35	11.0	250.7	Experimental
V19	1943-4	Jumo 213E	1750	34	5.5	33	5.5	196.5	Experimental
V20	1943	Jumo 213A	1750	34	5.5	31	1.0	196.5	Experimental
V20/U1	1943	DB 603L	1750	34	5.5	31	1.0	196.5	Experimental
V21	1943	Jumo 213A	1750	34	5.5	31	1.0	196.5	Experimental
V21/U1	1944	DB 603L	1750	36	1.0	35	5.5	210.9	Experimental
V22	1943	Jumo 213A	1750	34	5.5	31	1.0	210.9	Experimental
V23	1943	Jumo 213A	1750	34	5.5	31	1.0	210.9	Experimental
V25	1943	Jumo 213A	1750	34	5.5	31	1.0	210.9	Experimental
V29	1943	DB'603G	2000	34	5.5	31	1.0	196.5	Experimental
V29/U1	1944	Jumo 213E	1750	47	4.5	35	1.5	250.7	Experimental
V30	1943	DB 603G	2000	34	5.5	31	1.0	196.5	Experimental
V30/U1	1944	Jumo 213E	1750	47	4.5	35	11.0	250.7	Experimental
V31	1943	DB 603G	2000	34	5.5	31	1.0	196.5	Experimental
V32	1944	DB 603G	2000	34	5.5	31	1.0	196.5	Experimental
V32/Ul	1944	Jumo 213E-1	1750	47	4.5	35	1.5	250.7	Experimental
V32/U2	1944	Jumo 213E-1	1750	47	4.5	35	1.5	250.7	Experimental
V33	1943	DB 603G	2000	34	5.5	31	1.0	196.5	Experimental
V33/U1	1944	Jumo 213E	1750	47	4.5	35	1.5	250.7	Experimental
V34	1943	BMW 801F	2000	34	5.5	29	4.5	196.5	Experimental
V35	1943	BMW 801TU	2000	34	5.5	29	4.5	196.5	Experimental
V36	1943	BMW 801F	2000	34	5.5	29	4.5	196.5	Experimental
V42	1943	BMW 801D-2	1700	34	5.5	29	4.5	196.5	Experimental
V45	1943	BMW 801D-2	1700	34	5.5	29	4.5	196.5	Experimental
V47	1943	BMW 801D-2	1700	34	5.5	29	4.5	196.5	Experimental
V51	1944	BMW .801D-2	1700	34	5.5	29	4.5	196.5	Experimental
V53	1944	Jumo 213A	1750	34	5.5	33	5.5	196.5	Experimental
V54	1944	Jumo 213A	1750	34	5.5	33	5.5	196.5	Experimental
V55	1944	Jumo 213F-1	1750	34	5.5	33	5.5	196.5	Experimental
V56	1944	Jumo 213F-1	1750	34	5.5	33	5.5	196.5	Experimental
V57	1944	Jumo 213F-1	1750	34	5.5	33	5.5	196.5	Experimental
V58	1944	Jumo 213F-1	1750	34	5.5	33	5.5	196.5	Experimental
V59	1944	Jumo 213F-1	1750	34	5.5	33	5.5	196.5	Experimental
V60	1944	Jumo 213F-1	1750	34	5.5	33	5.5	196.5	Experimental
V61	1944	Jumo 213F-1	1750	34	5.5	33	5.5	196.5	Experimental
V62	1944	Jumo 213F-1	1750	34	5.5	33	5.5	196.5	Experimental
V63	1944	Jumo 213F-1	1750	34	5.5	33	5.5	196.5	Experimental
V64	1944	Jumo 213F-1	1750	34	5.5	33	5.5	196.5	Experimental
V65	1944	Jumo 213F-1	1750	34	5.5	33	5.5	196.5	Experimental
V66	1944	BMW 801TS/TH	2000	34	5.5	29	4.5	196.5	Experimental

ARMAMENT & EQUIPMENT	PROTOTYPE OF:	OTHER INFORMATION
FuG7	–	Empty wt. 5,530-lbs; Gross wt. 6,948-lbs.
2 x MG 17, 2 x MG 131, FuG 7, Revi 12.c	–	Empty wt. 5,530-lbs; Gross wt. 6,948-lbs.
–		Without engine.
2 x MG 17	Fw 190A-0	–
4 x MG 17; 2 x MG/FF	Fw 190A-0	–
4 x MG 17; 2 x MG/FF	Fw 190A-1	–
4 x MG 17; 2 x MG/FF	Fw 190A-1	–
4 x MG 17; 2 x MG/FF	Fw 190B-1	–
2 x MG 17; 2 x MG 151	Fw 190C-0	–
2 x MG 17; 2 x MG 151	Fw 190A-2	–
2 x MG 17; 2 x MG 151	Fw 190A-2	–
–	Project	Long-span project only.
2 x MG 17; 2 x MG 151	Fw 190D-9	–
–	Fw 190C-1	Fitted with Hirth turbo-blower.
–	Fw 190C-1	Fitted with Hirth turbo-blower.
–	Ta 152H-0	–
–	Fw 190Wbl	Exptl: Ta 153.
Engine-gun MK 103	–	–
–	–	–
2 x MG 151; 2 x MG 17	–	–
1 x MK 213; 4 x MG 151, FuG 25, 16ZY	Ta 152C-0	–
2 x MG 17; 2 x MG 151	–	–
–	–	–
Engine-gun MK 103, 2 x MG 17, 2 x MG 151	–	–
–	Fw 190C-1	Fitted with Hirth turbo-blower.
–	Ta 152H-0	GM-1
–	Fw 190C-1	Fitted with Hirth turbo-blower.
–	Ta 152H-0	–
–	Fw 190C-1	Fitted with Hirth turbo-blower.
–	Fw 190C-1	Fitted with Hirth turbo-blower.
–	Ta 152H-0	Gross weight 10,538-lbs.
Engine-gun MK 213, 2 x MG 151/15	Ta 152H-0	–
2 x MG 131, 2 x MG 151	Fw 190C-1	Fitted with Hirth turbo-blower.
–	Ta 152H-l	Gross weight 11,508-lbs.
	Fw 190A-9; F-9	–
2 x MG 131, 4 x MG 151	Fw 190A-7; A-8; F-9	–
2 x MG 131, 4 x MG 151	Fw 190A-9; F-9	–
2 x MG 151	Fw 190A-5/U2	–
2 x MG 131, 2 x MG 151	Fw 190A-6/R4	GM-1
2 x MG 131, 4 x MG 151	Fw 190A-8	GM-1
2 x MG 131, 2 x MG 151, 2 x MK 108	Fw 190A-6;A-7/R2	–
2 x MG 131, 2 x MG 151, 2 x MG 151 or MK 108	Fw 190D-9/D-10	–
2 x MG 131, 2 x MG 151	Fw 190D-9	–
2 x MG 131, 2 x MG 151	Fw 190D-11	Fitted with MW-50.
2 x MG 151, 2 x MK 108	Fw 190D-11	Fitted with MW-50.
2 x MG 151, 2 x MK 108	Fw 190D-11	Fitted with MW-50.
2 x MG 151, 2 x MK 108	Fw 190D-11	Fitted with MW-50.
2 x MG 151, 2 x MK 108	Fw 190D-11	Fitted with MW-50.
–	Fw 190D-11	Fitted with MW-50.
–	Fw 190D-11	Fitted with MW-50.
1 x MK 108, 2 x MG 151	Fw 190D-12/R11	–
1 x MK 108, 2 x MG 151	Fw 190D-12/R11	–
1 x MK 108, 2 x MG 151	Fw 190D-12/R11	–
1 x MG 151, 2 x MG 151	Fw 190D-13/R11	–
2 x MG 131, 2 x MG 151, ETC 504, FuG 16	Fw 190F-15	–

Appendix C Fw 190 and Ta 152 Projects and Variants

AIRCRAFT Type	Year	ENGINE Type	hp	SPAN ft. ins.	LENGTH ft. ins.	WING AREA (Sq. ft.)	PURPOSE
Fw 190 V67	1945	BMW 801TS/TH	2000	34 5.5	29 4.5	196.5	Experimental
V68	1945	Jumo 213E	1750	34 5.5	35 1.5	209.9	Experimental
V69	1944	BMW 801D	1700	34 5.5	29 4.5	196.5	Experimental
V70	1944	BMW 801D	1700	34 5.5	29 4.5	196.5	Experimental
V71	1944	Jumo 213F	1750	34 5.5	33 5.5	196.5	Experimental
V72	1944	BMW 801TS	2000	34 5.5	29 4.5	196.5	Experimental
V73	1944	BMW 801TS	2000	34 5.5	29 4.5	196.5	Experimental
V74	1944	BMW 801TS	2000	34 5.5	29 4.5	196.5	Experimental
V75	1944	BMW 801D	1700	34 5.5	29 4.5	196.5	Experimental
V76	1944	Jumo 213F	1750	34 5.5	33 5.5	196.5	Experimental
V77	1944	Jumo 213F	1750	34 5.5	33 5.5	196.5	Experimental
V78	1944	BMW 801D-2	1700	34 5.5	29 4.5	196.5	Experimental
V79	1944	BMW 801D-2	1700	34 5.5	29 4.5	196.5	Experimental
V80	1944	BMW 801D-2	1700	34 5.5	29 4.5	196.5	Experimental
Fw 190 A-0	1941-3	BMW 801C-0	1600	33 10	28 10.5	196.5	Fighter
A-l	941-2	BMW 801 C-l	1600	33 10	28 10.5	196.5	Fighter
A-2	1941-2	BMW 801 C-2	1600	34 5.5	28 10.5	196.5	Fighter
A-3	1941-3	BMW 801D-2	1700	34 5.5	28 10.5	196.5	Fighter
A-3/U1	1943	BMW 801D-2	1700	34 5.5	28 10.5	196.5	Heavy Fight/Bomb
A-3/U3	1942	BMW 801D-2	1700	34 5.5	28 10.5	196.5	Fighter/Bomber
A-3/U4	1942-3	BMW 801D-2	1700	34 5.5	28 10.5	196.5	Recon.-Fighter
A-3/U7	1942-3	BMW 801D-2	1700	34 5.5	28 10.5	196.5	Fighter-Bomber
A-4	1941-2	BMW 801D-2	1700	34 5.5	28 10.5	196.5	Fighter
A-4/U1	1941-2	BMW 801D-2	1700	34 5.5	28 10.5	196.5	Heavy Fight/Bomb
A-4/U3	1941-2	BMW 801D-2	1700	34 5.5	28 10.5	196.5	Ground Support Fighter
A-4/U8	1941-2	BMW 801D-2	1700	34 5.5	28 10.5	196.5	Long Range Fight/Bomb
A-5	1942	BMW 801D-2	1700	34 5.5	29 4.5	196.5	Fighter
A-5/U2	1943	BMW 801D-2	1700	34 5.5	29 4.5	196.5	Night Fighter/Bomber
A-5/U3	1943	BMW 801D-2	1700	34 5.5	29 4.5	196.5	Ground Support Fighter
A-5/U4	1943	BMW 801D-2	1700	34 5.5	29 4.5	196.5	Recon.-Fighter
A-5/U8	1943	BMW 801D-2	1700	34 5.5	29 4.5	196.5	Long Range Fight/Bomb
A-5/U9	1943	BMW 801D-2	1700	34 5.5	29 4.5	196.5	Fighter
A-5/U10	1943	BMW 801D-2	1700	34 5.5	29 4.5	196.5	Fighter
A-5/U11	1943	BMW 801D-2	1700	34 5.5	29 4.5	196.5	Heavy Fighter
A-5/U12	1943	BMW 801D-2	1700	34 5.5	29 4.5	196.5	Heavy Fighter
A-5/U13	1943	BMW 801D-2	1700	34 5.5	29 4.5	196.5	Long Range Fight/Bomb
A-5/U14	1943	BMW 801D-2	1700	34 5.5	29 4.5	196.5	Torpedo-Fighter
A-5/U15	1943	BMW 801D-2	1700	34 5.5	29 4.5	196.5	Torpedo-Fighter
A-5/U16	1943	BMW 801D-2	1700	34 5.5	29 4.5	196.5	Ground Support Fighter
A-5/U17	1943	BMW 801D-2	1700	34 5.5	29 4.5	196.5	Ground Support Fighter
A-6	1943	BMW 801D-2	1700	34 5.5	29 4.5	196.5	Fighter
A-6/R1	1943-4	BMW 801D-2	1700	34 5.5	29 4.5	196.5	Heavy Fighter
A-6/R2	1943-4	BMW 801D-2	1700	34 5.5	29 4.5	196.5	Heavy Fighter
A-6/R3	–	BMW 801D-2	1700	34 5.5	29 4.5	196.5	Heavy Fighter
A-6/R4	1943	BMW 801D-2	1700	34 5.5	29 4.5	196.5	Fighter
A-6/R6	1943-4	BMW 801D-2	1700	34 5.5	29 4.5	196.5	Fighter
A-7	1943	BMW 801D-2	1700	34 5.5	29 4.5	196.5	Fighter
A-7/R1	1943	BMW 801D-2	1700	34 5.5	29 4.5	196.5	Heavy Fighter
A-7/R2	1943-4	BMW 801D-2	1700	34 5.5	29 4.5	196.5	Heavy Fighter
A-7/R6	1943-4	BMW 801D-2	1700	34 5.5	29 4.5	196.5	Fighter
A-8	1944	BMW 801D-2	1700	34 5.5	29 4.5	196.5	Fighter

ARMAMENT & EQUIPMENT	PROTOTYPE OF:	OTHER INFORMATION
2 x MG 131, 2 x MG 151, ETC 504, FuG 15	Fw 190F-16	–
Engine-gun MK 103, 2 x MK 103 (wing roots)	Ta 152B-5	Rebuilt from Fw 190V53.
X-4, PKS 12	–	–
X-4, PKS 12	–	–
1 x MG 151, 2 x MG 151	Fwl90D-13/R11	–
2 x MG 131, 2 x MG 151	–	Fw 190A-8 with PKS 12.
2 x MG 131, 2 x MG 151	Fw 190A-8	–
2 x MG 151	Fw 190A-8	Revi 242, Gunpack MK 108.
SG 113A	–	–
1 x MG 151, 2 x MG 151	Fw 190D-14	–
1 x MG 151, 2 x MG 151	Fw 190D-14	–
2 x MG 151	–	Fw 190F-8 with AG 140.
2 x MG 151	–	Fw 190F-8 with AG 140.
2 x MG 151	–	Fw 190F-8 with AG 140.
4 x MG 17, 2 x MG/FF	–	Weight empty 7,003-lbs; loaded 8,491-lbs;
4 x MG 17, 2 x MG/FF, FuG 7a	–	Range 582 miles. Maximum speed 322-mph,
2 x MG 17, 2 x MG 151, 2 x MG/FF, FuG 7, FuG 25	–	Cruising speed 278-mph.
2 x MG 17, 2 x MG 151, 2 x MG/FF, FuG 7, FuG 25	–	Gross weight 8,500-lbs.
2 x MG 17, 2 x MG 151, 2 x ETC 501	–	–
2 x MG 17, 2 x MG 151, 1 x ETC 501	–	Gross weight 8,600-lbs, Range 565 miles,
2 x MG 17, 2 x MG 151, 2 x Rb 12-5/7 x 9	–	Ceiling 36,800 ft. Maximum speed 413-mph
2 x MG 17, 2 x MG 151, 1 x ETC 501/ER4	–	at 20,400 ft.
2 x MG 17, 2 x MG 151, 2 x MG/FF, FuG 16Z, FuG 25	–	–
2 x MG 151, 2 x ETC 501		
2 x MG 17, 2 x MG 151, 1 x ETC 501	Fw 190F-1	Gross weight 9,500-lbs; Max speed 418-mph at 20,400 ft.
2 x MG 151, 1 x ETC 501, 2 x 300 Litre Tanks		Gross weight 10,500-lbs, Max speed 352-mph, range 800 miles.
2 x MG 17, 2 x MG 151, 2 x MG/FF, FuG 16Z, FuG 25		Gross weight 8,990-lbs; Max speed 410-mph at 20,700 ft. Range, 435 miles. Ceiling 34,500 ft. Time to 26,300 ft, 12$\frac{1}{2}$ minutes.
2 x MG 151, 1 x ETC 501, 2 x 300 Litre Tanks		
2 x MG 17, 2 x MG 151. 1 x ETC 250, 1 x 300 Litre Tank	Fw 190F-2	Alternatively, 1 x ETC 500.
2 x MG 17, 2 x MG 151, FuG 17, 2 x Rb 12-5/7 x 9	—	–
2 x MG 151, 1 x ETC 501, 2 x 300 Litre Tanks	Fw 190G-2	–
2 x MG 131, 2 x MG 151	Fw l90A-7; A-8; F-8	–
2 x MG 17, 4 x MG 151	Fw 190A-6	–
2 x MG 17, 2 x MG 151, 2 x MK 103	Fw l90A-8/R3;F-8/R3	–
2 x MG 17, 2 x MG 151	Fw 190A-8/R1; A-6/R1	–
2 x MG 151, 1 x ETC 501, 2 x Fw racks, bombs, or tanks	Fw 190G-3	Gross weight 10,250-lbs, with 2 x 300-litre
2 x MG 151, 1 x LTF5b	–	tanks 11,500-lbs; Max speed
2 x MG 151, 1 x LT 950, ALSK 121	–	312-mph.
2 x MG 17, 2 x MG 151, 2 x MK 108	–	–
2 x MG 17, 2 x MG 151, 2 x 2 ETC 50	Fw 190F-3	Gross weight 9,100-lbs, Max speed 405-mph, at
2 x MG 17, 4 x MG 151, FuG 16Z-E, FuG 25	–	20,700 ft. Range 480 miles. Ceiling 34,000 ft;
2 x MG 17, 6 x MG 151	–	Time to 26,300 ft, 13$\frac{1}{2}$ minutes.
2 x MG 17, 2 x MG 151, 2 X MK 108	–	–
2 x MG 17, 2 x MG 151, 2 x MK 103	–	Project only.
–	–	GM-1.
2 x MG 17, 2 x MG 151, 2 x Wfr Gr. 2-cm	–	–
2 x MG 131, 4 x MG 151, FuG 16Z-E, FuG 25	–	Gross weight 9,250-lbs.
2 x MG 131, 6 x MG 151	–	–
2 x MG 131, 2 x MG 151, 2 x MK 108	–	–
2 x MG 131, 2 x MG 151, 2 x Wfr Gr. 21-cm		Empty weight 7,680-lbs, Gross weight 9,680-lbs, Max speed 402-mph
2 x MG 131, 4 x MG 151, ETC 501, FuG 16Z-r/FuG 25a		at 20,700 ft, Range 658 miles. Ceiling 32,700 ft; Time to 26,300 ft, 14$\frac{1}{4}$ minutes; landing speed, 100-mph.

Appendix C   Fw 190 and Ta 152 Projects and Variants

AIRCRAFT Type	Year	ENGINE Type	hp	SPAN ft	ins.	LENGTH ft	ins.	WING AREA (Sq. ft.)	PURPOSE
Fw 190A-8/U1	1944	BMW 801D-2	1700	34	5.5	29	4.5	196-5	Fighter-Trainer
A-8/R1	1944	BMW 801D-2	1700	34	5.5	29	4.5	196-5	Heavy Fighter
A-8/R2	1944	BMW 801D-2	1700	34	5.5	29	4.5	196.5	Heavy Fighter
A-8/R3	–	BMW 801D-2	1700	34	5.5	29	4.5	196.5	Heavy Fighter
A-8/R7	1944	BMW 801D-2	1700	34	5.5	29	4.5	196.5	Assault Fighter
A-8/R8	–	BMW 801D-2	1700	34	5.5	29	4.5	196.5	Assault Fighter
A-8/R11	–	BMW 801TU	2000	34	5.5	29	4.5	196.5	All-weather Fighter
A-8/R12	–	BMW 801TU	2000	34	5.5	29	4.5	196.5	All-weather Fighter
A-9	1944	BMW 801TS/TH	2000	34	5.5	29	4.5	196.5	Fighter
A-9/R8	–	BMW 801TS/TH	2000	34	5.5	29	4.5	196.5	Assault Fighter
A-9/R11	–	BMW 801TS	2000	34	5.5	29	4.5	196.5	All-weather Fighter
A-9/R12	–	BMW 801TS	2000	34	5.5	29	4.5	196.5	All-weather Fighter
A-10	–	BMW 801 F	1700	34	5.5	29	4.5	196.5	Fighter Bomber
Fw 190B-0	1943	BMW 801D-2	1700	34	5.5	29	4.5	196.5	Fighter
				40	4	29	4.5	218.5	Fighter
B-l	–	BMW 801D-2	1700	34	5.5	29	4.5	196.5	Fighter
Fw 190C-0	1943	DB 603A-1	1700	34	5.5	31	1.0	196.5	High Altitude Fighter
C-l	1943	DB 603G or A-1	2000	34	5.5	31	1.0	196.5	High Altitude Fighter
Fw 190D-9	1944	Jumo 213A	1750	34	5.5	33	5.5	196.5	Fighter
D-9/R11	1945	Jumo 213A	1750	34	5.5	33	5.5	196.5	All-weather Fighter
D-10	1944	Jumo 213A	1750	34	5.5	33	5.5	196.5	Fighter
D-11	1944	Jumo 213E	1750	34	5.5	33	5.5	196.5	Fighter
D-11/R20	–	Jumo 213E	1750	34	5.5	33	5.5	196.5	Fighter
D-11/R21	–	Jumo 213E	1750	34	5.5	33	5.5	196.5	Fighter
D-12	1945	Jumo 213E	1750	34	5.5	33	5.5	196.5	Fighter
D-12/R5	–	Jumo 213E	1750	34	5.5	33	5.5	196.5	Fighter
D-12/R11	–	Jumo 213E	1750	34	5.5	33	5.5	196.5	All-weather Fighter
D-12/R21	–	Jumo 213E	1750	34	5.5	33	5.5	196.5	All-weather Fighter
D-12/R25	–	Jumo 213EB	1750	34	5.5	33	5.5	196.5	All-weather Fighter
D-13/R5	–	Jumo 213F	1750	34	5.5	33	5.5	196.5	All-weather Fighter
D-13/R11	–	Jumo 213F	1750	34	5.5	33	5.5	196.5	All-weather Fighter
D-13/R21	–	Jumo 213F	1750	34	5.5	33	5.5	196.5	All-weather Fighter
D-14	–	DB 603F	1750	34	5.5	33	5.5	196.5	Fighter
D-15	–	DB 603F	1750	34	5.5	33	5.5	196.5	Fighter
D-15/R11	–	DB 603F	1750	34	5.5	33	5.5	196.5	All-weather Fighter
Fw 190E-1	–	BMW 801D-2	1700	34	5.5	29	4.5	196.5	Recon. Fighter
Fw 190F-1	1942	BMW 801D-2	1700	34	5.5	28	10.5	196.5	Ground Support Fighter
F-2	1942-3	BMW 801D-2	1700	34	5.5	29	4.5	196.5	Ground Support Fighter
F-3	1943	BMW 801D-2	1700	34	5.5	29	4.5	196.5	Ground Support Fighter
F-3/U3	–	BMW 801D-2	1700	34	5.5	29	4.5	196.5	Torpedo Fighter
F-3/U4	–	BMW 801D-2	1700	34	5.5	29	4.5	196.5	Night Ground Sup. Fighter
F-3/U5	–	BMW 801D-2	1700	34	5.5	29	4.5	196.5	Ground Support Fighter
F-3/U14	–	BMW 801D-2	1700	34	5.5	29	4.5	196.5	Torpedo Fighter
F-3/R1	1943	BMW 801D-2	1700	34	5.5	29	4.5	196.5	Ground Support Fighter
F-3/R3	1943	BMW 801D-2	1700	34	5.5	29	4.5	196.5	Ground Support Fighter
F-4	–	BMW 801D-2	1700	34	5.5	29	4.5	196.5	Ground Support Fighter
F-5	–	BMW 801D-2	1700	34	5.5	29	4.5	196.5	Ground Support Fighter
F-6	–	BMW 801D-2	1700	34	5.5	29	4.5	196.5	Ground Support Fighter
F-7	–	BMW 801D-2	1700	34	5.5	29	4.5	196.5	Ground Support Fighter
F-8	1944	BMW 801D-2	1700	34	5.5	29	4.5	196.5	Ground Support Fighter
F-8/U1	1944	BMW 801D-2	1700	34	5.5	29	4.5	196.5	Aux. LR Fighter/Bomber
F-8/U2	–	BMW 801D-2	1700	34	5.5	29	4.5	196.5	Torpedo Fighter
F-8/U3	–	BMW 801D-2	1700	34	5.5	29	4.5	196.5	Torpedo Fighter
F-8/U14	–	BMW 801D-2	1700	34	5.5	29	4.5	196.5	Torpedo Fighter

ARMAMENT & EQUIPMENT	PROTOTYPE	OTHER INFORMATION
2 x MG 131	Fw 190S-8	–
2 x MG 131, 6 x MG 151	–	Gross weight 9,900-lbs.
2 x MG 131, 2 x MG 151, 2 x MK 108	–	GM-1, Gross weight 10,300-lbs.
2 x MG 131, 2 x MG 151, 2 x MK 103	–	GM-1, Project only. Gross wt 9,830-lbs.
2 x MG 131, 4 x MG 151	–	–
2 x MG 131, 2 x MG 151, 2 x MK 108	–	–
2 x MG 131, 4 x MG 151, PKS 12, FuG 125	–	Gross weight 9,685-lbs.
2 x MG 131, 2 x MG 151, 2 x MK 108, PKS 12, FuG 125	–	Project only.
2 x MG 131, 4 x MG 151	–	Gross weight 9,750-lbs.
2 x MG 131, 4 x MG 151, or 2 x MG 151, 2 x MK 108	–	Project only.
2 x MG 131, 4 x MG 151, PKS 12, FuG 125	–	Gross weight 9,755-lbs, Project only.
2 x MG 131, 2 x MG 151, 2 x MK 108, PKS 12, FuG 125	–	Project only.
2 x MG 131, 2 x MG 151; 2 x MG 151 or MK 108, ETC 503	–	Project only.
2 x MG 17, 2 x MG 151	–	GM-1.
Werk Nr 0046 Large wing—no weapons	–	GM-1.
2 x MG 17, 2 x MG 151, 2 x MG/FF	–	GM-1.
2 x MG 131, 2 x MG 151, 1 x MK 103	–	Gross weight 9,575-lbs.
2 x MG 131, 2 x MG 151, 1 x MK 103	–	Gross wt 9,575-lbs; Hirth turbo-blower.
2 x MG 131, 2 x MG 151, ETC 504, MW/B4	–	–
2 x MG 131, 2 x MG 151, PKS 12, FuG 125	–	–
1 x MK 108, 2 x MG 151	–	–
2 x MG 151, 2 x MK 108, MW 50	–	–
2 x MG 151, 2 x MK 108, MW/B4, PKS 12	–	Project only.
2 x MG 151, 2 x MK 108, MW/B4, PKS 12, FuG 125	–	Project only.
2 x MG 151, 1 x MK 108, MW High Pressure	–	–
2 x MG 151, 1 x MK 108, MW High Pressure	–	Project only.
2 x MG 151, 1 x MK 108, MW 50, PKS 12, FuG 125	–	–
2 x MG 151, 1 x MK 108, MW High Pressure, PKS 12	–	Project only.
2 x MG 151, 1 x MK 108, MW High Pressure	–	Project only.
2 x MG 151, 1 x MG 151	–	Project only.
2 x MG 151, 1 x MG 151, PKS 12, FuG 125	–	–
2 x MG 151, 1 x MG 151, MW High Press., PKS 12, FuG 125	–	–
2 x MG 151, 1 x MG 151, MW High Pressure	–	–
2 x MG 151, 2 x MK 108, MW High Pressure	–	Project only.
2 x MG 151, 2 x MK 108, MW High Press., PKS 12, FuG 125	–	Project only.
–	–	Project only.
2 x MG 17, 2 x MG 151	–	–
2 x MG 17, 2 x MG 151, ETC 501/ER 4	–	–
2 x MG 17, 2 x MG 151, 4 x ETC 50	–	–
2 x MG 17, 2 x MG 151, BT 1400	–	Project only.
2 x MG 17, 2 x MG 151	–	Project only.
2 x MG 17, 2 x MG 151	–	Project only.
2 x MG 151, LTF5b	–	Project only.
2 x MG 17, 2 x MG 151, 4 x ETC 50, 1 x ETC 501/ER 4	–	–
2 x MG 17, 2 x MG 151, 2 x MK 103	–	–
2 x MG 131, 2 x MG 151, 2 x 2ETC 50, 1 x ETC 501	Fw 190F-8	ER 4 Project.
2 x MG 131, 2 x MG 151, 2 x 2ETC 50, 1 x ETC 501	Fw 190F-9	Project.
2 x MG 131, 2 x MG 151, 2 x 2ETC 50, 1 x ETC 501	Fw 190F-10	Project.
2 x MG 131, 2 x MG 151	–	–
2 x MG 131, 2 x MG 151, 2 x 2ETC 50, FuG 16Z-Y	–	–
–	–	Similar to Fw 190G-8.
2 x MG 151, ETC 503/2 x BT 400, or I x BT 700	–	Project only.
2 x MG 151, BT 1400	–	–
2 x MG 151, LTF5b	–	–

Appendix C   Fw 190 and Ta 152 Projects and Variants

AIRCRAFT		ENGINE		SPAN		LENGTH		WING	PURPOSE
Type	Year	Type	hp	ft	ins.	ft.	ins.	AREA (Sq. ft)	
Fw 190F-8/Rl	1944	BMW 801D-2	1700	34	5.5	29	4.5	196.5	Ground Support Fighter
F-8/R2	1944	BMW 801D-2	1700	34	5.5	29	4.5	196.5	Ground Support Fighter
F-8/R3	1944	BMW 801D-2	1700	34	5.5	29	4.5	196.5	Ground Support Fighter
F-8/R5	–	BMW 801D-2	1700	34	5.5	29	4.5	196.5	Ground Support Fighter
F-8/R13	1945	BMW 801D-2	1700	34	5.5	29	4.5	196.5	Night Ground Supp. Fighter
F-8/R14	1945	BMW 801TU	2000	34	5.5	29	4.5	196.5	Torpedo Fighter
F-8/R15	–	BMW 801D-2	1700	34	5.5	29	4.5	196.5	Torpedo Fighter
F-8/R16	–	BMW 801D-2	1700	34	5.5	29	4.5	196.5	Torpedo Fighter
F-9	1944-5	BMW 801 F	2000	34	5.5	29	4.5	196.5	Ground Support Fighter
F-9/R13	–	BMW 801TS	2000	34	5.5	29	4.5	196.5	Night Ground Supp. Fighter
F-9/R14	–	BMW 801TS	2000	34	5.5	29	4.5	196.5	Torpedo Fighter
F-9/R15	–	BMW 801TS	2000	34	5.5	29	4.5	196.5	Torpedo Fighter
F-9/R16	–	BMW 801TS	2000	34	5.5	29	4.5	196.5	Torpedo Fighter
F-10	1945	BMW 801F	2000	34	5.5	29	4.5	196.5	Ground Support Fighter
F-15	1945	BMW 801TS	2000	34	5.5	29	4.5	196.5	Ground Support Fighter
F-15/R1	1945	BMW 801TS	2000	34	5.5	29	4.5	196.5	Ground Support Fighter
F-16	–	BMW 801TS/TH	2000	34	5.5	29	4.5	196.5	Ground Support Fighter
F-16/R5	–	BMW 801TS/TH	2000	34	5.5	29	4.5	196.5	Ground Support Fighter
F-17	–	BMW 801TS/TH	2000	34	5.5	29	4.5	196.5	Ground Support Fighter
Fw 190G-1	1942-3	BMW 801D-2	1700	34	5.5	28	10.5	196.5	L Range Fighter/Bomber
G-2	1942-3	BMW 801D-2	1700	34	5.5	29	4.5	196.5	L Range Fighter/Bomber
G-3	1943	BMW 801D-2	1700	34	5.5	29	4.5	196.5	L Range Fighter/Bomber
G-3/R1	–	BMW 801D-2	1700	34	5.5	29	4.5	196.5	L Range Fighter/Bomber
G-3/R5	1944	BMW 801D-2	1700	34	5.5	29	4.5	196.5	Aux. Ground Supp. Fighter
G-4tp.	1944	BMW 801D-2	1700	34	5.5	29	4.5	196.5	L Range Fighter/Bomber
G-8	1944	BMW 801D-2	1700	34	5.5	29	4.5	196.5	L Range Fighter/Bomber
G-8/R4	–	BMW 801D-2	1700	34	5.5	29	4.5	196.5	L Range Fighter/Bomber
G-8/R5	1944	BMW 801TU	2000	34	5.5	29	4.5	196.5	Aux. Ground Supp. Fighter
G-9	–	BMW 801F	2000	34	5.5	29	4.5	196.5	L Range Fighter/Bomber
G-10	–	BMW 801F	2000	34	5.5	29	4.5	196.5	L Range Fighter/Bomber
Fw 190S-5	–	BMW 801D-2	1700	34	5.5	29	4.5	196.5	Fighter/Trainer
S-8	–	BMW 801D-2	1700	34	5.5	29	4.5	196.5	Fighter/Trainer
Wb-1	–	Jumo 213A	1750	34	5.5	33	5.5	196.5	Fighter
Ta 152V6	1945	DB 603L/LA	1750	36	1.0	35	5.5	210.9	Experimental
V7	1945	DB 603L/LA	1750	36	1.0	35	5.5	210.9	Experimental
V8	1945	DB 603L/LA	1750	36	1.0	35	5.5	210.9	Experimental
V9	–	Jumo 213E	1730	36	1.0	35	1.5	210.9	Experimental
V13	–	Jumo 213E	1730	36	1.0	35	1.5	210.9	Experimental
V14	–	Jumo 213E	1730	36	1.0	35	1.5	210.9	Experimental
V15	–	Jumo 213E	1730	36	1.0	35	1.5	210.9	Experimental
V16	1945	DB 603LA	1750	36	1.0	35	5.5	210.9	Experimental
V17	1945	DB 603LA	1750	36	1.0	35	5.5	210.9	Experimental
V18	–	DB 603LA	1750	36	1.0	35	5.5	210.9	Experimental
V19	1945	Jumo 213E	1730	36	1.0	35	1.5	210.9	Experimental
V20	1945	Jumo 213E	1730	36	1.0	35	1.5	210.9	Experimental
V21	1945	Jumo 213E	1730	36	1.0	35	1.5	210.9	Experimental
V22	–	DB 603L	1750	36	1.0	35	5.5	210.9	Experimental
V23	–	DB 603L	1750	36	1.0	35	5.5	210.9	Experimental
V24	–	DB 603L	1750	36	1.0	35	5.5	210.9	Experimental
V25	1944	Jumo 213E	1730	47	4.5	35	1.5	210.9	Experimental
V26	1945	Jumo 213E	1730	47	4.5	35	1.5	250.7	Experimental
V27	1945	DB 603LA	1750	36	1.0	35	5.5	250.7	Experimental
V28	1945	DB 603LA	1750	36	1.0	35	5.5	210.9	Experimental

ARMAMENT & EQUIPMENT	PROTOTYPE OF:	OTHER INFORMATION
2 x MG 131, 4 x MG 151, 4 x ETC 50	–	–
2 x MG 131, 2 x MG 151, 2 x MK 108	–	–
2 x MG 131, 2 x MG 151, 2 x MK 103	–	–
2 x MG 131, 4 x MG 151	–	Project only.
2 x MG 131, 1 x ETC 501, 2 x ETC 503, FuG 25, FuG 16ZS	–	Also jettisonable 300-litre tank
2 x MG 151, ETC 502/LTF5b, PKS 12, FuG 25, FuG 16ZS	–	–
2 x MG 151, ETC 502/BT 1400, PKS 12	–	Project only.
2 x MG 151, ETC 502/BT 700, PKS 12	–	Project only.
2 x MG 131, 4 x MG 151	–	–
2 x MG 131, ETC 501, FuG 25, FuG 16ZS	–	Also 2 x 300-litre tanks.
2 x MG 151, ETC 502/LTF 5b, PKS 12	–	Project only.
2 x MG 151, ETC 502/BT 1400, PKS 12	–	Project only.
2 x MG 151, ETC 502/BT 700, PKS 12	–	Project only.
2 x MG 131, 2 x MG 151, 2 x MK 103, 4 x ETC 70	–	Project only.
2 x MG 131, 2 x MG 151, ETC 504, FuG 16ZS, TSA 2d	–	–
2 x MG 131, 2 x MG 151, ETC 504, 4 x ETC 50	–	–
2 x MG 131, 2 x MG 151, ETC 504, FuG 15	–	Project only.
2 x MG 131, 2 x MG 151, ETC 504, FuG 15	–	Project only.
2 x MG 131, 2 x MG 151, ETC 504	–	Project only.
2 x MG 151, 1 x ETC 501, 2 x 300 litre tanks in racks	Gross weight 10,480-lbs, Max speed 350-mph. Cruising speed 290-mph, Range 648 miles.	
2 x MG 151, 1 x SC 500, + 2 x 300 litre tanks	Messerschmitt Racks, Cruising speed 278-mph. Range 960 miles.	
2 x MG 151, 1 x SC 500, 3 x SC 250 + 2 x 300 litre tanks	Focke-Wulf Racks, Gross weight 10,480-lbs, Max speed 355-mph, Cruising speed 262-mph. Range 396 miles basic.	
6 x MG 151, 1 x SC 250	–	Project only.
2 x MG 151, 1 x SC 250, 4 X SC 50	–	–
2 x MG 151, ETC 501	–	–
2 x MG 151, ETC 501/SC 250, 2 x 300 litre tanks	–	Cruising speed 296-mph; Range 733 miles.
2 x MG 151, ETC 501	–	Project only.
2 x MG 151, ETC 501, 4 x ETC 50	–	–
2 x MG 151, ETC 501	–	Project only.
2 x MG 151, ETC 501	–	Project only.
–	–	–
–	–	–
2 x MG 131, 2 x MG 151, 1 x MK 108	–	–
1 x MK 108, 4 x MG 151	Ta 152C-0	–
1 x MK 108, 4 X MG 151	Ta 152C-0/R11	–
1 x MK 108, 4 x MG 151, Revi EZ42	Ta 152C-0/EZ	–
1 x MK 108, 2 x MG 151	Ta 152E-1	Cancelled 1944 – static tests only.
1 x MK 108, 2 x MG 151	Ta 152E-1	Cancelled 1944.
1 x MK 108, 2 x MG 151	Ta 152E-1	Cancelled 1944.
1 x MK 108, 4 x MG 151	Ta 152C-0, C-l	Cancelled 1944.
1 x MK 103, 4 x MG 151/15	Ta 152C-3/R11	–
1 x MK 108, 4 x MG 151	Ta 152C-3/R11	–
1 x MK 108, 4 x MG 151	Ta 152C-0	Cancelled 1944.
1 x MK 103, 2 x MK 103	Ta 152B-5/R11	–
1 x MK 103, 2 x MK 103	Ta 152B-5/R11	–
1 x MK 103, 2 x MK 103	Ta 152B-5/R11	–
1 x MK 103, 2 x MK 103	Ta 152C-4	Cancelled 1944.
1 x MK 103, 2 x MK 103	Ta 152C-4	Cancelled 1944.
1 x MK 103, 2 x MK 103	Ta 152C-4	Cancelled 1944.
FuG 16ZY, GM-1, FuG 25	Ta 152H-1	Cancelled during construction; wings to Fw 190V32/U1, Empty wt: 8,880-lbs;
1 x MK 108, 2 x MG 151	Ta 152H-1/R11; H10	Gross weight 11,520-lbs.
1 x MK 103, 2 x MG 151/15	Ta 152C-3	–
1 x MK 103, 2 x MG 151/15	Ta 152C-3	–

AIRCRAFT		ENGINE		SPAN		LENGTH		WING	PURPOSE
Type	*Year*	Type	hp	ft	ins.	ft	ins.	AREA (Sq. ft)	
Ta 152A-1/2	–	Jumo 213A	1750	36	1.0	35	9.5	210.9	Fighter
B-0	–	(*see last column*)	1750/2000	36	1.0	35	5.5	210.9	Fighter
B-1/2	–	(*see last column*)	2000/1750	36	1.0	35	5.5	210.9	Fighter
B-3	–	Jumo 213A	1750	36	1.0	35	1.5	210.9	Ground Supp. Fighter
B-4	–	DB.603LA	1750	36	1.0	35	5.5	210.9	Fighter
B-5	1945	Jumo 213E	1750	36	1.0	35	1.5	210.9	Heavy Fighter
B-5/R11	1945	Jumo 213E	1750	36	1.0	35	1.5	210.9	Heavy Fighter
C-0	1945	DB 603L	1750	36	1.0	35	5.5	210.9	Heavy Fighter
C-O/EZ	1945	DB 603L	1750	36	1.0	35	5.5	210.9	Heavy Fighter
C-0/R11	1945	DB 603L	1750	36	1.0	35	5.5	210.9	Heavy Fighter
C-1	–	DB 603L	1750	36	1.0	35	5.5	210.9	Heavy Fighter
C-1/R11	–	DB 603LA	1750	36	1.0	35	5.5	210.9	Heavy Fighter
C-1/R 14	–	DB 603LA	1750	36	1.0	35	5.5	210.9	Torpedo Fighter
C-1/R 31	1945	DB 603LA	1750	36	1.0	35	5.5	210.9	Fighter
C-2	–	DB 603LA	1750	36	1.0	35	5.5	210.9	Fighter
C-2/R11	–	DB 603LA	1750	36	1.0	35	5.5	210.9	All-weather Fighter
C-3/R11	1945	DB 603LA	1750	36	1.0	35	5.5	210.9	All-weather Fighter
C-4	–	DB 603LA	1750	36	1.0	35	5.5	210.9	Fighter
E-0/,-1	1945	Jumo 213E	1730	36	1.0	35	1.5	210.9	Recon.-Fighter
E-1/R 1	1945	Jumo 213E	1730	36	1.0	35	1.5	210.9	Recon.-Fighter
E-2	–	Jumo 213E	1730	48	7.5	35	1.5	253.0	High Alt. Recon.-Fighter
H-0	1944	Jumo 213E	1730	47	4.5	35	1.5	250.7	High Altitude Fighter
H-0/R11	1945	Jumo 213E	1730	47	4.5	35	1.5	250.7	All-weather Fighter
H-1/R11	–	Jumo 213E	1730	47	4.5	35	1.5	250.7	All-weather Fighter
H-1/R21	–	Jumo 213E	1730	47	4.5	35	1.5	250.7	All-weather Fighter
H-1/R31	–	Jumo 213E	1730	47	4.5	35	1.5	250.7	All-weather Fighter
H-2	–	Jumo 213E	1730	47	4.5	35	1.5	250.7	All-weather Fighter
H-10	–	Jumo 213E	1730	47	4.5	35	1.5	250.7	Recon.-Fighter
S-1	–	Jumo 213E	1730	36	1.0	35	5.5	210.9	Fighter Trainer
Project	–	Jumo 222A/B	2500	36	1.0	34	9.0	210.9	Experimental
Project	–	Jumo 222E/F	2500	36	1.0	35	0.0	210.9	Experimental

ARMAMENT & EQUIPMENT	PROTOTYPE	OTHER INFORMATION
2 x MG 151, 2 x MG 151, FuG 24	–	Project only.
1 x MK 103 or 108 (engine) + 2 x MG 151 or MK 103 or 108 (wings)	–	Project only; engine Jumo 213A or DB 603G
–	–	Project only; engine DB 603G or Jumo 213E
–	–	Project only.
–	–	Project only.
1 + 2 x (ie, 1 + 2 MK 103.) MK 103, MW 50	–	–
1 + 2 x (ie, 1 + 2 MK 103.) MK 103, MW 50, FuG 125, PKS 12	–	–
1 x MK 108, 4 x MG 151, ETC 503	–	–
1 x MK 108, 4 x MG 151, Revi EZ42	–	–
1 x MK 108, 4 x FuG 125, PKS 12	–	–
1 x MK 108, 4 x MG 151, ETC 503	–	Project only.
1 x MK 108, 4 x MG 151, FuG 125, LGWK 23	–	Project only.
2 x MG 151, ETC 504/LTF 5b	–	Project only.
1 x MK 108, 4 x MG 151/20	–	–
1 x MK 108, 4 x MG 151	–	Project only.
1 x MK 108, 4 x MG 151, FuG 125, FuG 16ZY	–	Project only.
1 x MK 103, 4 x MG 151, FuG 125, FuG 16ZY	–	–
1 x MK 103, 4 x MG 151, 2 x Wfr Gr. 21cm, FuG 15	–	Project only.
1 x MK 108, 2 x MG 151, Rb 75/30, FuG 15, MW 50	–	–
1 x MK 108, 2 x MG 151, Rb 50/18, FuG 15, MW 50	–	–
2 x MG 151, 1 x MK 108, GM-1	Ta 152H-10	–
1 x MK 108, 2 x MG 151, ETC 503	–	Empty wt 8,620-lbs; Gross wt 10,400-lbs.
1 x MK 108, 2 x MG 151, FuG 125, LGWK 2	–	–
1 x MK 108, 2 x MG 151, FuG 125, LGWK 2, GM-1, MW 50	–	Empty wt 8,875-lbs; Gross wt 11,520-lbs.
1 x MK 108, 2 x MG 151, FuG 125, LGWK 2, GM-1, MW High Press.	–	Project only.
1 x MK 108, 2 x MG 151, FuG 125, LGWK 2, GM 1	–	Project only.
1 x MK 108, 2 x MG 151	–	Project only.
1 x MK 108, 2 x MG 151, Rb 50/18, FuG 15, MW 50	–	Project only.
–	–	–
–	–	Empty wt 8,988-lbs; Gross wt 10,803-lbs.
–	–	Empty wt 9,208-lbs; Gross wt 11,023-lbs.